Baroness

NADINE DE ROTHSCHILD

SAVOIR-VIVRE

in the 21st century

*A guide to the art of living in France, for the French
...and like the French*

Littlefox Press – Melbourne

Savoir-Vivre in the 21st Century

*The art of living in France, for the French…
and like the French*

Copyright © 2015 Nadine de Rothschild

Translation ©2015 Christine Mathieu
Foreword © 2015 Christine Mathieu
English language edition by Littlefox Press
PO Box 816 Kyneton Vic 3444 Australia
ISBN 978-0-9925562-1-1

Original French edition published by
Editions Robert Laffont
Copyright © 1991 Editions Laffont
Le Bonheur de séduire, l'art de réussir, savoir-vivre aujourd'hui
ISBN 978-2724265897 (1991)
Second edition published by
*Le Bonheur de séduire, l'art de réussir: le savoir-vivre
au XXIème siècle (2001)*
ISBN 978-2221095959

This edition:
Cover design Littlefox Press
Photograph courtesy of Baroness Nadine de Rothschild

To my sister

Nadine de Rothschild

SAVOIR-VIVRE

The art of living

Translated and annotated by

Christine Mathieu

TABLE OF CONTENTS

FOREWORD
by Christine Mathieu

VII. CUSTOMS AND GOOD MANNERS

VIII. SAVOIR-VIVRE AND LOVE AFFAIRS

FOREWORD

Christine Mathieu

Nadine de Rothschild, the illegitimate daughter of a factory worker and an unknown father, began factory work at age fourteen. In her late teens, she was the muse of artist Jean-Gabriel Domergue who introduced her to the world of the arts. Nadine Tallier had a successful acting career in both the theatre and the cinema. Her beauty, personality and charming manner earned her the admiration of many, among them the celebrated poet-singer Georges Brassens, whom she rejected! Nadine Tallier entered nobility, in 1961, when she married the Baron Edmond de Rothschild, head of the banking group based in Geneva. The Baroness has no doubt that her romance and her marriage were enabled by her own gift of *savoir-vivre*.

Charming and provocative, Nadine de Rothschild embodies *savoir-vivre à la Française*. She has made it her personal journey (among other worthy causes) to instruct her French speaking compatriots in France and also in Switzerland where she lives, on the rules and practices of *savoir-vivre*. These rules, she believes, hold the key to her own success and to the happy-ever-after ending of her own fairy tale. Whether she is appearing on radio, television, in the newspapers, or she is publishing another book, Nadine de Rothschild does not leave people indifferent. Mention the Baroness, and you are sure to initiate a lively discussion on the merits of politeness, personal respect and the prejudices of class and gender… indeed, at the core of the controversy lies the question asked by Mary Wollstoncraft at the time of the French Revolution: are our manners the offspring of a true and sincere morality, or are they but "painted substituted morals"? [1] For Nadine de Rothschild, *savoir-vivre* is undeniably founded in self-respect and sincere consideration for others.

When Nadine de Rothschild writes, the French read, and they talk. She has her supporters and also her critics who either find her too conservative or too open-minded, and yet others who perhaps protest a little too much, that she is irrelevant. Or as one critic put it during a television talk show: "It is not that I disagree with what you say, it is that the way you say it makes me feel like doing the contrary."

With calm equanimity, the Baroness looks upon these objections, no matter how forcefully or rudely they are put to her, just as she looks at herself with quirky humour. "I have been poor and I have been rich. In the final count, rich is better."

Whatever the controversies, Nadine de Rothschild's *Le savoir-vivre au XXIeme siècle* found a large readership in France. And it is presently enjoying much success in Chinese translation, in the world's oldest civilization. *Savoir-Vivre in the 21st Century* is the first translation of Nadine de Rothschild's work in English language.

Savoir vivre, in French, means literally "knowing how to live". The phrase has passed into English in the original French and in its hyphenated noun form: *savoir-vivre*. To have *savoir-vivre* is more than knowing about etiquette, it is also more than having good manners. It is an art of living but

---

[1] See Daniel O Neill: *The Burke-Wollstoncraft debate: Savagery, Civilization, Democracy*, Penn State University Press, 2007, p.175.

more than the art of living – *l'art de vivre*. *Savoir-vivre* is about all of those things: it is consideration for others, elegance, social grace coupled with kindness and respect for everyone. *Savoir-vivre* is a pragmatic, moral and aesthetic approach to living with others and with oneself.

Savoir-vivre in the 21st Century was written for French readers, and more specifically, for French women. With lively authority and more than a little humour, Nadine de Rothschild speaks to her readers directly, and she broaches every possible topics: the contents of the ideal wardrobe (for both women and men), the etiquette and traditions of marriage and other ceremonies, when and how to write a letter or an email, when to turn off your mobile phone, how to address a lawyer, the pope or a member of the medical profession, why one should tip taxi drivers and waiters, what is a good and an exceptional wine, and how to choose the right wine for the right dish – but also how to raise children responsibly, form an enduring couple, forgive an unfaithful spouse, invite a same-sex couple to your country house, and how to avoid or, when all else fails, to manage a divorce. The resulting book is both a practical guide to social living and a personal reflection on the meaning of life in the 21st century.

But what can a guide to a good French life, written by a French author for French women, bring to English language readers?

To begin with, Nadine de Rothschild's book addresses a hot topic: what is happening to manners and consideration in this new world of entitlement, of narcissistic preoccupations, instant communication and instant gratification? No doubt Australian readers will recognise their own dismay in Nadine de Rothschild's take on the degradation of public and social behaviour among some of her countrymen and women. Although she advocates not only French but also conservative (or indeed, as some see it, not conservative enough) solutions to the problems of modern living, this book may stimulate for Australians the sort of conversation it initiated among the French. And after all, whether one agrees or not with the author, a good dose of advocacy for mutual respect is unlikely to place anyone at great risk!

But this book is also, and perhaps more so, of interest to those who are curious about France and French culture.

Australians and Americans often express the wish to visit France, to spend extended time there and to live like the French. A number of my own friends and acquaintances have done just that and they have returned home enchanted by their experience. Others, however, have tried and felt somewhat disappointed. A few have even returned embittered, convinced of French unfriendliness, rudeness and ... *arrogance*.

Perhaps, Nadine de Rothschild's chiding of her badly behaved, rude and inconsiderate compatriots will bring solace to the Francosceptics who venture to read this book! Francophiles, meanwhile, will find in her words a window onto French culture, traditions and contemporary modes of life and values. And beyond such anthropological interests, English speaking readers will find a practical guide to behaviour *When in France...* and food for thought on what may or may not constitute a good life.

A guide to French manners and social expectations

Savoir-vivre in the 21st century is a practical guide; not a chronological narrative. Readers may therefore approach the various chapters according to their personal interests and needs. To the Australian readers who intend to travel in

France, this guide offers practical advice on travelling, tipping, on making a restaurant booking, and reserving a hotel room with the best of social graces and patience. To the Francophiles who are contemplating living in France among the French – friends, in-laws or relatives – the book gives precious advice regarding laws, traditions, social rules and social expectations in virtually all situations. Nadine de Rothschild advises on the organisation of a dinner with friends and family; she details the etiquette of formal functions; what to serve, what to do and what to wear at a dinner party, a wedding reception, a funeral; how to address various persons in their professional capacities – janitors, hairdressers, accountants, lawyers, medical personnel, taxi drivers and high dignitaries. Australian tourists may never find themselves in need of the correct form of salutation to write to the archbishop of Paris in French, but life is filled with the unexpected, and in the meantime, nothing is lost by knowing how to…

Many Australian readers will no doubt find the highlights of this book in the chapters on food and wine. For knowing about food and wine in France is not only a measure of an individual's cultural capital, of their social standing and personal credibility, it is an art universally practiced. Australian food lovers will be delighted by the Baroness's advice on the laws of gastronomy: the marriage of wine and food, the etiquette of food sharing, the aesthetics of setting a table for an intimate dinner party or for a large celebration.

Cross-cultural reflections and interest

At first glance, there are significant and at times baffling differences between the French and English speaking cultures – which are not to lump the former or the latter together, as there are also significant differences within. But broadly speaking, the French are Latin, Cartesian and anti-authoritarian – all three at once. Which is to say that they are driven by powerful and at times contrary forces: emotional passion, intellectual curiosity and reason coexist with a love of order and a desire for chaos. The French are romantic in love and realistic in marriage. Their passion for food and wine is matched by their contempt for excessive consumption of both. Idealised notions of freedom and individualism compete with a profound attachment to traditions which for their part rarely go unquestioned or uncriticised.

In this book, Nadine de Rothschild admonishes her compatriots for a certain lack of *savoir-vivre* in the public space. Indeed, the French often find it easier to be polite than to be civic minded. Politeness facilitates face-to-face, respectful connections between persons, but in the larger urban centres, where the public space is by nature impersonal, individual behaviours are more easily led by self-centred opportunism. The same person who would not dream of entering a shop without acknowledging and greeting the shopkeeper, may feel no pangs of conscience jumping a queue – a shocking deed in the Anglo-Saxon order of things. Thus, a foreign visitor may well experience the French at their best by being a guest in their homes than as a guest in their country…

All cultures of course value respect for others, or at least all cultures value respect for *some* others. Not all cultures, however, establish standards of respect according to the same rationale. Three rules govern traditional French notions of social consideration: discretion, formality and charm. Readers will find that these themes run through this practical guide to good living, whether Nadine de Rothschild is discussing what you should keep in the ideal wardrobe, how to behave with your tax accountant or how best to lie to

vi

your spouse when conducting an extra-marital love affair. Discretion, formality and charm are the golden rules by which all French individuals are expected to live in "good society".

Discretion

It is a fair generalisation to say that the French love nothing more than good food, good wine, good conversation and the opportunity to appreciate the charms of the opposite sex. Good conversation being incompatible with deafening environments, they seek quiet restaurants where they keep their voices appropriately low (in fact, speaking loudly is perceived as a significant mark of impoliteness in all social situations). And since good food cannot be appreciated in a hurry, the French may spend hours at the dinner table. Finally, if wine frees the tongue and sharpens the wit, it must not be allowed to cloud the mind or lead the tongue astray.

For Nadine de Rothschild, discretion *is* elegance. But as her readers will appreciate, elegance does not lie in moderation so much as in taking context into account.

Formality

French culture is at once formal and egalitarian. It has inherited formality from the court of Louis XIV and egalitarianism from the revolutionary clubs.

The equation of formality and respect in social exchanges is possibly the most likely area of cross-cultural misunderstanding between the French on one side, and Australians and Americans on the other. Nadine de Rothschild comments with dismay on the American habit of addressing people one barely knows, even significant public personalities by their first names or pet names (Honey!). In fact, this custom is even more pronounced in Australian culture where addressing someone by their first name is a mark of equal respect, as well as an acknowledgement of their individual person.

French people, however, show respect to others by adhering to prescribed degrees of social distance, and Australians who are especially informal, may easily misinterpret this as unfriendliness, coldness or snobbism. On the other hand, on being addressed by their first names, the French are likely to feel as some Australians of a certain generation do when receiving email from unknown and generally younger persons, headed by a disembodied *Hi!* – to which one immediately feels compelled to reply with a "Dear So and So, it is Ms Jane Smith to you!"

French formality is best understood as an extension of discretion. It is foremost a mark of respect for other people's personal boundaries, or at least, for what is generally recognised as personal boundaries. Secondly, but not least, formality is also an acknowledgement of a person's social rank.

Rank in French society is not necessarily, or solely, established by monetary success and social class. Rank is the mark of the professional, of the dignitary, the VIP, but also of the individual with extraordinary achievements: the dedicated artist, the artisan, scientist, writer... Good manners, Nadine de Rothschild tells her readers, require us to acknowledge the realities of social hierarchy with grace. This, no doubt, is one of the pills some of her detractors find difficult to swallow, but even those who disagree with the principle, generally defer to traditional etiquette and bow to such realities in their everyday lives. At any rate, the author never ceases to press the point that whatever special manners of address are owed to rank, all individuals deserve to be treated according to the fundamental rules of *savoir-vivre*. And *savoir-vivre* is to show impeccable respect to all persons, whatever their social circumstances.

In his *Manners in France*, published in 1780, the English travel writer John Moore noted that courtesy was applied to all and by all in France, unlike in English society, where politeness was the exclusive preserve of the upper classes – what Nancy Mitford, writing in the 1950s, would identify as the U and non-U behaviours of British society. But kindly as French manners were or appeared to be in the late 18th century, the revolutionary principles of Liberty, Equality, Fraternity instilled a whole new meaning into French notions of respect. Equality abolished all feudal privileges, nobiliary titles and ranked forms of address. In 1793, the revolutionary government went as far as to decree not only the mandatory use of the word *citoyen* but also that the informal "*tu*" form, to reflect the new egalitarianism (in a similar vein, the communist revolutions of the twentieth century would mandate the term comrade). Although the latter measure was abrogated within two years, egalitarian ideals endured. Indeed, Alexis de Tocqueville wrote that the French had sacrificed Liberty to Equality.

More than two centuries later, French egalitarianism still enjoys taking pot shots at social rank and formality. In a verbal fight, the French are quick to reach for their speech registers to draw on either formality or informality in reverse of what circumstances would command, so as to add weight to their insults. Undoubtedly, degrees of vulgarity and verbal aggression have also become acceptable fare on French television and airwaves (to say nothing of the Internet) as has happened in other parts of the world. But the French prefer to attack formality in their imagination – in their films, plays, stand up comedies and novels – rather than in real life face-to-face situations. The displays of conspicuous familiarity in the media amount to a sort of un-elevated Punch and Judy show, which does not truly translate into normative behaviour.

Nadine de Rothschild, drawing the line at vulgarity, writes with indulgence of the young people who drop into informal speech as soon as they set eyes on each other and who wear their informality as a badge of honour. In some milieus, she also notes, informality is deemed to be "chic". On the other hand, she deplores the television interviewer who addresses a political figure or a famous person by her or his first name and surname, dispensing with formal titles or even with the simplest Madame or Monsieur.

Nevertheless, while many previously unacceptable social and verbal behaviours have become mainstream, the French have not cast out *all* traditional formalities. The young and very cool are as unlikely to slip into informal speech when addressing older persons, as they are unlikely to use formal speech with their peers. Unlike their American and Australian counterparts, French students would feel extremely uncomfortable addressing their university professors by their first names. Impolite or oafish individuals aside, the French continue to defer to age, gender, and professional position according to socially and culturally prescribed usages. Many of these usages are sufficiently complicated to necessitate formal learning and practice, and here lies the success of Nadine de Rothschild's books.

Charm

Charm is a game of subtle and inconsequential seduction played between members of the opposite sex, for the simple pleasure of enjoying the *différence*. Charm is the *modus operandi* of French social etiquette. The language of gendered courtesy is the language of politeness and it always gives women the higher ritual position. Although younger generations, feminists and anarchists surely regard as old hat *some* of the usages advocated by Nadine de Rothschild, much of traditional courtesy is proving enduring and remains prized by both sexes, at all levels of society, and by persons of all political persuasions. Gendered courtesy adds piquancy, playfulness and grace to French social relations. And the French have relatively little interest in single-sex social occasions. This too is an old habit, also observed by John Moore who marvelled at the fact that, at the end of a dinner party, French women did not withdraw to leave the men to serious conversation, but being just as knowledgeable on the sciences, the arts and politics, conversed on equal terms and to the satisfaction and happiness of all concerned.

Charm may or may not lead to a greater propensity for engaging in extra-marital sexual affairs: for the French are also idealistic and romantic and they have a profound belief in Love with a capital and undying L.

On the opposite side of the Channel, a favourite cliché holds that the French look upon extramarital affairs with equanimity. In fact, the French think of the probability, if not the inevitability, of infidelity with about as much serenity as they do the probability of catching a nasty illness (and let it be known that the national character is hypochondriac). An affair may be exhilarating for the unfaithful spouse but it is not much fun for the spouse who is cheated on. For Nadine de Rothschild, if an affair is a disaster, the real catastrophe is an affair that results in divorce. English language readers would be singularly disconcerted if they were to learn that the average French couple is not a *ménage à trois*. But readers can rest assured: Nadine de Rothschild will not disappoint them, although she will no doubt surprise them.

A note on translation

Nadine de Rothschild's style is direct, humorous, lively and chatty. She addresses her readers in the second person; giving advice, imagining a variety of scenarios and recounting anecdotes and personal stories. In this translation, I have attempted to retain her humour and conversational style, along with a certain "Frenchness" of tone. To the original text, I have also added a number of footnotes so as to fill in the necessary cultural contexts which may confuse English language readers, and which French readers would for their part take for granted. At times too, my notes draw the readers' attention to a significant point of cross-cultural difference.

In Chapter V, on the art of writing, I have adapted the English language text to preserve all the prescribed greetings, valedictions and other formulas in the original French alongside the English translation. My aim was to provide readers who are proficient in French with the language tools the author provided her French readers. The translation, of course, will be of interest to French speaking and non-French speaking readers alike.

Finally, this translation differs slightly from the original French book. Thus, along with minor points of edition, Nadine de Rothschild brought a few items of information up to date. A section on correct French grammatical usage was judged too arcane for the English language reader and was therefore omitted from this 2015 English language edition.

Christine Mathieu, Melbourne, 2015

If you want to succeed in life,
hang your dreams on a star...

Like all young girls, I began by dreaming about my life. Visions of beauty and luxury would transport me to far-away lands... sumptuous palaces, elegant and refined people... And I wished for a fairy to introduce me to this enchanted world. But when the fairy manifested, she appeared under such a strange aspect that I failed to recognize her. In my dressing room at the wonderful Théâtre des Variétés where I was playing a young Parisian girl of light morals in a play by Sacha Guitry, I happened on an old dusty book at the bottom of a wardrobe, no doubt left behind by an actress. So I took the book home with me, not knowing that it was going to transform my life; that it would give me the means of rising above my dreams.

I read and re-read this book as though it were a novel in which I was the main character. Through it, I presided over sumptuous meals while men in evening suits bowed to me, all the way to the ground. I lived amongst lilies and roses. Then, I opened my eyes and returned to my daily life and to

1

people who had nothing in common with the characters in my book – who possessed none of their language, manners, or exquisite politeness.

And I asked myself: Can people like these characters be real? Am I destined to ever meet them? Would I even know how to please them?

No and no… For they had a knowledge I did not have, a knowledge I would have to acquire if I wished to behave as one should in any and all places and in any and all circumstances.

Fast forward ten years…

I have been invited to lunch at my future mother-in-law's. I cannot but notice that she is observing me with insistence and I understand that I am being examined, that this is the most perilous test of my life. Under the keen eye of this grand lady of severe demeanour, I am experiencing a feeling of vertigo – I am standing on the edge of a precipice. I will never forget this experience. During the entire luncheon, the situations I had rehearsed for years in my imagination were now echoing like musical chords. And I had learned these chords from *Le Savoir-Vivre,* written by my fairy godmother, the marquise Louise d'Alq. Thanks to her, I was about to acquire an art of living more beautiful than what I had imagined in my wildest dreams.

What would become of road, sea or air traffic without the codes that regulate them?

What would social life be without the codes of good manners?

When two boats cross one another at sea, they greet each other. When two people meet in the street, they too exchange greetings. At every moment of our lives, we submit to a code of conduct with its own signals, its green and red lights, its stop signs and danger warnings. If we do not respect this code, we risk accidents that may well cost us our career or our happiness.

The fact of the matter is, we may accumulate a considerable amount of knowledge, the most prestigious diplomas, and have travelled to all continents, but we will remain stowaways if we forget to pack in our luggage the only passport that opens every frontier and every heart. This passport is *le savoir-vivre.*

From generation to generation, the transmission of *savoir-vivre* has been passed on by women. Therefore, in the first part of this book I have addressed young girls and women principally.

It would be impossible to make an inventory of all the rules that constitute the ideal code of good manners. But if one reflects a little, this code rests on two essential foundations from which all else is derived. To know these foundations is to own the key that will open the right door, no matter where and no matter the circumstances. The first of these principles is, to my mind, respect for others; the second is the law of exchange or reciprocity. Nobody can always be giving or always be receiving: this one-way street is a dead-end street.

Readers will appreciate that every book, even a book about *savoir-vivre*, is an expression of the personality of its author. In the following pages, you will no doubt discover that although I like people of tradition, I do not like hypocrites. Thus, I have broached certain topics about real existence and which are part of every-day living with the frankness of a Mrs Shameless, and at the risk of creating some controversy, and of shocking traditional decency.

I have written this guide with a wish: that it may light a spark, ignite your dreams, and paint your ambitions with the colours of a brilliant life.

I

SAVOIR VIVRE WITH OURSELVES

In the order of civility and politeness, who deserves your respect in the first place? Can you guess? You, of course. The more respect you have for yourself, for your person, and the more you will know how to respect others. I am entirely convinced that it is impossible to respect others if we have no self-respect.

Therefore, before we do anything else, we must build for ourselves the most positive self-image, in every possible ways and by every possible means. This standard can change your life.

But what is self-respect?

Let us start at the beginning. Firstly, you must consider yourself worthy of every care and attention.

You deserve the best and will not be content with a "That will do". Because it will not do!

So, take care of yourself, make yourself happy, treat yourself to simple pleasures. I have often noted that, unlike men who are so easily accepting of their own pleasures, women tend to be rather hard on themselves: They punish themselves, deny themselves, and hold themselves back. Women seem to give to others by taking from themselves, by denying themselves.

Now, you would not think of catching up with your friends in a stained or crumpled dress, with your hair in a mess. And you may have noticed that a bad sense of dress leads to a downwardly slippery type of scepticism and the eternal: "What's the point?" What is the point of dressing nicely? What is the point of going out? What is the point of travelling? What is the point of being alive?

Failure in the rules of elegance or simply in those of hygiene (do I need to mention the benefits of a daily shower?), even in a small way, can quickly lead to a failure in other areas of life: less rigor in the choice of your dress or shoes and next, there goes the discipline in your thoughts, in your choice of leisure activities, in your friendships, and in your morality…

If you choose the path of least effort, you will have ever fewer reasons to be satisfied with yourself. I would never serve tea to my guests in a chipped cup. And so, why would I do to myself, something I would not do to another?

This evening, if you are dining alone, before coming home, buy yourself a flower, or a nice little dessert, something that brings you pleasure. And if you are out of perfume, don't wait until it is your birthday in the hope that someone will think of offering you some as a gift.

Don't wait. Life passes too rapidly. Become a fulfilled and radiant woman, even if you live on your own. In any case, dependence is always a risk. Take charge of yourself, you are perfectly capable of it: you have already cared for your children, your husband, your parents. Show yourself the kindness and attention you show them.

And above all, never sink into self-pity. Do not revel in the narration of your health issues, or work or family. You will gain nothing by this and only lose your power. A difficulty, a failure can be overcome if we have the will to take responsibility.

And if you should make a mistake (indeed who doesn't?) don't judge yourself too severely, don't accuse yourself of being incompetent or incapable. Remember Spinoza's words: "Remorse is a second failing". Accept yourself as you are, as your birth, your education and the story of your life have made you.

To live well with ourselves, we need one commandment: *Love Thyself.*

FEMININE ELEGANCE

One evening, during a dinner party, I asked my friends what positive changes they would expect a book on *savoir-vivre* to bring to people's lives.

Serge, a writer and aesthete, replied: "Nadine, if your book could only teach people to be clean and correctly dressed, you would be acting for the public good!"

Now, this would be a mission impossible. Of course, I have no ambition to change the world or to reform society. Who could? Rather, I add my voice to the voice of others, in the hope to rally a few of you to the pursuit of a word so beautiful that it has become international: *élégance*.

Classical theatre obeyed three rules: the unity of time, the unity of action, and the unity of place. Elegance too obeys three rules: the rule of age, the rule of timeliness, and the rule of context.

Is *élégance* the same as fashion?

Take a dress, for example. On a young woman, the look may be sublime, on a woman of forty, ridiculous. A sense of dress does not develop in a vacuum, it obeys the law of liquids: clothes take on the shape of the body they cover. In the evening, unless a woman is twenty, she should not go out in jeans or a short jacket, and when attending a wedding, even if the ceremony takes place at mid-day, she should be dressed for the occasion.

Indeed, following fashion blindly leads to excesses and signals a lack of imagination.

In France, the President of the Republic remains in Paris until 14 July to watch over our armies marching on the

Champs-Elysées, and on 23 July, the fashion *pasionaria* fly in from all the corners of the earth to Paris, to watch, not very far from the Champs-Elysées, the catwalk presentations of our great designers. Indeed, to each, his or her parade!

I follow fashion, but with small steps. And I have shown exemplary loyalty towards Pierre Cardin's dresses and ensembles. For years now, I have had them cut and re-cut, with the smallest alterations, from a variety of fabrics and in a variety of hues.

What to wear, when and where...

Re-reading the original edition of the present book which was first published in 1991, I got a good sense of how much fashion had changed in only one decade. By 2001, the little chiffon dress which I had recommended as an essential item, had made way for the pant-suit which is now so ubiquitous that it has become a virtual uniform. I would be looking in vain to find one of our many women now in government office exposing the curve of a calf! And what a pity!

But fashion moves so fast, that today in 2015, my advice risks becoming…"unfashionable" within only a few months. Therefore, I will limit my advice to essential rules and the basics.

I will not speak of sweaters, tee-shirts or skirts, and only briefly mention blouses and accessories. And I will leave the rest of the discussion to the writers of the fashion magazines who so excel in guiding their readers' desires and choices at the return of the seasons.

Dresses

Always choose quality over quantity. It is better to possess a single dress that is well cut and of irreproachable quality than three mediocre outfits. When you trust in what you are wearing, your demeanour reflects your self-confidence and emanates a natural ease. If your wardrobe is limited, choose darker colours for winter: black, grey, dark green, red. Then move to white or pastels, light hues: pink, sky blue or light green. In summer, all colours and prints are suitable.

The little black dress

Over the past forty years, the black dress has been unbeatable; in today's language we call it a "must-have". The black dress dresses up the eighteen year old girl as well as the woman of eighty. It is the most elegant of all dresses, the dress we can wear in all confidence. Black can match and uplift jewellery of whatever colour or shape. Black also goes with any accessory: belts, shoes, bags, or scarves, be those red, blue, brown, green, pink, yellow, violet, white or turquoise... With black, no colour needs be excluded.

At what hour of the day may one begin to wear black? Well, unless it is of satin, silk, crêpe or velour, as early as 9:00 am. There is no limit placed on jerseys, woollens, gabardines, knits, cashmere, cotton, poplin, or linen...

Tailored suits (pants or skirts)

The basis of a wardrobe is the tailored suit. Not one but three: a casual suit, a dressier ensemble for lunch and one for the evening (the latter preferably in black). Classic ensemble for daywear may be in tweed, jersey, wool if Armani, twill or knit, in either a single colour, hounds-tooth, tartan, or Prince of Wales.

The evening dress

Short evening dresses have flair and chic. However, Yves Saint Laurent's long black evening velour and lace dresses made a dazzling come-back at the turn of the millennium. In summer, an evening dress should be a feast of colours – fireworks!

Blouses

Poplin, foulard, jersey, and silk should be worn in the daytime. And linen, cotton, or viscose in summer. Printed silk and satins are suitable for a luncheon, and at dinner, choose from silk crepes, muslin, damask, brocades, and brochés.

Trousers

Today, all women wear pants. To be perfectly honest, only the slimmest of women, and only those over five feet five, can truly look elegant in trousers. However, the comfort that trousers provide is unbeatable and all of us succumb to it, myself included.

Jeans

Jeans have become an institution, like refrigerators and televisions. Men, women, children, babies, the elderly, the destitute and the billionaires have all worn, are all wearing or will be wearing jeans. One does not fight against an institution, one bears with it.

Coats

In France, the word and the thing have been replaced among the young by *la doudoune*, the down or puffer jacket.
An elegant woman, however, has several coats:
- a sporty, casual coat – with or without a belt – in taupe, brown, dark green, red or beige,
- a dress coat, in a dark black, dark grey or flamboyant red,
- a raincoat, Burberry style,
- a fur lined cloak, in an outer gabardine either in beige, brown or olive green, lined with fur from rabbit to sable.

Cape

May be either in wool or cashmere; soft, warm and light, it is the most elegant of feminine attire.

Tips and manners

- Do not lift your dress or coat when sitting down.

11

- When buying a coat, take your husband along with you, for discreet and reliable advice. Too often, women dress to please other women even though they actually wish to be attractive to men.
- When in the store, before trying on a garment that you must step into, take your shoes off, to avoid dirtying or catching the hem with your heels. In the same vein, before trying on a dress or a blouse, to make sure you don't leave traces of make-up, ask the salesperson for a piece of muslin to cover your face. This should avoid any unpleasantness.

Accessories

Accessories, shoes and bags, are an important part of my wardrobe. Being a romantic, I welcomed the return of the hat: I love *lace veils* and toques, scarves and capes. But it is with jewellery that I am truly playful. I wear jewellery, real and false, at all hours of the day!

Hats

And I love hats. I wear hats in all seasons, summer and winter, and I buy them wherever I happen to be, except in London. I find the hats in London incomparably ugly.

In winter, fur hats even faux lend beauty to a plain face, conferring upon it the Slavic charm of an Anna Karenina. The black toque has always been for me the most sensual symbol of femininity. Borsalino hats can only suit a casual dress. In summer, I wrap a cotton scarf around a straw hat, a *cache-misère* that saves daily blow-drying.

Shoes

The foot, it is said, has erotic power. Perhaps this is indeed true. What is certain, however, is that shoes play a primordial role in elegance: if the heel of your shoe is worn, or its toe is scratched, this is the end of it. A shoe must be impeccable, with impeccable shine. It must also not be too tight, nor too broad or too flat, nor so high as to destabilise your walk, which renders one ridiculous.

I like my shoes, unlike my handbags, to be of the same colour as my dress or suit. The brown and black Chanel escarpins are suited to almost every style of dress.

Moccasins or small boots go well with a casual sporty outfit. Evening shoes, with strass, beads, or sequins should only be worn in the evening as the name implies. In summer, flat pumps, sandals, and open shoes rather than the classic shoe, are good for fun and imagination.

Running and sport shoes

American women, who can be more concerned with comfort than with elegance, have transmitted to us the virus of the running shoe! For sports, hiking, shopping, and for the health of your back, sport shoes are simply marvellous. In leather and suede, and in colour, they can be almost elegant. And after years of resistance, even the great designers Hermès and Gucci have finally conceded to the obligation of designing sport shoes for their women clients.

13

Handbags

The handbag you are carrying should be made of the same material as the shoes you are wearing. You should not wear leather shoes with a suede handbag, or lizard shoes with a crocodile bag, even if they are in the same tones. However, you may wear black kid leather shoes and carry a red, blue, green, or purple kid leather bag.

This said, even the most exclusive of leather designers have to bow a little to trends and fashions, and all have become more playful.

Evening bags

In a small format, evening bags are made of satin, velvet, lamé, strass, beaded or tapestry fabrics. My personal preferences lean towards the pochette, in velour, satin or suede and in the brightest colours.

Belts

They are potentially the architectural element of a dress, a skirt or trousers. However, unlike a man's belt which actually serves the purpose of holding up trousers, a woman's belt attracts the eyes of the onlooker, especially if the waist that it is encircling is slim. But then again, who would ever think of bringing attention to a thick waist. A good wardrobe should contain several belts, in classic and casual styles. Today, belts can also be true works of art.

Gloves

Whatever happened to the pretty little white gloves, in lace, Marcella, or kid leather that always returned in summer? Do they now exist only in our imagination? Did the practice of sports and the love of tanned skin consign the gloves to the dress museum? Only the winter gloves, in either wool, kid leather or suede, and usually lined with cashmere or silk, have remained with us.

Should gloves be the same colour as the shoes you are wearing? The answer is yes, your gloves should be the same colour as your shoes.

Scarves

Scarves quietly accumulate in our wardrobes over the years. We keep them all, even those we no longer wear because each has sentimental value, attached to a memory; this scarf was offered to you by your husband, this other by your mother or your daughter or son, or a beloved... It is in any case impossible to do away with it! Where should you wear a scarf? In town, in the country, on the beach or in the mountains: anywhere will do! Scarves will cheer a dark outfit and soften its severity.

Knitted scarves

Whether in wool or cashmere, knitted scarves have become the number one accessory. Ever longer, you can roll them around the neck several times over. And today, even men ask to be given knitted scarves on their birthdays!

Pochettes

Pochettes add class to a tailored dress-suit. I often used my husband's as I found them brighter than mine. But lace pochettes also have a charm which fully satisfies my appreciation of femininity.

Handkerchiefs

As for the handkerchiefs: please do keep tissue paper in your bathroom, not in your handbags! Reclaim the small squares of batiste and lace your great-grandmothers used to own; in your spare time, embroider your initials, and before placing them in your handbag, remember to add a tear drop of perfume.

Medals and Decorations

Men no longer have the monopoly on decorations and medals. Women also obtain the Légion d'Honneur, academic honours, and other decorations including foreign medals. Medals and decorations are worn on a ribbon attached to a buttonhole, or on the shoulder of a dress.

Perfumes and eau de toilette

Imagine what a canvas painted by a grand master might look like without a frame. No doubt, you will find the work superb but you will more than likely be inclined to think that something is missing, that the work is somehow incomplete. The same applies to an elegant woman who is not wearing perfume. Perfume exalts all of the senses, converses with the imagination, courts sensuality, calls for a kiss, wakes emotions and sentiments, and infuses memories.

But to wear a perfume is not enough: you must find the right perfume, a perfume that agrees with your skin, your personality, your profession. A heady sensual brunette may not wear the same perfume as a Scandinavian blonde or an Irish red-head. A medical doctor does not wear the perfume of a cover-girl. You must therefore experiment with several perfumes before settling on *your* perfume, the perfume with which you will become identified. Unless, of course, you find pleasure in infidelity, as I do. Yes, I change my perfume regularly; I leave and I return to perfumes, as boredom or interest take my fancy.

Only married men have reason to fear perfumed women, because their own spouses will no doubt pick up the scent on the collar of their shirt and remember *L'Heure bleue* by Guerlain or *Eau* by Issey Miyaké... As to the (im)morality of this story: Gentlemen, you had better offer your mistresses the same perfume you offer your wives!

I might not be Sherlock Holmes but I do have a nose. And I did once discover that such a liaison had occurred, one weekend, under my own roof, thanks to a trace of perfume hovering in the air. Entering the bedroom where one of my guests (a bachelor) had stayed, I found irrefutable proof of the crime: the perfume of the lady in black. And so, ladies, if you do not wish the murderer to be uncovered, make sure the weapon has disappeared!

But even a faithful woman's perfume should be discreet. We must always use perfume with moderation. Perfume should neither announce our arrival, nor stubbornly remain in the room after our departure. Perfume ought to follow you as your shadow.

Where should you apply perfume? Behind the ear, on the wrist, between your breasts.

When should you wear perfume? Perfume is only suitable for evening and night life. In the morning, wear eau de toilette. In the countryside, wear eau de toilette also and with great moderation, and nothing at all when in the wilderness.

Savoir-vivre and jewellery

Over the years, a woman will accumulate jewellery. While she may well dispose of a ring or a necklace without a hint of regret, she will no doubt hold onto her precious pieces for the rest of her life. The more advanced in years she is, the more meaningful her jewels are to her. When at forty, she no longer feels right wearing the little gold broach with the three pearls her young husband had offered her on their first wedding anniversary, or the delicate ring of white silver with the minuscule sapphire she had bought during a trip to Bali, she will keep them at the bottom of her jewellery box, as nostalgic keepsakes. Or she will offer them to her daughters when they are old enough to wear them. This is how jewellery passes from mother to daughter or to daughter-in-law.

Jewellery should be worn according to time and circumstances: a few pieces in the morning. For a weekend in the country, wear casual jewellery, either a watch, a *gourmette* [2] or a simple chain. No sonorous or showy jewellery should ever be worn when visiting a sporting facility, a place of worship or a hospital.

If you have very beautiful jewellery, whether it is costume jewellery or real gems, observe the rule of never wearing a lot of them at one time. A woman covered in rings, necklaces and bracelets lacks elegance. In the same vein, if you are hosting a party, keep your choice of jewellery discreet so as not to eclipse your women guests. Should one mix real gems and paste? There are two schools of thought, the school of the purists and that of Coco Chanel who enjoyed, with a little perversity, wearing the purest of pearls with cheap chain necklaces. I shall leave it up to you to choose your side on the matter.

What jewellery should we wear during the day?

- At a casual lunch in a bistro: you may wear a thick gold or silver necklace, or a chain necklace with stones and matching earrings, but do not add bracelets or rings to the mix.
- At an elegant lunch: you may wear several rows of pearls real or false, and either white or coloured, or a necklace with small and multi-coloured stones as for example, white, pink or red coral, turquoise, lapis lazuli, or a torsade of tourmaline. Your earrings

---

[2] A gold chain with a small badge, which is often inscribed with the first name of its owner.

should match the dominant hue of your necklace. Add rings but no bracelets. You may also swap the necklace for a pretty broach with hard stones, pinned on the lapel of your dress-suit or on the sleeve of your dress.

- To a cocktail or dinner: if you are wearing a black dress, you may allow yourself more jewellery. But on a printed or brightly coloured dress, you should limit yourself to a few reasonably sized coloured pieces. And remember that when in doubt, it is always best to wear less than to risk wearing too much.
- In the evening: with a long evening dress, you should never wear a watch, even a diamond incrusted watch: for time stops during a ball or a party. A few larger pieces go well with a simple dress in a single colour.

Rings

Rings deserve a special mention. At the risk of displeasing many, I would advise women to wear rings only if they have fine elegant hands and long supple fingers. Today, precious and semi-precious stones are mounted on yellow gold. But diamonds will keep their brilliance whether they are set in a gold or platinum ring.

Wedding rings

They may be of yellow or white gold and consist of either a single ring or triple interlaced rings. In the north of France, they are worn on the right hand, and in the south of France as in all the other Latin countries, they are worn on the left hand.

Diamond wedding rings, which were once worn only at cocktail or dinner parties, may now be worn throughout the day.

A stone for every woman
and
a symbol for every stone

- Garnets symbolise love and loyalty and belong to January.
- Amethysts are symbols of sincerity and belong to February.
- Rubies are omens of passion and thunder to be offered in March.
- Sapphires and diamonds share the month of April, the first is a symbol of true friendship, the second a symbol of eternal love.
- Emeralds herald the month of May and a happy love life.
- Agates and coral bring to the woman born in June long life and a brilliant career.
- August is under the influence of Lapis Lazuli, the symbol of matrimonial fidelity.
- Chrysolites protect women born in September from the madness of passion.
- Aqua-marines are the stones of hope and preside over October.
- To those born in November, topaz promise prosperity… but also infidelity.
- Turquoises symbolise friendship, and malachites forecast successes for all we undertake in December.
- And never forget that there is no stone more precious or more beautiful than your smile.

Advice to young women

You may feel a tad resentful that your mother fought to acquire the gender equality that you can now take for granted. Ever since the victory of the Women's Liberation Movement, men, you complain, have abandoned courtesy. But perhaps, as a reaction, have you perhaps ceased to act in a feminine manner? In your tom-boyishness, have you not encouraged them to become a little less considerate?

I believe that it is not too late to take a few steps back, to reinstate the rituals of seduction, and for women to regain their privileged status. For this to happen, however, women need to forgo familiarity, triviality, despondency and all vulgarity.

Why not cultivate mystery, secrets, false indifference and even a little frivolity? Do not give yourself up at the first flutter of the heart: learn to be desirable. Marilyn Monroe is still one of your idols? Try to imitate her inimitable femininity.

Here is a little advice on etiquette:

- ❖ Do not stand when a young man comes to greet you, but hold out your hand first. However, always wait until an older person holds out her hand to you before shaking.
- ❖ Do not smoke in the street, and never hold your cigarettes to your lips when speaking, greeting someone or dancing; at dinner, do not light up while you are eating. Always wait until coffee has been served before smoking.
- ❖ Do not take the first seat in a living room, wait until the other women have sat down. The same goes for

the dinner table, wait until your parents and grandparents are seated before sitting down yourself.

❖ Do not slouch when sitting in an armchair or a sofa, and don't put your feet on the coffee table! Keep your back straight, do not cross your legs, or spread your knees, even when you are wearing pants. Keep your knees together with your feet slightly crossed.

❖ You should stand when accepting a glass or a plate from a person who is older than you. You must offer to help the hostess who has invited you, or your mother, to serve the tea and refreshments, as well as to set and clear the table.

❖ When a young man helps you with your coat, thank him with a pleasant smile and say: Thank you, Jean-Philippe...

❖ If you really must hitchhike, only ever accept rides from women.

❖ To sit in a car with elegance, you need to sit at an angle first and then bring your legs into the car by turning your hips. To get out of the car, bring your legs out first, keeping your knees together, place your feet on the ground first. A woman in pants has often a tendency to adopt masculine movements, to sit with knees apart, or with a leg on top of a knee, or with her feet on the table – all of these are truly regrettable postures.

❖ Women tend to drive more cautiously than men, but they also have a tendency to forget that the most beautiful machines must be maintained, and that a beautiful car should be cleaned. Don't leave your clothes, tennis rackets, or empty bags on the seats, or an odd shoe, paper or plastic wrappings, or empty cigarette boxes on the floor of the car.

❖ Your car should be as neat and as clean as your bathroom or your kitchen. Don't make the person who is taking the seat next to you do your housework before she or he can find a place to sit.

Savoir-vivre and femininity

This summer, on the beach in Biarritz, I spent some time observing a young couple, aged no more than twenty-five. I watched their backs, as they stripped off their clothes with the natural grace of noble savages.

They took off their identical grey tee shirts; they removed their identical faded jeans, their worn out sandshoes, their socks, red and green, respectively. They both had very short hair, but in the same style, although one head was lighter than the other. They were both very thin and almost androgynous, so that in their nakedness, I could not tell from looking at their backs which was the woman and which was the man – I even wondered if they were not a couple of boys or girls. One of them had on his arm, a tattoo of a winged heart. Ah, that is the man! I thought. But I was wrong, the winged heart belonged to Eve emerging from the waters! Where was the charm of seduction? On what wings of desire had flown the dreams and fantasies of love?

Femininity, I do admit, is a prism with an infinite number of mirrors. Femininity may take on a myriad aspects, ranging from extreme modesty to extreme immodesty. Some men will tell you that a nun in a habit and under a large hat is desirable. Grace Kelly who set off millions of heartbeats never revealed a breast. But the immodesty of Brigitte Bardot in Vadim's *God Created Woman* caused such a profoundly

24

disturbing scandal that an entire generation of young people identified with it.

This said, when an older woman lacks modesty, her bearing becomes somewhat insolent or aggressive, and it will put one off or even frighten. Seduction is a mystery, but mystery is also one of the major ingredients of seduction. In order to seduce Herod, Salomé had wrapped herself in seven veils. Among all of the women I have met, those whose lives were triumphant were not especially beautiful. Beauty provokes a strong emotional response which, like all other emotions, eventually quietens and fades away. Sooner or later, the wonder of the first encounter dissipates like mist before the sun. If beauty is without charm, it soon ceases to have an effect.

No one can choose to be beautiful: beauty is a gift, bestowed or not, but to some extent, we can choose to be charming, because charm can be cultivated, developed, and so charm can blossom.

MASCULINE ELEGANCE

London is still the capital of masculine elegance. Italian and French couturiers have class, imagination, and brio. But the English have something more, they have tradition. And this, translated into dry or soft, high quality fabrics, and style gives us Fashion pronounced with a certain upper-lip. Madame, if you would like your husband to look like a Gentleman of the City, dress him in London.

But what should his wardrobe contain?

What to wear

In town

- A dark grey flannel suit
- A Prince of Wales suit
- Harris Tweed grey
- A gabardine suit, either in beige or tobacco
- A dark blue blazer with a pair of grey flannel trousers
- A very dark blue suit.

A suit should never be brown. Brown should be reserved for sport clothes. The three-piece suit is little worn these days. The vest has been replaced by a woollen or cashmere vest either dark blue, wine coloured, grey, light blue, or yellow.

Shirts

All striped or plain coloured poplin shirts with cuffs must be worn with cuff-links. The cuff should not be more than two or three centimetres longer than the jacket sleeve. Remember that a man whose cuffs cover half of his hands looks ridiculous.

Shirts with buttoned up collars are for casual wear. Short-sleeved shirts should not really be worn under a jacket, and especially so in winter time.

Overcoats

- A dark blue overcoat
- A grey overcoat
- A camel hair overcoat (for men over 180 cm tall)
- A Loden
- A raincoat
- No fur coat
- And do not forget the parka jacket, it is indispensable.

Casual suits

- A tweed jacket to be worn with corduroy pants
- A linen suit
- A cotton suit
- Jeans – suitable so long … so long as a man is slim enough, and he has a flat stomach.

27

Once upon a time, in England, at the end of dinner, at the point when women left the dining room, men removed their tailcoats which they handed over to their footmen, and they put on their smoking jackets. After smoking the last cigar, they took off this garment and dressed again in their suit jackets. They then re-joined the ladies without fear of incommoding them with the smell of cigar smoke.

The most elegant smoking jackets are made of *grain de poudre*, in Barratea, either in wool or mohair or in one of the other fine wools. The jackets are black with folded cuffs in either mat satin or ottoman. In summer, the smoking jacket may be of white silk and the pants of a black gabardine in light wool. The jacket is worn over a simple or finely pleated white shirt with musketeer cuffs, a black bow-tie, and a belt.

Socks are black (preferably not transparent) and the shoes are in black patent leather. Add to this a white or playful pochette. The lapels of a suit can be highlighted with a few pearls. Pearls or enamel may also complement the smoking jacket.

A man in a smoking jacket should never wear a casual or sporty wristwatch, whilst a suit requires a pocket watch.

Accessories

Ties

Did you know that our French word for tie, *cravate*, comes from the word *croata*? In other words, it originates in Croatia where it was once worn by cavalry soldiers. But it is now a universal accessory that reflects the taste and the personality of the man who wears it. The tie can be creative or traditional, it can reveal a man's indifference to dress or identify a keen dresser, suggest an audacious or a timid man. One of the world's most famous makers of ties is Croatian, and his label is… Croata.

Madame, you may offer the man of your life a silk tie, or foulard, in cashmere, silk or wool. But your taste and your responsibility may be contested. Be cautious and accept the idea that your husband may wish to exchange it. As for you, Monsieur, remember that you should wear a tie with the colours and patterns of a club only if you belong to that club. In summer, swap your tie for a kerchief.

Bowties

Perhaps, bowties have become even more traditional than ties. Unless they are on television, young men rarely wear them.

Pochettes

These are the only fun and casual element of the masculine dress. Today, there is no requirement to match the pochette to the tie.

Handkerchiefs

A white batiste handkerchief is always worn in the breast pocket, and must be folded horizontally.

Cuff-links

They should be in a classic style and not look like large pieces of money or be otherwise ostentatious. Passementerie cuff-links can be worn with coloured shirts.

Socks

I measure the elegance of a man by looking at his socks. When his socks are too short, even the most beautiful man appears a lot less so. Socks must reach the knees. Socks should never be white (unless one is playing tennis or sailing), transparent or made of synthetic material; the sock must be made of Scottish thread, fine wool or cashmere. Socks should match the colour of the pants or the shoes.

Shoes

- Buckled or laced shoes
- Moccasins

Choose either leather, suede, box leather: black, brown, yellow. Do not wear snake, crocodile or ostrich leather.

Belts

To go with a city suit, a belt should be in black, brown or ochre box leather. The buckle, which can be either in silver or "gold", should not carry the initials of a famous designer.

Hats

- A felt hat for those who love Humphrey Bogart
- A hunting cap
- A fur hat for those who suffer from the cold.

Jewellery

- A wedding ring is not a piece of jewellery, it is a symbol that should never leave your finger.
- You may wear a signet ring if you have a coat of arms,
- A tie pin
- A pocket watch. I noticed recently, that young men are again wearing these.

Scent

After using after-shave, a man will add a subtle and masculine eau de toilette – but no flowery scents! A few drops on a handkerchief will do.

A man (especially if he is no longer young) should not be seen wearing the following:

- A singlet or tee shirt visible under the shirt: you will give the impression of an old fashioned gentleman afraid of the cold.
- Short-sleeved shirts under a jacket
- *Gourmettes* (chain bracelets)
- Chains around the neck
- Rings (except for a signet ring)

- After the age of sixty: a kerchief-less open neck shirt under a jacket
- A shirt with a lace jabot under a smoking jacket
- His coat of arms on his handkerchiefs, undergarments or bathrobe. A coat of arms is embroidered on bed sheets, tablecloths and napkins, and initials are embroidered on a handkerchief or a shirt.

Advice for young men

If you are shy (all young men are shy), you have all the more reasons to be proficient in social etiquette and *savoir-vivre*. For you will never find yourself stepping into a *salon* filled with unfamiliar persons, feeling at a loss, paralysed, not knowing what you should say or do. The greater your *savoir-vivre*, the faster you will overcome your shyness.

❖ When entering a room during a reception or a formal party, make sure that you are first introduced to the hostess and the host. You can also introduce yourself, giving your first name and your surname. You may kiss the hostess' hand and give a ceremonious bow.

❖ Never hold out your hand to a young woman, or indeed to either a woman or a man older than yourself. Bow slightly when taking the hand that is held out to you. And please, do not leave your left hand in your pocket.

❖ At a formal party, do not sit before anyone else, wait until all the women have taken a seat. You must stand up every time a woman walks into the room where you are seated, and also when a woman leaves the table. Stand when she returns to sit at the table. At home, wait until your grandparents and your parents are seated before taking your place at the table.

❖ When a woman sits at your table, help her pull out her chair, and then move it in towards her as she is sitting down.

❖ At a formal party, if you befriend a young woman, do not exchange business cards, rather write each other's details in your respective agendas.

❖ On the other hand, we exchange business cards when we meet someone in the street or in a public or professional space. In any case, it is up to the young man to call on the young lady first, either by writing or telephoning.

❖ If you are seated when a young woman comes to greet you, you must immediately stand up, and shake the hand that she is holding out to you – you do not kiss the hand of a young woman. At the door, you move to the side and let her pass before you, except when entering a restaurant: Here you should go first. When walking together on the footpath, you should walk closest to the curb. Your lady friend has the high ground.

❖ When walking upstairs in the company of a lady, you should go first – for once upon a time, it would have been scandalous for a man to catch even a glance of a woman's ankle. Today, skirts have almost disappeared but the rule is still with us! Going downstairs, you should also precede the lady so as to catch her in your arms if she happens to trip.

❖ A young man should help a young lady with her jacket or her coat.

❖ Do not dance, speak or greet anyone with a cigarette hanging on your lips. Do not eat while smoking. And finally, don't squash your cigarette butt in your plate, on the floor or on the lawn – use an ashtray.

❖ Never light up in the room of a sick person.

❖ Stand up to take up a plate or a glass that a person who is older than you is holding out to you, and help with clearing the table. Doing the dishes is no longer a woman's prerogative!

❖ If you invite a young woman to dance, you should accompany her back to her table; if you invite her out, you should see that she gets home safely.

❖ If you have been invited to a weekend in the country, help your hosts with mowing the lawn, pruning, shopping, cleaning the car, or moving garden furniture. Be a pleasant and useful guest.

❖ If you practice a sport, abide by the rules of your club and your trainer. Follow safety regulations and wear appropriate clothing. Remember to play fair: the man who knows how to lose is more admirable than the man who wins at all cost.

II

SAVOIR-VIVRE

AND

LIFE'S EVENTS

THE ENGAGEMENT

What has become of the Engagement? Today, could we still find a father dressed in striped blue trousers and cream-coloured clothes paying a visit to prospective in-laws, and asking for the hand of the young lady on behalf of his son?

I recently asked a friend of mine, most definitely a member of the high bourgeoisie, if he would succumb to such a custom. To this, he answered: "*Me*, go to a young woman's home, decked out in this ridiculous manner, to ask for her hand on behalf of my son? Surely, you are joking! Although, it might occur to me to send an email or a fax!"

His reply both amused and disappointed me. And I am still convinced that in the provinces, among the great and ancient families, the tradition of the Engagement is maintained. At any rate, it is certainly permissible today for the young man to engage in this enterprise on his own behalf. And the meeting with his future father-in-law may well take place in the latter's office, rather than at the young lady's home.

The engagement party

When parents grant their daughter's hand to their future son-in-law, custom requires that the two families (especially if they have not as yet been introduced) should get together over lunch or dinner. If the event is small and intimate, the bride-to-be's parents cover the cost. If the event is a large party and many people are invited, then the cost of the reception should be shared by both families. The groom-to-be, his relatives and friends, send bunches of white or pastel coloured flowers in the morning.

The young man offers the engagement ring to his future bride in private, before lunch or dinner. She will wear this ring for the rest of her life. At least, we certainly wish her to do so.

Parents, grandparents, siblings and their spouses take part in the engagement celebrations. The place of honour at the table is reserved for the woman's grandparents. The engaged couple should be at the head of the table and seated next to each other. [3] The young man's parents will reciprocate by giving a dinner or a luncheon within a month of this first celebration.

During the engagement dinner, either the young man himself or his mother introduces the future bride to their side of the family and friends. A future mother-in-law introduces her future son-in-law.

Should one send out notices of the engagement?

Yes, and both families should write the announcement on the same card.

---

[3] Note that in French etiquette, the places of honor are not at the head of the table, but at the centre, on opposite side of the table. In other words, the host and hostess (or the guests of honour) do not preside over the table as is done in Anglo-Saxon cultures, but sit among their guests.

> *Monsieur and Madame Philippe Poiré*
> *Monsieur and Madame Jacques Bonan*
>
> *are pleased to announce the engagement of their*
> *children, Sophie and Marco*
> *January 2002*
>
> 116, rue de La Boétie   Villa Marina
> 75 008 PARIS   56, rue des Maltais
>   Carthage

On an engagement card, the young woman's name is always announced before the young man's. In other words, one always writes Sophie and Marco and never Marco and Sophie.

If the families are organizing a reception, the invitation should read as follows:

> *Monsieur and Madame Philippe Poiré*
> *Monsieur and Madame Jacques Bonan*
>
> *are pleased to invite you to the engagement of their*
> *children, Sophie and Marco*
> *Sunday 7 January 2002, beginning 3 pm*
>
> **R.S.V.P.**   116, rue de La Boétie
>   75 008 PARIS

Evidently, the card must provide the address of the reception. If only one family is inviting, then the invitation card shows only the name of the family hosting the engagement party.

> *Monsieur and Madame Philippe Poiré*
> *are pleased to invite you*
> *to the engagement of their*
> *daughter Sophie*
> *to Monsieur Marco Bonan,*
> *Sunday 7 January 2002,*
> *beginning 3 pm*
>
> **R.S.V.P.**
> 116, rue de La Boétie
> 75 008 PARIS

The engagement may also be announced in the society pages of the newspaper.

On several occasions while in London, I was told the story (which I am about to recount for all it is worth) of a dinner that the famous writer Barbara Cartland gave for her step-granddaughter's eighteenth birthday. The hostess had convened the most brilliant young persons which British gentry could supply. The evening was a great success, and everyone was wondering which of the young men would be the lucky chosen one.

At dawn, when Diana, the queen of the evening, was taking leave of her friends, she tripped on the stairs, and only just managed to get hold of.... ? Of nothing less than her tragic destiny, the Prince of Wales himself, the heir to the throne.

Breaking up an engagement

Sometimes an engagement is broken, perhaps, only days before the wedding. In this case, the betrothed must announce their decision personally and without intermediaries. Firstly, and before anyone else, they must notify their parents and other intimates and do this in person. If wedding invitations have already been posted, a notice should be inserted in the newspapers to inform all concerned persons that the wedding has been postponed to a later date. Everyone will know the true signification.

There is no need to give the precise reasons for the breakup, it is enough to say "personal reasons". The young woman gives her ring back to her fiancé along with the valuable presents. Both return the wedding gifts which they received ahead of time.

THE WEDDING

The happiest day of your life has arrived! While weddings no longer have the pomp and solemnity they once commanded, the wedding day remains a unique event, a symbolic frontier beyond which individuals are transformed. Make sure your wedding day (your *first* wedding day) remains one of your most precious memories, and the most beautiful of all parties.

Everything there is to know about marriage and weddings

When to marry and how old?

A young woman may marry at age fifteen, with the consent of her parents. If her parents refuse to give their consent, the President of the Republic can grant a dispensation of the legal minimal marriageable age at the young couple's request and on the basis of some serious reason. Otherwise, she can marry when she reaches her legal majority, at eighteen years of age. Young men may marry at eighteen.

Ten days before the wedding date, the wedding bans are published at the Town Hall of the municipality where the couple intends to reside. The bans announce the planned wedding date along with the couple's family names, first names, professions, current residences and intended residence. Note that the civil service celebrant cannot proceed with the publication of the marriage bans until the couple has provided:

1) x-rays and HIV tests,
2) a birth certificate issued within the past three months, and
3) the forms provided with the "Guide for future married couples" (which will be given to the couple by the Town Hall). These forms must be filled and signed.

In principle, widowed and divorced persons cannot remarry within three hundred days after either the death of their spouses or the divorce.

The marriage contract

The dowry (in cash and kind) has disappeared. However, parents can nevertheless endow their children with either cash or real estate upon their marriage. The marriage contract, drawn and signed before a solicitor, allows the couple to agree on what property they will hold in common and which will remain in their individual possession. The solicitor provides advice on the basis of the partners' professional standing and personal wealth.

Should they decide not to marry under contract, they will be subject to the law of January 1966 and the community of acquisition, under which property and wealth acquired in common are automatically held jointly. Each spouse thus retains the sole property of goods, real estate and wealth acquired prior to the marriage, along with other goods and properties, as for example, personal gifts, legacies or inheritance which have been acquired individually.

When both spouses have substantial independent wealth, solicitors always advise the couple to draw a marriage contract separating their respective wealth and property. In the case of an eventual divorce, this avoids disputes and petty arguments.

The wedding invitations

Usually, the couple's parents send out the wedding invitations at least a month prior to the wedding day. But how should they organise the guest-list for the wedding?

The best method is for parents, in-laws, the groom and the bride to begin by each drawing up their own list. Once this is done, they can meet one evening or during a weekend to draw a final common list from these four individual lists. The point of the exercise is to make sure that no-one, relative, friend or connection, has been forgotten. Once this final list has been established, it is split in half.

The first half lists all the people you wish to communicate your coming wedding to. The second and shorter list includes all the persons you wish to actually invite to the wedding reception, which will take place either after the civil ceremony or the religious ceremony.

The invitation to the wedding ceremony is either printed or etched on two doubled sheets of velum, or on a unique, larger sheet, formatted Italian style; the left-hand inner sheet is reserved for the bride's family while the right-hand sheet is the groom's. The paper should be white or (better) ivory, the font is simple and italicised.

On the second sheet, the groom's parents announce their son's coming wedding in the same manner as given below. They include their own address. The parents or their children's honorary and official titles, their awards and medals (French uniquely), or their university titles and grades are indicated where appropriate.

> *Monsieur and Madame André Champigny[4]*
> *have the honour of announcing*
> *the wedding of their daughter*
> *Mademoiselle Sophie Champigny*
> *to*
> *Monsieur Julien Sorel.*
> *You are cordially invited to the wedding mass*
> *which will be celebrated Friday 28 June 2002 at 3:30 pm*
> *in the church of Notre-dame de l'Assomption*
> *Villeneuve-le-Comte*
>
> 116, rue de La Boétie
> 75 008 PARIS

If there is no religious ceremony, the invitation to the wedding ceremony ends in this manner:

You are cordially invited to the wedding ceremony
at the Town Hall of the 3rd arrondissement,
2 rue Eugène-Spuller,
Thursday 31 January 2002 at 3:00 pm.

---

[4] The names of living grandparents can also feature at the head of the invitation. [Author's note]

The invitation to the wedding reception

Both the bride's and the groom's mothers' names are included, and printed on a card of Bristol-board:

Madame André Champigny
Madame Paul Sorel
will hold a reception in the Salon of
the Cercle de l' Union Interalliée
23 rue du faubourg Saint-Honoré
75008 PARIS ; from 5:00 pm to 8:00 pm
wishing for a reply prior to 15 May 2002

116, rue de La Boétie
75 008 PARIS

If only one of the mothers-in-law has organised the wedding reception, then only her name should appear on the invitation card.

If the groom or the bride's parents are divorced, the invitation to the wedding ceremony includes both of these parents' names, but the mother's name precedes the father's.

Madame Jeanne Daronval
Monsieur Edouard Lenormand
Monsieur and Madame Lacombe

Each family sends their own invitations. They place their sheet in first position. The card with the invitation to the

44

reception is slipped inside the invitation to the wedding ceremony. Evidently, all the wedding invitations, letters and cards, are ordered from the same printer, with matching paper, card stock, and printed in the same format.

The cost of the wedding, including the cost of the wedding invitations to the ceremony and to the reception, is halved between the two families rather than shared *pro rata*. However, if one of the families is wealthier than the other, they may choose to cover the entire cost of the reception.

Newspaper announcements

The text of the invitation may be published in the newspaper, a few days before the wedding date. This extends the invitation to the wedding ceremony to distant relatives.

Replying to an invitation

We reply to a wedding invitation as soon as we have received it. The reply is sent to the groom and the bride or to their parents to congratulate them. If an invitation ends with RSVP or "Wishing for a reply before ...." we reply with congratulations and thanks, and if we cannot attend, we reply with congratulations and regrets. Avoid replying by using a visiting card: a personalised letter is always more appreciated.

Notices sent after the wedding day

> *Monsieur Jacques Darsonval*
> *and Madame née Mathilde Bernadeau*
> *wish to let you know of their recent wedding*
> *celebrated at a small private ceremony*
> *Friday 19 April 2002 in Nevers.*
>
> 16, rue du Parc
> 580000 NEVERS

The wedding rings

The couple choose their wedding rings together but the young man purchases both of them. All styles are suitable: triple rings, rings in a round, gold, guilloche, diamond studs... but the simple gold ring still has its faithful supporters.

The wedding gifts

Wedding gifts may be sent either during the engagement period or after receiving the wedding invitation. It is advisable to enquire whether the bride and groom have made a wedding list, and in which store it is held. Relatives can purchase a more significant and princely gift jointly. Only parents and grandparents can write a cheque as a wedding present, whilst white goods are offered only by intimate friends or close relatives.

Note that it is absolutely socially unacceptable to bring a wedding gift on the wedding day itself.

46

The gift is always accompanied by a visiting card conveying your good wishes and congratulating the couple. Cards should not be silent (i.e. stating only your name) but should always contain a personal message.

Flowers should be sent on the morning of the ceremony, either to the bride's address or to the reception.

Whenever I find a beautiful object in a beautiful store or at an auction, I purchase it and place it in a cupboard designated as "Weddings". Every year I send a hundred or so wedding gifts to the children of friends or professional relations. This requires organization and I have established four procedures:

- Like everyone else, I consult the wedding lists as this is the simplest way to go about it.
- I choose a two person setting for lunch, and order several of those.
- To wine lovers, I send a coffret containing a Bordeaux magnum, a carafe and two wine glasses.
- And I keep all these objects in the "Wedding cupboard"! When I know one of the future spouses personally, I attach a personalised note and another small gift, such as a small ashtray of hard stone, or a glass in a crystal of Bohemia, an antique etching, a silver picture frame.

A couple belonging to the Parisian high bourgeoisie once offered a superb 18th century German silver cutlery set to their daughter, on the occasion of her wedding. Invited to dinner at the young woman's home, at a later date, they noticed a new object on the mantlepiece. Out of politeness, they enquired about the creation.

"It's a *compression*" answered their son-in-law triumphantly. "And we owe it to you. Out of your simple silver, out of this mass of spoon ware, César has fashioned a great work of art."

Giving thanks

The engaged couple send a letter or a card to thank everyone who has sent them a gift, not matter its value. If the couple received presents only a few days before the wedding ceremony, they can send their thanks after the honeymoon. The couples should never thank anyone by telephone, but always in a letter, in which they will have the good taste of mentioning the present made to them and of showing that it gave them great satisfaction. And finally, they should never send an identical standardised letter to dozens of persons, as the son of one of my friends did recently. His uncles and aunts had the disagreeable surprise of receiving letters headed with "*Cher monsieur*" and "*Chère madame*".

The civil wedding ceremony[5]

The civil ceremony takes place at the Town Hall. It is a public event, and the doors of the wedding hall must remain open throughout. Present at the ceremony are the parents, close relatives, close friends, godparents and one or two

---

[5] In France, a legal wedding must be celebrated in a civil ceremony conducted at the *mairie* (townhall). Hence, people wishing for a religious wedding participate in two ceremonies: the civil ceremony and the religious ritual. [Translator's note]

witnesses for each spouse. One should never refuse the honour of acting as a witness for the bride or groom.

The fiancée enters the hall at her father's arm. The groom follows at his mother's. The mother of the bride is accompanied by her son-in-law's father. After the spouses have given their consent, the mayor declares them husband and wife. The young bride (who stands at her husband's right) first signs the civil register, using her maiden name. Note that the law now allows a married woman to retain her maiden name. After she has signed, her husband joins his name to hers, he is followed by the two or four witnesses who then add their signatures to the register. Civil ceremonies often occur in groups. So, in order to be guaranteed an individual wedding, it is important to apply to the Town Hall in plenty of time. In Paris, it is 'chic' to marry on a Friday.

If there is no religious ceremony, the wedding rings are presented by one of the witnesses who is seated in the first row immediately behind the bride and groom. The witness hands the rings over to the mayor after the fateful and emotional "I now declare you man and wife".

A collection is taken for the various charities organised by the municipal council. Then, the wedding party leaves the Town Hall as handfuls of rice are showered on the newlyweds.

If the civil ceremony is immediately followed by the religious ceremony, either at the church, temple or synagogue, the bride will arrive at the Town Hall in her full wedding dress, with her veil, her long train, and the little round bouquet which her fiancé has sent her. If not, the bride will wear a short tailored dress, a hat (mandatory) and gloves. Her dress is white or pastel.

49

The groom wears a very dark suit. All the guests are dressed elegantly, especially if a luncheon or a cocktail party is planned after the civil ceremony.

In Muslim weddings, the bride and groom will exchange vows in front of their witnesses. An imam may also perform the ceremony. The marriage is announced at the wedding feast. Brides may wear white or opt for a scarlet traditional dress, the *shalwar-qameez* threaded with gold.

The religious wedding ceremony

In the Church, weddings can be celebrated any day of the week except for Sundays and Good Friday.

At the Synagogue, weddings may be celebrated everyday but Saturday.

The guests are the first to arrive, followed by the members of the family. As a rule, the bride enters the church last, on the right arm of her father (or another relative if she is an orphan). She looks straight ahead, without acknowledging anyone. The groom enters at his mother's left arm and takes his place before the altar, on the right kneeling-chair.

The bride and groom each have two or even three witnesses who stand on either side of them at the altar. In general, the witnesses at the religious ceremony should not be the same persons who accompanied the couple during the civil ceremony. After the blessing, the groom takes the wedding rings out of his pocket. He then places both rings on a tray which the priest holds in front of him. The husband puts the wedding ring on his wife's left-ring finger. She is not wearing any other ring, not even her engagement ring: she will put the latter back on her finger after the wedding ceremony.

Little girls and boys, the flower girls and pages or other young relatives are in charge of collecting for the church's charities.

The register is signed in the sacristy or the choir. The bride signs her name first, then her husband, followed by the witnesses.

Congratulations and good wishes

The couple and their parents can be congratulated before the altar, in the chapel or outside the church, on the porch. The bride lifts her veil and kisses the good wishers who are crowding around her.

Note: Never kiss the hand of the bride – you may extend a handshake, a small bow, and (especially if many guests are present) offer a few words.

Exiting the church

The husband leads the wedding party out of the church, with his wife at his left arm, followed by his mother who is walking at the arm of his father-in-law; his mother-in-law and father are next.

If the groom is in the army or in the cavalry, his companions may form a *"haie d'honneur"*, lining up on either side of the couple's path and brandishing their swords or their riding whips.

The veil

According to tradition, after the religious ceremony, the bride cuts a piece of her veil (if it is made of tulle) to give to her unmarried girlfriends, so that they may find a husband within the following year. She gives her bouquet to her closest friend. In rural areas, the bride's garter is sometimes auctioned to the guests, and as the price rises, so do the emotions and the fun.

In the Synagogue, guests are offered paper cones filled with *dragées* (sugared almond sweets). In the church, the couple are showered with rice as they leave the church.

Dressing for a wedding: la toilette

Today, outside of royal weddings, the wedding cortege and the maids of honour are rarely seen.

Yet, the young maidens of old, with their long dresses, white gloves and flower crowns made a beautiful and romantic tableau. As did the young men with their dark suits, white shirts and ties in a single colour.

The bride's dress should be made of lace, damask, moiré, plain satin or brocade, zibeline, taffeta. The veil is of tulle or lace, long as a dream.

The bride wears covered satin pumps (the pumps are never open or in kid leather); stockings are flesh coloured. She wears either short or long gloves in angel skin.

The bride wears a pearl necklace and ear-rings but no rings or watch. On her wedding day, time does not exist....

The bride's dress may be long, with a train. If the bride wears a short dress, her veil must also be short.

The bride may also wear a tailored white dress-suit with a small white hat and veil. If so, she will complement those with white pumps and gloves.

The bride should never carry a handbag or even a small purse. She simply tucks her small handkerchief inside one of her gloves.

She carries only a small bridal bouquet, white or pastel, (not a large bunch of flowers across her arms).

A bride's make up should suit her maidenly status. It should be soft and nuanced. Her lipstick should be light, never bright red, and her perfume is discreet.

At a grand wedding, the groom wears a morning coat or suit.

The morning coat is a tailcoat of a lighter or deeper shade of grey which must be worn with gloves, a grey top hat (matching the coat) and black patent leather shoes.

A suit is worn with a white bow tie, a starched white shirt with a hard collar, and a white vest. The groom should wear a gusset watch (a wristwatch is not acceptable with this formal attire).

More simply, the groom may prefer a dark blue or black suit, with a white shirt, grey silk tie, black shoes (and in this case never patent leather), tall black socks (not see-through).

Whatever he chooses to wear, the groom always wears a white carnation flower in his buttonhole.

Graduates of Polytechnique, officers, prefects, and members of the academies (if they are still young) marry in their uniforms showing off their medals and decorations.

The photographer

The photographer is the indispensable witness. It is up to him to fix for times to come the events and details of this most important day: Aunt Jeanne's flowery hat, the worried smile of the little page-boys, the moment the wedding ring was slipped on your finger, the look exchanged before the wedding kiss. What would become of both our memory and our memories if it were not for these photographs?

The married couple will post the photographs of their wedding ceremony to their parents and intimates friends, either in an envelope with a small note attached, or in an album of several pages.

The honeymoon away

Where the newly married couple choose to spend their honeymoon depends on the time and financial resources at their disposal. But whether they go to Bali or to Nogent, their honeymoon should have all the colours and promises of the rainbow. Upon their return, parents, witnesses and friends will invite them, to thank them for the wedding reception.

COMMON LAW UNIONS

Your daughter, your nephew, your grandson may well live together without being formally married. Indeed, couples in common law marriage relationships are ever more numerous. In 1968, they represented only 3% of the French population and were recruited from amongst old anarchists. They are now more than 13%. They are generally under thirty-five years old and are from all social classes.

In the past, unmarried couples often legitimised their situation at the birth of their first child. This is no longer the case: 40% of persons who have chosen to live in a de facto marriage have children. And under the law of 3 January 1972, a child born out of wedlock has the same legal rights as a legitimate child, provided that both parents have acknowledged their maternity and paternity. No doubt, this explains, at least in part, why common law relationships are now competing with institutional marriage. Another reason might be the increase in the divorce rate (one couple out of three).

Young people sometimes decide on a free living arrangement to spare themselves the eventual experience of petty arguments and a court decision – or so they say. Finally, divorced persons might also prefer to live in de facto relationships so as not to re-live the painful experience of a divorce or a separation.

It remains that the lives of common law spouses are in all aspect comparable to the lives of legally married couples. The parties can buy property in joint names, and each can have access to the other's bank account, and when they separate, the custody of children and alimony payments give rise to the same difficulties.

De facto couples announce the birth of their children according to the same rules of *savoir-vivre* as married couples. While de facto partners usually print visiting and business cards in their own names, they nevertheless send invitations and announcements in both of their names: "Sophie Brandy and Marco Chasles have the pleasure of announcing the birth of their son Ulysse".

We reply to these invitations with a single card of congratulations and good wishes, and write the names of both parents on the envelope.

On the other hand, when a couple has only just moved in together, it is usual to send individual dinner invitations to them on two separate cards, even though their addresses are identical. These newly established partners are also expected to reply individually.

Savoir-vivre and de facto partners

Does one live better in a marriage or in a de facto relationship? I asked this question to several married women and de facto wives.

None was entirely satisfied with her situation.

The first complained of a loss of freedom; the others, after sometime, of a lack of security. Although de facto wives usually added that living as a couple without formal obligation gave their commitment greater value: every day that went by, they and their partners were together because they chose to.

Perhaps, these are idealised statements, not entirely true to life. No doubt, routine and habit weigh equally upon married and de facto couples. Still, it is true that in a de facto relationship, conjugal rights and obligations are of a moral order only, thus obliging partners to greater mutual respect.

Perhaps, couples who live together without a social contract show greater qualities than couples who are protected by the law, and their union may be stronger for this. "Love," as the poet says, "sings well only when it is free." A few famous couples, Jean-Paul Sartre and Simone de Beauvoir, André Malraux and Louise de Vilmorin, Elsa Triolet and Aragon journeyed together for the long haul, in spite of a few storms, and they poured their talents and their efforts into making their lives as successful as their works.

To conclude, *savoir-vivre* with a de facto spouse is about taking risks and about living up to the difficult commitment of not expecting commitment. This means living up to the ideals of liberty – hers and his – on a daily basis, and not allowing one's freedom to conflict with the other's. It is about living love in the present, without a safety net.

EXPECTING A CHILD

At last, the event you have been waiting for, for months, and upon which all your dreams and hopes now crystallise, has arrived. The medical tests and your doctor are categorical: you are expecting your first child. Nothing can compare to the joy now flowing through you. You first run to your husband to give him the news, since he is almost as concerned as you are. In the coming days, you will perhaps keep this promise of a new happiness between the two of you.

Later, you announce the happy event to your parents, your parents-in-law, and your grandparents. If they live in the same town as you do, you will not tell them by telephone, or by writing. You will visit them or invite them into your home so as to give the event all of its due significance.

As the days go by, you announce the news to your more intimate friends, and close relatives. If you already have a child, he or she might well be the only person not to rejoice at the announcement! For your child will soon have to share you with a little brother or sister. You will need therefore to increase your tender attention, and reassure her that she will always remain your first born child. Gradually, you will bring the child to develop positive sentiments towards the one she is bound to perceive (and rightly so) as a usurper. If you have more than one child, no doubt your children have already come to terms with not having you solely to themselves.

Your husband, your parents celebrate you and surround you with a thousand gestures of attention… Try not to take advantage of the privileges acquired through your current condition. Above all, remain happy, active, vivacious.

The birth of a child

When a close friend has a baby, it is usual to go and visit her in hospital only after consulting her, and after deciding on the date and time with her.

It is best not to remain too long in her room, and of course, not to smoke. Other don'ts: don't kiss the baby and don't recount your own experiences of childbearing or stories of difficult births. You can give her your present personally without a visiting card attached. And since flowers are not allowed in either private or public hospitals, you can send flowers after the mother and her baby have returned home.

It is best to send pink or white roses, pastel flowers with only a mild perfume. Avoid lilies, wattle and other flowers with heady scents.

Choosing a name

This is up to the parents, but it is thoughtful to consult parents and grandparents on the matter. Children are usually given three names one of which is the name of a forebear. As a general rule, the first born son is given either his father or his grandfather's first name. In the same vein, a first born daughter is given the first name of her maternal grandmother or maternal great-grandmother. A second daughter is given her paternal grandmother's or paternal great-grandmother's first name. The names given to a child may also include the name of his or her godparent.

One last word of advice: don't burden your child with an overly eccentric first name or a name which will risk, once the child goes to school, attracting his comrades' mockery, or silly nicknames. Also, stay away from overloaded names as for example, Venus or Adonis.

Announcing the birth of a child

A birth is such a happy event that we want to announce it to everyone on the spot. And so we can let friends and family know by telephone.

The formal announcement is either printed or etched, and preferably on white Bristol card without flourishes: no need for hearts, ribbons, or little birds nesting. The announcement is intended for a large circle of acquaintances. The announcement card is in a larger format than the visiting card; it should also match the envelope. It is sent within ten days of the baby's birth. The recipients should reply by letter (handwritten and not typed) within a week.

A notice placed in the society pages of a newspaper may be phrased in the following manner:

Monsieur Jacques Darley and Madame, née Gelane, are happy to announce the birth of .....

On the other hand, the announcement card will be headed as follows:

Monsieur et Madame Jacques Darley are happy to....

Godfathers and godmothers

In Christian families, prior to the birth of a child, it is customary to choose a godfather and godmother. Persons who are offered this role see in such a request the evidence of trust, but they are also conscious of a lifelong obligation. In accepting a godchild, godparents commit to raising the child, should his or her parents pass away. To become a godparent therefore is to commit to a lifetime of providing attention, care and advice to the child. Given this, one should not feel offended if certain persons, either because they are too tired or too busy, refuse our offer. Godparents should be of a similar social milieu, have the same religion and level of education as parents. They should also be mature and responsible.

If your baby's godparents have never met, invite them to dinner so as to introduce them to one another. Through your child, godfather and godmother have now established an important connection.

On the day of the baptism, the godfather offers his godson a silver object (a cup, plate or cutlery set) or a gold *gourmette*: a chain bracelet with a small badge on which the name of the child is engraved. Furthermore, the godfather will remember to offer a gift to the child's godmother: a scarf, or a bibelot will be appreciated. It is the godfather's responsibility to buy the boxes of *dragées* [sugared almonds] which are customarily offered to the child's parents and grandparents. The child's parents, for their part, purchase paper cones filled with *dragées* which are distributed to the guests during the baptismal ceremony.

The godmother offers her godchild a baptismal dress, a silver object, or a gold chain.

RELIGIOUS RITUALS

Baptism

A child is usually baptised within a few months of his birth. The baptism takes place in the church of the town where either the child was born or where his parents were born.

At this ceremony, women dress elegantly and soberly: no low cut blouses or dresses, no bare arms, except in summer when in the country; men are in dark suits.

Today, it is the mother – or sometimes, although it is unusual, the godmother – who holds the child over the baptismal fonts. It is up to the father (or to the godfather) to hand over the envelope containing the contribution made to the priest. If the child's health is fragile, the Catholic Church allows a private baptism to take place in either private or public hospital, or at the family home.

In the Reformed churches, Adventist and Lutheran, baptism is not a dedicated ceremony and it therefore takes place during the weekly services. In the Protestant worldview, baptism is not a sacrament leading to redemption but a liturgic act.

The Baptists baptise their brethren when they have reached adult age. Among them, baptism stems from the faithful's decision, not his or her parents'.

The reception

The baptismal reception is often very simple: a dinner with parents, relatives and close friends. If the priest is on intimate terms with the family, he is also invited and given the place of honour. But the child's father and mother nonetheless preside over the meal.

The new-born child is brought to the dinner party for a few moments only, when the guests raise a toast (and the party *will* refrain from wetting the baby's lips with Champagne under the pretext that it should bring him or her good luck). Cups filled with *dragées* are placed on the table in the salon and the dining room. *Dragées* are also offered to neighbours and domestic staff.

When catering for a large number of guests, the hosts set up buffets, and provide tables and chairs for the comfort of older persons. Alternatively, parents sometimes prefer to invite guests to a beautiful afternoon collation which ends with Champagne.

Circumcision

Jewish families celebrate the seventh day after the birth of a child with a brilliant and hearty party. Through the Brit (or covenant) the male child bears within his flesh the mark of his belonging to the religion of Abraham. Today, circumcision, the removal of the prepuce, is often performed by a surgeon in the hospital, rather than by the traditional *Mohel*. The Brit is followed by a grand reception during which an orchestra and singers invite the guests to rejoice. The guests are in their most elegant attire. They send a gift to the new-born either on the eve or on the day of the ceremony.

The Muslim circumcision (*khitan*) is also performed in hospital by a surgeon, at least seven days after the birth of the child. This ritual comes along with a similarly cheerful party.

Confirmation

Protestants pledge their Confirmation at fourteen years of age. However, like the Communion, the Confirmation is not a sacrament. It is a liturgic act where the minister pronounces these words: "May the Lord confirm you in the covenant of your baptism."

Communion or the profession of faith

Communion exists in both the Jewish and the Christian religions, but they have different meanings. Among Catholics and Protestants, the Communion remains a simple and relatively private event. Boys and girls wear the *aube* (the traditional white robe) as required by the Church. After the mass, they offer their priest, parents, teachers and friends holy images on the back of which they have inscribed their names, the name of their church and the date of the communion. After the ceremony, the family invites relatives and close friends to an intimate dinner which has none of the trappings of a society event. The communicant is seated between his godfather and his godmother. The parents preside at the table, with the grandparents at their sides. A beautiful bunch of white flowers adorns the table, to stress the fact that this day is not an ordinary day.

Some families, however, prefer to invite children, relatives and teachers to afternoon snacks and drinks after vespers. And yet others invite their relations to lunch the Sunday following the Communion.

Whatever the choice of event, it is the communicant's mother who sends the invitations, either in a letter or a card.

The gifts

Custom requires grandparents to offer their grandson or granddaughter a watch. Godparents give a mass book, a rosary or a crucifix. During the two weeks preceding the ceremony, friends send CDs, DVDs, a camera, cufflinks, books... or, on the day of the luncheon, white flowers.

Only the Communion (profession of faith) requires a formal dinner. By contrast, the Confirmation is entirely a private event.

The Bar-mitzvah

Among the Jewish people, the Bar-mitzvah is a decisive stage in a boy's life; from this day onwards, the boy is responsible before God for his actions. This ceremony therefore symbolises that he has reached adult age (although he is only thirteen) and that he belongs to the community of men. During the months leading to the ceremony, the boy has learned Hebrew and he is now able to read from the Torah, the large parchment scroll rolled on two rods, where the five books of the Pentateuch are inscribed: Genesis, Exodus, Leviticus, Numbers, and Deuteronomy. There is an especially moving moment at the closure of the ceremony, when the adolescent has the immense privilege of carrying the Torah in his arms and with his precious burden approaches the congregation; every person then lays a hand on the sacred scroll. After the prayers at the Synagogue, a dinner is given for the extended family, followed by a brilliant evening reception where dozens of guests dance to the sound of the orchestra.

Sephardic communities (originally from Spain and North Africa) often organise unforgettable feasts. Relatives and friends compete in elegance and the young communicant may well receive more presents on this occasion than he will receive on his wedding day.

THE YEAR'S FESTIVITIES

Christmas

Nowadays, in almost every home, people erect Christmas trees, because Christmas is now a universal feast and, above all, it has become a children's festival. On that night, we all believe in one same Father Christmas who will come loaded with presents for everyone.

How should we prepare for Christmas?

It is best to draw a list of all the people we want to offer gifts to at the very start of December (this way we are more likely to remember everybody). Next, come the difficult questions. "What to buy for whom? What would make them happiest?" Finding a beautiful gift is an art that requires time, care, thought ... and money. But not only money. For example, imagine that one of your friends mentioned to you that she is renovating, and fitting in new wardrobes, then, why not offer her a dozen or twenty-four velvet covered coat-hangers? No doubt, she will be touched by your thoughtfulness.

Children and godchildren of course are given the presents they have wished for and have been waiting for, sometimes for months – toys, and more toys, and preferably no useful gifts like clothes, or a school-bag or a lamp... On the other hand, adults: parents, relatives and friends will no doubt welcome useful gifts – as for example, the latest model food processer, mobile phones or electronic notebooks. After the long search for gifts, comes the purchase of ribbons and gift-wrapping paper. A golden or shiny paper, a large bow, and a pretty Christmas card complement the pleasure of giving and receiving.

The presents are placed at the foot of the tree decorated with glass balls, garlands, lights, and silver and gold tinsel. A wreath made of pine branches, dried flowers, pinecones and red and green ribbon is hung on the front door of the apartment. A large bundle of mistletoe hangs on the door of the living room, and there is a garland of holly on the dining room.

Christmas Eve dinner

The table is decorated in the colours of holly, with a red or green tablecloth, red or green candles (tonight, no white candles), small bouquets of anemones or Christmas roses, large ribbons and bows tie the napkins, and little father Christmas figurines are placed all over the table.

The dinner takes place at one's parents or grandparents. The traditional menu includes oysters, a turkey stuffed with chestnuts and presented with small black and white pudding sausages, the *bûche de Noël*[6] for desert or sometimes a pudding.

---

[6] The *bûche de Noël* [Christmas log cake] is the traditional French Christmas cake. It is a genoise or sponge cake rolled in a cylinder shape, filled and covered with butter cream (chocolate, coffee, ganache, etc); decorated with meringues so as to look like a log with little mushrooms growing on it. The cake hails from the Yule Log, which was burned on Christmas Eve in various parts of Europe, and originate in the ancient and pre-Christian celebrations associated with the Winter solstice. The Yule Log is centuries old, but the *bûche* is a 19th century invention. [Translator's note]

The entire evening is focused on the children and everything revolves on making them happy. Divorced parents ought to spend Christmas together, in a state or renewed peace or at least a state of truce.

New Year's Day

New Year is a secular festival celebrated more noisily than Christmas, with friends rather than with parents and family, and more often than not at a restaurant, in a cabaret, or on a Caribbean beach rather than at home. It is an evening of dreams and nostalgia, a fragile frontier between what has been and is disappearing and what is in sight and will be.

For New Year's Eve dinner, first choice goes to gold decorations. The order of the night goes to anything glittery and shinny, from the napkins to the tablecloth as well as the decorated holly and pine cones. Sparkling cutlery and white porcelain plates. Women wear low cut dresses, jewellery, and sophisticated hairstyles. A little madness is welcome: petticoats, masks, balloons. Guests are offered small gifts: a pouch, a broach, a bowl, horoscope, books, cassettes, a good bottle of wine or other drink, rare teas….

The meal may be served as a buffet if the guests are numerous. It may include salmon, tarama, smoked eal or trout, Russian pickles, fresh cream, (nicely hot) blinis, zakuskis, dark rye bread, bread with cumin seeds, light rye bread and iced vodka … flowing! Vodka will quickly warm up the atmosphere!

If the theme is purely Russian, the hosts complement the meal with a Beef Stroganoff (prepared the day before) seasoned with red chilli and paprika. The meal ends with a ginger sorbet and various sweets.

At the stroke of twelve, Champagne!

Everyone gets a kiss, and first of all your partner. If we spend New Year's Eve at home, we phone parents and friends!

And the music begins! Gypsy or other, never mind, all that matters is the exhilaration and the promise of a radiant future!

If the party lasts into the early hours of the morning, you may need to put up the few friends who celebrated a little too joyously to be able to go home!

Incidentally, did you remember to let your neighbours know you would be hosting a New Year's Eve party, and with music? When you wish them a Happy New Year the next morning, don't forget to apologise for the noise you caused! Past one in the morning, it may also be worth lowering the volume on your music player and moderating your enthusiasm.

Easter and Easter

The Jewish Easter or Pessah (Passover) commemorates the exodus of the enslaved Jews from Egypt and the renewal of the Jewish nation. During the seven days of this festival, Jewish people do not eat wheat flour or leavened bread but an unleavened bread called *matzoh*.[7]

Well before the beginning of Easter, every Jewish house where the tradition is maintained, is cleaned from top to bottom, often even repainted, and all cooking utensils are

---

[7] Because *matzah* is unleavened, it resembles more a thickish and large wafer than bread. Matzah may be made from either wheat, barley, spelt, rye and/or oats. [Translator's note]

70

renewed or plunged in boiling water. The great Spring cleaning prepares the members of the household for renewal.

On the first day of Passover, the extended family sits at the table, around the father, and so begins the *seder*, the ritual meal. The head of the family reads the story of the exodus, the Haggada, as he distributes the bitter herbs (*maror*), whose bitterness recalls the centuries of slavery and the unleavened bread, the "bread of humility" as yeast, the leavening (swelling) agent, is the symbol of pride.

To partake in the *seder* and absorb each of its ingredients, is to partake in the history, culture and symbolism of the Jewish people. The first commandment says: "I am Yahweh, your God who guided you out of Egypt, the land of slavery." According to writer Gérard Haddad, the exodus from Egypt is both a symbol of biological birth, "the expulsion of a smaller and radically different body from the wounded body of Egypt" and also equally the birth of our individuality, our own volition and hope.

If you are invited to Passover at the home of a practising Jewish friend, do not bring pastries, as wheat flour should not be taken across the threshold of the house; and do not be surprised to be served only *matzoh*[8]. You will also be served a delicious dish of lamb and vegetables.

For Catholics, Easter is the most important religious festivals. "Jesus-Christ lives" call the bells of Rome and Christendom – and on this day they are rung at full swing. Those who go to Church only once a year usually attend the Easter Mass.

At Easter, we offer chocolate eggs or painted wooden eggs, brightly decorated (those are specialities from Central

---

[8] Note that a French meal is never served without bread – baguette or other *pain*. [translator's note]

71

Europe and Russia), and in the country, people hide eggs in their gardens for the children to go hunting for them.

Ramadan

Ramadan occurs on the ninth month of the Muslim calendar. It is a period of fasting, praying and charity-giving, and the most important religious and communal event for Muslims. During Ramadan, people commonly fast during the day and eat between sunset and sunrise, they also spend time with family and friends.

May first

We offer Lily of the valley: husbands to their wives and sons to their mothers. This small good luck charm is a token of either affection or friendship and women expect this much from you, Monsieur! Also, remember to bring a flower to your colleagues and your secretary. And if you are absent from home and work, leave it to Interflora to send flowers for you.[9]

---

[9] May first, the International Labour Day, is an important secular festival in France. Labour days were first acknowledged in the 18th century to celebrate the achievements of workers. In 1889, the Second Socialist International declared the *1er Mai* a day of protest and part of the ongoing struggle towards the eight hour working day. The French Senate finally granted the eight hour day in April 1919 and officialised 1st May as a secular holiday. Nadine de Rothschild's recommendations show how universalized the festival is today. [Translator's note]

Mother's day and father's day

No child ever forgets Mother's Day. And every mother should remember to hang on their bedroom wall, or to place on their bedside table, the gift her child has fashioned for her at school with the greatest of efforts and care, a token of every child's immense affection and love for their mother. The first drawing my son offered me, when he was three years old, still hangs on my bedroom wall.

Father's Day is also becoming an institution, and we have discovered that fathers we had never suspected of emotional neediness, are infinitely touched by the loving fuss made of them on this day.

Grandmother's day

The writers who have painted a negative portrait of their mothers are neither rare nor few. Hervé Bazin's *Folcoche* (from his novel *Viper in the Fist*) is perhaps one of the most terrifying. But in spite of all my efforts, I have not found a novelist who failed to love his grandmother. Why do we keep sweet, even exquisite memories of our grandmothers? Because, unlike young mothers, grandmothers are neither impatient nor in a hurry. And they seemingly never tire of re-reading or re-telling the stories which children never tire of hearing. A grandmother's indulgence is limitless. And a grandmother's joy lives in the smile of her grandson, her granddaughter, in the small head leaning against her shoulder.

There is a special and exclusive bond between a child and a grandmother, because a true "Nanny" is incapable of reprimanding, she can only reward. She always says yes.

Every time my mother scolded me, for just or unjust reasons, I would run into the arms of my grandmother who would always dry my tears with kisses, tender words, or a lolly.

A grandmother's *savoir-vivre* lies in her subtlety, in that she refrains from monopolising her darling little ones, and never attempts to draw to herself the affection which a child has for her mother. Also, it is well to remember that every child has at least two nannies; they should not compete for the position of preferred grandmother.

Florists are thoughtful persons and they were quite right in instituting a grandmother's day in March. To all Nannies: "Happy grandmother's day!"

And… when are we going to celebrate a grandfather's day?

Birthdays and other individual celebrations

Everyone knows how important birthdays are to children, for they talk about it weeks in advance of the event, their thoughts returning time and again to the presents they are hoping to receive, to the cake and the candles. We could never deprive our children of this party, of the joy of inviting their school friends and their cousins, no matter how taxing we sometimes find it.

Take photos at every birthday and keep them safe: they are precious. Later, you will find yourself looking over them with a great deal of emotion. Every family should have a photo and video library, a record of its history in images. Memory can be such a good liar, it is prudent to entrust it to an archival record.

Our husbands' birthdays are as sacred as our own. Let's celebrate this special day with an intimate candle-light dinner, an outing to the cinema, or an unexpected present. There are so many ways to make someone special feel happy. Champagne, a pretty tablecloth, two candles and a smile are all we need to transform a simple meal into a lovers' dinner.

It is your husband's fiftieth birthday, how about a little oom-pah and a dance? Fifty years, half a century … this is a pill that requires a bit of help to swallow. Coming to terms with the thought that he is no longer a young man turns his hair white. So, reassure him, let him know that he has never been more handsome (which is probably true), that maturity is the most beautiful stage of life. If you love him, don't try and teach him acceptance, never say: "That's life, we all get old…" because he is quite prepared to believe that everyone does get old… except him!

Women have one advantage over men; unless one is an oaf, no one ever asks how old a woman is and in any case, women always celebrate their age and never reveal it. And unlike men, women can lie with astonishing confidence and self-control. Every year, their children get younger and they hide the grandchildren. What robust health!

Once at a child' birthday party, someone asked the age of the young hostess. "Thirty-six" she replied without a tremor of hesitation. A little voice behind her rose in protest: "But Mummy, that can't be, you've been thirty-six several times already!"… Beware of close relatives!

The birthdays that should never be neglected are:

Your grandparents', parents' and parents-in-law's; your husband's birthday, your children's, your son and daughter-in-law's, your brothers', your sisters', your brothers and sisters-in-law's; then also, your god-children's, your best friend's, your close friends and finally close associates and colleagues!

At the start of the year, when you begin your new diary, keep note of everyone's birthday so that you won't risk making a mistake. Use your electronic diary to keep track of the birthdays or name days (patron saint days) of your family and friends and to remind you on the day.

LIFE'S UNHAPPY EVENTS

Savoir-vivre : divorce and separation

"Is it not an affliction dreaded as death when a companion identical to yourself turns into an enemy?" (*Ecclesiastes*)

I believe divorce is a scourge. The sexual revolution, the widespread generalisation of permissive morality, and the policy reforms that created a right to divorce, have turned divorce into a social trend and a fashion. At the risk of shocking you, I believe that divorce inflicts as much damage on children as drug abuse. And the damage is all the more pernicious that it is not immediately visible.

I remember my nephew Cédric complaining to his mother: "Mummy, my friends at school have two daddies, how come I only have one?"

The normal couple has become abnormal.

Many couples, at some point in their married life, think of separating – and after contemplating the potential destruction of their common wealth, decide not to severe the conjugal bonds, and instead make the effort of re-establishing harmony, as far as possible.

Others, however, speed towards divorce even when they have been married only a short time, without even glancing back, and without a thought about the consequences their break up might have on their children. They may take it all in their stride; even call it a friendly separation.

There is no such thing as an elegant divorce – and no one knows this better than lawyers. Indeed, it is always a good idea for married couples not to share a lawyer, even when there is no conflict between the spouses.

When someone tells me that he is in the midst of an amiable separation, I know he is in a state of delusion, and that conflicts are going to manifest soon enough: conflicts about the custody of the children, the amount of alimony, the sharing of the property and goods. In fact, a couple can tear each other apart even if there is nothing to be shared!

Come what may, once they are divorced, ex-spouses with children must maintain bonds and mutual obligations which divorce does not do away with. This also requires *savoir-vivre*.

One should never, under any circumstances, criticise an ex-spouse or place all blame upon him or her; and one should never speak of years of common life as lost years, or consider one's marriage as a failure.

With divorce, everyone suffers: you, your children, your family, your friends. Do not add to the pain by putting either your family or your friends in a position where they must be with you or against you.

Do not force your friends and family into two camps: your allies, those who are united under your flag, and your adversaries who have gone over to the enemy side. The people who loved you when you were a couple will continue to love you now that you are no longer together. Give them the freedom to invite you and your ex-spouse into their homes at different times.

I have known so many couples who have divorced, remarried, and then lived the best years of their lives together, that I can only recommend to anyone considering a separation, to proceed with caution. Who-ever knows what the future holds?

Children of divorce

As soon as a family has split in two, children are torn between their mother and their father. Going from their mother's house to their father's at the weekend is profoundly disturbing; and poor performances at school are the first sign of children's suffering.

What can be done? Surround them, during the period of adjustment, with double the attention and care. Both parents must reassure them and never allow them to perceive their own anxieties. Their parents' anxiety is unbearable to children who are in need of a strong parental image.

No doubt too, a mother will find it difficult to accept the thought that her children love their father's new wife. But she should feel safe. A child may acquire a new family, new brothers and sisters, a new house, but the affection which a child feels for his step-mother can never equate the love he feels for his mother.

The end of life

In Hebrew, the word for cemetery is *Bel Alamin* "the house of the living". Is this to exorcise the anxiety of dying? To announce the coming of the Messiah, the resurrection and eternal life? It is true that believers look upon death with serenity. To them, death is a passage towards light.

However, the loss of a loved one is the most difficult event to bear, it is something that plunges us into the depth of a grief that only time can blunt, and ever so slowly.

Nowadays, sick people often die in hospital. That is one more reason why we need to be at their side and assist them in their last moments, surrounding them with our presence and our love. If they are practising Catholics, we must respect their wishes and call a priest to administer the last sacraments.

The body is washed by the family or a nun, or more commonly by the staff at the funeral parlour.

In the Christian religion, the deceased are dressed in their best clothes, while among the Jews and Muslims, they are naked under the shroud. "From dust you came and to dust you will return" says the Bible.

But whatever their religion, family members stand by the departed night and day during the period of wake.

The departed's decorations and medals are pinned on a cushion and placed on the coffin, where they remain until the journey to the cemetery.

The formalities

A death is reported to the municipal council within twenty-four hours. To obtain a burial permit, it is necessary to present a death certificate drawn by a physician, a number of pieces of identification, and the deceased's *"livret de famille"*.[10]

---

[10] The *livret de famille* is a booklet issued by the government to all French married couples. De facto couples obtain a *livret* at the birth of their first child. The *livret* contains official copies of extracts from the birth and marriage certificates of parents and children. Divorces and separations are also recorded. The *livret de famille* was instituted in 1877 after arson destroyed the Parisian civil register during the revolutionary Commune of 1871. The *livrets* held by individual citizens, act as a supplementary depository of civil records. [Translator's note]

The death notice

No one sends individual death notices anymore. Family and friends are informed by telephone and a notice is placed in the obituaries of a newspaper.

> *Madame Roger Bourdin née Rosalyn Meret-Dufour*
> *Monsieur and Madame Jean-Paul Vannier and their*
> *children[11]announce, in their grief, the passing of*
> *Monsieur Roger Bourdin Professeur at the Collège de*
> *France on 2 December 2002, aged 52 years.*

> *A religious service will take place at the church of*
> *Saint-Ferdinand- des-Ternes, 27 rue d'Armaillé 75017*
> *PARIS, Friday 4 December at 15:00.*
> *Burial will be at the Père Lachaise cemetery, on the*
> *same day at 16:30.*

Condolences

Families and friends offer condolences to the grieving family as soon as the death has been announced and before the funeral. They may come to the family's house or to the hospital mortuary.

A member of the family welcomes the visitors.

Highly sensitive persons sometimes prefer not to bow before the body of the deceased. Instead, they meet with the members of the family who are assembled in the living room. A few words are enough. One should abstain from excessive demonstrations of grief as well as from off-hand or casual

---

[11] The names of family members may be added to this list.
[Author's note]

comment. Silence and reflection are expected. It is in poor taste to ask the grieving family for details, either of the "last moments" or of the illness. One should not linger but retire silently, guided by a member of the family, back to the door.

Our attendance at a funeral ceremony and burial does not dispense us from sending written condolences. The letter, always handwritten, should be sent within three days of the death notification. Condolences are sent in a letter, not a card.

If you are out of the country, you may also send a telegram to the family, and if you are an intimate of the grieving family, you will write a letter within a few days.

Funerals

Formal mourning is almost never worn nowadays. Widows in long veils are only seen in American movies. This said, one should nonetheless attend a funeral in a sober and sombre attire. No bright colours, flashy jewellery, or obvious make-up. Friends should be as soberly elegant as the family.

It is best to entrust the organisation of a funeral and funeral ceremony to a funeral parlour. Their staff knows better than anyone the smallest points of etiquette and the respect due to the departed.

If you were not on intimate terms with the departed, it is enough to convey your condolences to the family either at the departed's home in accordance with the Jewish or Muslim faith, or at the church in accordance with Christian observances. Among the Catholic, the bereaved family receives condolences in the sacristy. Men lead the people who have come to pay their last respects and who form a line as they approach the family. It is important to remain brief, to shake a hand or kiss a cheek without expressing one's grief verbally, as this part of the ceremony is especially difficult for the family. If formal condolences have been omitted from the funeral ceremony, mourners enter their names and addresses on the register provided for the purpose at the entrance of the church.

Savoir-vivre requires you to wait at the front of the church before leaving, until the funeral cortege has started for the burial ceremony.

Close family or friends accompany the departed to the cemetery. They present their condolences to the family after the burial.

Flowers

Should the departed have requested, before dying, not to have flowers or wreaths at his or her funeral, we must honour their wishes.

Otherwise, *savoir-vivre* requires us to send flowers, a cushion or a wreath, together with a few words on a visiting card, when the body is first taken from the home and taken to the funeral parlour.

Cremation

Increasing numbers of people are cremated and cremation is now accepted by both the Catholic and the Protestant churches. A cremation is a long and painful ceremony. The family must wait until it is over, in a chapel located near the crematorium. Afterwards, the family receives the ashes in an urn. If the departed expressed the wish to have their ashes scattered in a favourite place, the family obliges their last wishes. If the departed left no instructions, the urn can be sealed in a niche at the crematorium, where the departed's name, dates of birth and death will be inscribed.

Replying to condolences

It is not acceptable to thank people in a communiqué published in the press, in order to avoid answering condolences personally. You must write a letter to every person who sent you one. If you received many letters, you may space your writing over several weeks.

A white letter paper, or white letter cards with a fine black border are in order. Today, envelopes are entirely white.[12]

Social outings and mourning

Mourning no longer interrupts one's professional life or physical fitness program, life simply returns to normal. However, it is not only usual but socially expected that grieving persons withdraw from social engagements for several weeks.

When attending the wedding of a relative, grieving persons must remove their mourning clothes for the occasion and wear appropriately light attire.

---

[12] Up until three or so decades ago, French custom required death notices to be sent in an envelope bordered with a thick black line. [Translator's note]

The mass or prayers at the end of the mourning year

The mass and/or the prayers held for the dead are announced in a newspaper notice or in a letter addressed to close relatives and friends. To attend this ceremony is to show respect for the family as well as loyalty and attachment towards the departed.

So as not to end on a sad note, I will recount these words attributed to Juliette Achard. Her husband, Marcel Achard, author of the famous comedies *Patate* and *Jean de la Lune* was a renowned skirt-chaser, as unfaithful as he was witty. As she stood before his grave, about to throw a rose on his coffin, Juliette sighed despondently: "From now on, I will always know where to find him".

And I will conclude with this ironic word from a friend: "To have a sizable attendance at your funeral, you have to die between 15 October and 15 December, because in August, there's no one left in Paris." On second thought, he added, "A funeral is the only society event where anyone can attend uninvited".

All Saints Day

On 1st and 2sd November, it is customary to visit the grave of parents or friends, to remember the departed, to bring flowers and to maintain the graves. Some people still avoid attending merry social events on these days.

III

SAVOIR-VIVRE AND FAMILY

No one knows how love comes to lovers. For love comes without announcing itself and may come at any moment.

Love is Lady Luck waving the magic wand that brings us joy, a taste for happiness – and wakes the wildest dreams sleeping within us.

Love is too marvellous and fantastic; too complicated and too complex to be explained.

What does love add to life? First of all, it adds colours. A woman in love no longer sees the world in shades of grey: neither the weather nor people are grey or dull. And love breaks our narrow limitations, draws us out of our shells, inspires us, touches us like divine breath. Love, this oh so sweet bond transforms two beings; the loving silences, the loving gazes, the sighs, the laughter, the starts of sentences uttered suddenly and the light that dances in the eyes, and that glowing complexion.

Savoir-vivre in love is to be prepared to take risks, to flout caution and age, to accept love's suffering and to "die" for it.

Savoir-vivre in love is to love the other more than we love ourselves, to give everything and to forgive everything.

Savoir-vivre in love is to have the strength and courage to admit our weaknesses, to bare our hearts, and to admit that we are in love.

SAVOIR-VIVRE AND THE FAITHFUL COUPLE

Men and women are fundamentally different; biologically (our chromosomes differ), psychologically (we have different reactions), intellectually (we reason differently).

The geneticist Albert Jacquard believes that there are two human races: the race of men and the race of women. Hence, we find it difficult to live together and impossible to live without each other.

Everyone wants to find in the other what is lacking within themselves, and so we run after the eternal dream, the desire to find unity, to recover our original plenitude.

The game of the sexes is a game of opposition: it is a fascinating game of extreme fecundity but it is also a game that changes over time.

At twenty

Passion is the order of the day, everything seems easy and life is full of promises. We live together because we love each other, because we are beautiful, because we share the same dreams, the same illusions, the same hopes.

There is mutual admiration, respect, loyalty, generosity, and optimism. Everything is cause for laughter. We make love to life itself – we are "drunk on youth". The young couple is a true miracle.

Then, the years pass, children are born and passion begins to recede, morphing into a beautiful memory which we speak of with some nostalgia. Passion makes way for tender love, for team spirit, for the balance of forces, and a new regime: the sharing of tasks and responsibilities.

Neither side enforces its authority, each makes itself heard, respected. We still love each other, but we know now that love is neither easy, nor so natural.

At forty

Half way through life we reach the age of certainty and satisfaction. A woman is never more beautiful, more charming and more radiant than she is at forty. Her children are self-reliant, her relationship with them is enriching, no longer work. She can spend more time on her career and on her projects. She involves herself in new interests. She has never been more enterprising and has never felt more confident of her eventual success.

At forty, we know whether or not we have made the right choices and the right decisions. But dreams have given way to reality. We practice a politic of respect and courtesy, the two pillars of married life, which protects or blunts conflicts. Our respective personalities have developed and strengthened the stability of our family. But when the time comes to add up the sum total of our married experience, stormy weather looms – and on the horizon we see: disillusionment, lies, nagging melancholia, delays, carelessness. We are now alone because the children have left home, and suddenly, we discover that we don't really get along, that we no longer communicate very well. We no longer have so much to talk about. And we begin to wonder if perhaps we made a mistake; perhaps we even begin to talk about breaking up.

At sixty and beyond

Thank Heaven, we are still together, and we now share the same pleasures of life. We know that life is not eternal, that life is precarious and fragile, except for the love and tenderness we feel for our grandchildren. We also know our spouses so intimately. We have gone through so many challenges together that our mutual flaws, so irritating in the past, are now filling us with tenderness.

This is the time for leniency and understanding. We still feel love, but the passion begun with a glass of Champagne has landed in a pretty cup of chamomile tea.

SAVOIR-VIVRE AND IN-LAWS

Savoir vivre with your parents-in-law

One does not set a trap for a fly with vinegar, and the same goes for a mother-in-law. When your turn comes to be a mother you will understand that it is not easy to share your darling son with another woman. In the meantime, in order to please your mother-in-law, you need to make use of all your charms, and be especially patient and attentive. It is much easier to win over your father-in-law's affections as he sees in you another daughter.

When you are invited to dinner at your parents-in-law, bring flowers, cigars, chocolates, jams or *petits-fours*. Find out what they like so that you can offer them something to their taste.

Don't be in a hurry to leave the party. Take the time, after coffee, to listen to the tales of their travels, the incidents of their daily lives, and yes, again and one more time, the details of their son's birth, his studies and his achievements. Don't shock them with your style of dress or the freedom of your conversation.

Honour their dinner table, their wine cellar, even if you are on a slimming diet and you don't like alcohol. And finally, don't hold back your compliments.

Remember their birthdays, return their dinner invitations, and when you are hosting your mother-in-law, take extra care of the table, the menu, your dress – as if you had invited a high society guest or a Very Important Person. If your husband is away for work or other professional purpose, ask your mother-in-law to come with you to the theatre or to the cinema – and above all don't forget to walk or drive her back to her front door. It might take you time and require a lot of your attention to win over her heart, but one false move and you could lose it all.

And how should you address your mother-in-law?

When I was first married, it was the rule to address one's mother-in-law as "*Belle-maman*".[13] Today, young women address their mothers-in-law by their first names which is a friendly way of narrowing the generation gap.

Savoir vivre with one's daughter-in-law and one's son-in-law.

All mothers-in-law adore their sons-in-law, and nurture special bonds with them. They never forget their birthdays, they feed them delicious gourmet dinners, and bestow a thousand cares upon them. With their daughters-in-law, relations are not always as smooth. Oh Mother-in-law, if you

---

[13] The term for mother-in-law in French is "belle-mère" which literally means "beautiful mother". Father-in-law likewise is "beautiful father", and so forth. *Belle-maman* is modeled on the form of address *maman*, which can be translated into English as mother, mummy or mum depending on how it is pronounced. Common speech pronunciation gives the word *maman* an adult and affectionate feel equivalent to Mum in English. In fact, no self-respecting working class (or middle-class) individual would ever address his or her mother-in-law as *Belle-maman*, as this form is truly an upper-middle and upper class usage, but nonetheless the notion that in-laws are owed both respect and formality transcends class. Working and middle class people commonly address their in-laws as Madame Martin or Monsieur Boulanger – but not as Monsieur or Madame which would be cold and too distant. In many middle and working class families today, it is also acceptable to address in-laws by their first names while also maintaining the formal "vous". [Translator's note]

are truly concerned with your darling son's happiness, you must become your daughter-in-law's best ally. And above all, you must remain a discreet ally. Do not meddle with their conjugal live, do not criticize their way of life, their friends, or the way they bring up their children. Do not impose your presence upon them, do not insist on seeing them every Sunday. And never, ever criticise your daughter-in-law in front of her husband. Remember that she has given you what you most cherish in the world: your grandchildren.

SAVOIR-VIVRE AND CHILDREN

Culture is what we are left with when we have forgotten everything else, education is what we have left when everything else has been lost.

Education begins at birth (not so long ago, even newborns learned to be patient and wait three hours between bottle feeds), and education is practiced and perfected for the duration of our lives.

A child may be gifted with extraordinary beauty or intelligence, but if he is badly brought up, all his talents and qualities will be of little use as he will become odious. This child may grow up to keep, for the rest of his life, flaws of character and a lack of civility, which will make him undesirable.

It is a must to begin a child's education from a tender age, before he is even talking or walking.

Firstly, give your children good habits of cleanliness: taking a bath, brushing their teeth and their hair are daily rituals to which they must submit even if they do so while screaming and in tears. We owe hygiene to ourselves and to others, cleanliness must be inculcated from the start and suffer no exception. Hygiene is a quasi-military discipline. Children who have been taught to be clean from head to foot will remain so their entire lives.

There are a number of principles concerning hygiene, tidiness, and politeness which cannot bear any compromise or concession, and these hold until children become adolescents.

Obedience

Thankfully obedience is no longer inculcated with the cane or by locking children away. But have we not perhaps gone from excessive rigor to regrettable laxness? Today, parents sometimes appear reluctant to use their authority for fear of losing their children's love and affection. Yet, psychologists maintain that many of the emotional troubles which teenagers suffer from have their origins in the lack of parental authority. Don't hesitate to punish your son or your daughter, even sometimes by smacking their bottoms (though never in front of others),[14] should they have shown excessive rudeness. On the other hand, whilst you must not retreat from a power struggle, you must also retain your equanimity. The tragedy over, explain the reasons for your firmness and reassure the child that your affection is indestructible.

Politeness

As soon as he learns to speak, a child should learn to say: "Thank you *Maman*", or "*Bonjour Grand-père*", or "*Oui Madame*". But you will need to correct him and to remind him until he is able to associate, without prompting, the person speaking to him and the correct formula for thanking, greeting, accepting and refusing. A child needs to learn to speak without lowering his head, he needs to look at his interlocutor, and answer people with kindness.

---

[14] The author implies that the punishment is a demonstration of parental authority, and should not intend to humiliate the child. [Translator's note]

Table manners

A baby begins to eat on his own at eighteen months. And this is the time to begin teaching him to hold his spoon, to fill it with mashed vegetables or soup and bring it to his mouth without spilling and throwing its contents around the walls and on the ceiling. You need to have patience and kindness because it would not do at all for the baby to end his meals in tears or in a rage.

When a child is about four years old, she should be able to sit at the table with proper table manners. She should not eat with her fingers, she should finish what is in her plate, and not exclaim when a dish arrives on the table; "Yuck, I don't like that". Whenever she asks for water, she needs to add: "Please *Maman.*" She does not speak or drink with her mouth full of food, and she chews with her mouth closed.

Lunch and dinner, however, are often too long for a young child who should be excused from the table before cheese and desserts are served.[15] Small children can finish their meals later, either in the kitchen or in their bedroom.

Family meals should be happy and relaxed: the family meal is not the place for conjugal disputes, nor even for the shadow of a quarrel. We should also avoid worrying children

---

[15] French meals consist of several courses that are brought to the table in a specific order, unlike Anglo-Saxons meals which are presented to each person on a single plate. An every day meal is a simpler version of the dinners described by the author in Chapter VI. The simple family meal begins with a vegetable salad (crudité), or a plate of charcuterie (cold meats) or potage; then a meat, egg or fish dish which is either followed by, or served with, a cooked vegetable dish; a green salad is next; finally the meal always ends with cheese, followed by dessert. Hence, even a simple meal in France is a far more time consuming affair than in Australia, England or the US. [Translator's note]

by discussing the details of tragic news events. Everyone should talk about what they did today, and no one should monopolise either the conversation or the general attention. Children should not interrupt when another person is speaking, but certainly, nowadays children are entitled to speak and to be heard.

Your little ones, evidently, will take their place at the dinner table when your parents, siblings and in-laws come for dinner. What childhood memories would we have, without these wonderful extended family meals and their excellent food, their conviviality and affection?

On the other hand, when you invite friends over, it is best not impose your children's presence on them: the conversation and atmosphere can suffer for it.

Sports and leisure

Nowadays, children swim before they can walk and they take up sport when they are very young: cycling, judo, tennis, skiing, skating, volleyball, rollerblading, football, sailing, golf, and so forth. These activities make them robust and healthy, teach them endurance and team spirit. Children lose their shyness, and show more self-confidence. Take a boy who practices a sport and one who does not. The former has a good posture, holds his head high, and has natural, flexible movements. He behaves, moves and expresses himself with ease and comfort. The other hides his head between his shoulders, he is awkward, timid, and clumsy.

My son was only two years old when his father taught him to swim, and he was only barely older, when he could swim in rivers, lakes and the sea.

At four years of age, a child can already ride a pony and hold onto the reins. Horse riding, besides, teaches children to love and take care of animals.

However, a child is not only made of muscles. Children are full of imagination and creative forces, and we must give them the opportunity to express themselves creatively. Help your children develop these qualities through drawing, music, sculpture, dance, theatre.

Toys play an important educational role, and if you have the means to offer toys to your child, do not hesitate. Children engage in real conversations with their toys; they make up plays, and multiply the scenes; and they invent episodic stories just like real novelists.

But you also need to teach your children not to break their toys and to put them away before going to sleep, and although this may prove more difficult, you need to teach children to lend their toys to their friends and even to give them away to children who don't have their good fortune. Remember the organisations which collect toys for children in developing countries.

It is a good thing to encourage children to appreciate peaceful and safe toys; and to avoid trumpets and roller skates so as not to disturb neighbours' peace.[16]

Books or television? This is a debate that has agitated parents and educators for decades. The answer to this question is now evident, a child who sits in front of the television, his play station, or his computer simply does not

---

[16] Most French families live in apartments, and therefore within hearing reach of their neighbours, on either side, as well as above and below them. Keeping one's noise down is the most fundamental rule of polite apartment living, and children are always reminded by their parents to think of "the neighbours". [Translator's note]

read enough. To sit passively for hours, in front of a screen, while moving images, often violent and cruel, move before his eyes: this is enough to fill his sleep with nightmares. Parents must be absolutely intransigent on this count. Allow a few hours a week for children to use their play stations or other programmes which you will have chosen together.

Finally, parents need to take care of their language: we should banish all trivial and vulgar expressions from our own mouth for fear of hearing those coming out of our children's. Correct your children's grammar, enrich their vocabulary, teach them to look up words in the dictionary or to search for their extended meaning on the Internet.

Pocket money

A child is king of consumerism: lollies, comics, toys, DVDs, video games – ceaselessly going from one to the other. A child can ruin his parents in a single afternoon. The best way to teach him to moderate his excesses is to agree on a certain sum which he receives, for example, every Monday, and then leave it up to him to manage his spending. How much should you give him? Try to find out how much pocket money his friends receive, as your child should not have at his disposal a lot more, nor a lot less than his friends.

Americans reward children for the household tasks their children perform: so many dollars for mowing the lawn, so much for washing the car. I strongly believe that children should take part in domestic chores, but I find the idea of paying for this distasteful.

Children and school

If your four-year-old has developed habits of cleanliness, tidiness, and discipline, if your child is polite and cooperative, school will not seem a horrible prison. Your little children will not burst into tears when you leave them with their teachers in the morning. They will be prepared and ready to conform to the rules of communal living. At school, they will not only learn to read, write, count, and discover the history of the world, but to accept others as they are; they will learn tolerance and peace.

Encourage your children, by your own attitude, to respect their teachers, to always speak to her and about her politely; encourage them to take care of their books, not to damage them, tear or fold or write on the pages.

To develop your child's love of learning, help her do her homework, take an active interest in her learning, talk with her about the topics and subjects that interest her, awaken her curiosity, and answer her questions honestly and truthfully. And of course, do not make empty promises.

Take your child, as young as four, to the museum, to outdoor concerts, and puppet plays. As for the cinema, he will drag you there himself!

His absences at school should not be unjustified. If your child has school on Saturday morning, do not make him miss three hours of classes so that you can leave earlier to take the family away for the weekend.

Allow him to invite friends for after-school snacks, and accept their return invitations.

On the other hand, if your son fights with his school friends, do not interfere, let him learn to solve his differences on his own. If he has difficulties being accepted by others, explain to him that it is not always easy to be part of a group. It is never too early to acquire a sense of reality.

Savoir-vivre and teachers

If your child is a mathematical genius, it is thanks to you. But if she happens to be useless in arithmetic, it is her teacher's fault. And you will accuse the man of being incompetent, of favouring other students – surely, he dislikes your little darling.

You are right: some teachers are better than others, but do not forget that some students are also not as good as other students. And besides, no one can take credit for heredity!

What should you do if your Julien is getting poor results? To begin with, tell yourself that this is not a tragedy, nor a destiny, and that, next month, he could be at the head of the class.

The wise course of action is for you to side with his teachers; the respect you have for them will soon show in his behaviour. Children are bound to become aggressive and rebellious if their parents are constantly criticizing their school and the education system.

One of my friends complained to me about his child's teacher, who, according to him, had developed a strong dislike of little Charles-Henri and did not give him sufficient attention.

"What about your son, how does he behave towards her?" I asked him.

"Ah! Badly! He is defiant, restless, can't concentrate."

After some time, I asked about my friend's relationship with his wife (which I knew was strained). He confided that there were scenes at dinner, and that their arguments were not always over problems at school. There were accusations, reproaches and very harsh words.

"Do you think your child may be behaving with his teacher as you are with your wife? Perhaps, Charles-Henri is modelling on you."

My friend agreed that the tensions at home were upsetting his son and that these were probably at the root of his misbehaviour.

Your children's experience of school and their relationships with their teachers and schoolmates will be positively enhanced if you participate and show interest in school activities, if you attend parents' meetings, student evenings, if you know and meet with their teachers. Under no circumstances should you miss the end of the year school festival.

Pay close attention to your children's term or monthly progress reports so that you can follow up on either their achievements or their failings; and take the drama out of a school failure because it is bound to be a temporary setback.

Don't forget your own school days... School is a hard school, isn't it?

Your child's birthday

There is one day in the year which holds significance as none other for your son or your daughter, and they await this day with feverish expectation: Their Birthday. On that day, they are at the centre of the earth; family and relatives, friends, friends of friends come like the Three Kings, to deposit at their feet good wishes and more importantly, presents.

No one needs to hire the Trianon[17] at Versailles to organise an unforgettable birthday party. String your dining room with balloons, garlands, and masks and it becomes a dreamland.

---

[17] Marie-Antoinette's private residence at Versailles. [Translator's note]

On that special day, your child wants to have all the people he loves in his presence. So it is up to him, not you, to choose the school friends, the cousins, aunts and uncles, all those whose presence and whose presents matter to him.

Send birthday invitations on creatively designed cards, written in your child's name:

"Virgile looks forward to receiving Stéphanie on the occasion of his birthday, Saturday 20 June, from 15:00."

Make his favourite cake, place the candles on top and let it reign over the table. As to the party fun, let the child choose whether to organize an excursion to the circus, the *Guignol* (Punch and Judy), the zoo, a pop concert, or a fun park. All this depends on his age and his tastes. When your daughter is ten years old, she may prefer to dance to the sound of her favourite singers. Allow her to do so, even if the party causes you some inconvenience. It is a party, a celebration: it is a time for noise, joy and hyperactivity.

Your children's friends

School is made in the image of society: your child's schoolmates belong to various social strata. From the first day at school, friendships are born, and your child will tell you about Nour and Thomas with enthusiasm. He will ask you to invite them home. That is a good opportunity for you to meet his friends, and perhaps even their parents. When he is ten or twelve years old, you will need to take a more critical interest in the quality of his relations: from that age onwards, it is easy for children to be influenced by strong willed, strong minded peers, with either positive or negative consequences. If you are concerned with your children's choice of school friends, consult with their teachers. What is the point of hiding the fact that drugs are available in high schools, and deluding ourselves in the thought that only other people's children take drugs?

Useful know-how

- When you invite a school friend to your home, address the invitation to his or her mother, either by letter or telephone. Do not send the invitation directly to the child.
- Do not ask questions regarding the profession of a child's parents, or other private details regarding their lifestyle. Let children play together and let them be children together.
- If a child you have invited is returning home unaccompanied, telephone the parents when he or she leaves your house.
- Do not repeat in front of your children the clever things they have said, you may succeed in either stemming their spontaneity or in turning them into pretentious show offs.
- When your child is invited to an after-school afternoon tea or a birthday party, remember to reply to the parents by telephone, or in writing, to thank them. They will confirm that your son or daughter was indeed present.
- Give your child the habit of sending, if not letters, at least post-cards to his grandparents, uncles, aunts, and siblings, every time he goes on holidays. Encourage him to write rather than telephone. Also, write him long letters as soon as he is away from you.
- In all public spaces, in public transports, require your child to behave politely with everyone, to give up his

seat for adults without being prompted, to not run into people on the pavement (especially is he is rollerblading or pedalling his scooter), and to greet your friends by shaking the hand that is held out to him. He must not hold his hand out first.

- If an adolescent speaks to you in a formal manner, and addresses you with the formal you, return the civility.
- Finally do not wait to read the declaration of Children's Rights to observe the latter.

SAVOIR-VIVRE AND TEENAGERS

At about fourteen or fifteen, boys and girls enter into either latent or open conflict with their parents, whose opinions they no longer share. This is normal. We all lived through this rebellious period. But what is the best attitude to adopt when we are confronted with our own rebellious young people?

Should you oppose them and threaten them with your authority, you will achieve nothing less than poisoning or even breaking your relationship, and I do not believe that anyone wishes for this.

The best course of action is dialogue. Don't confront teenagers with your differences of opinion; rather, try to understand their perspective and if you do not agree with them, just tell them so. Learn to negotiate. Adolescence is a difficult age, and requires understanding and unconditional love. The passage from childhood to adulthood is a biological watershed which disrupts a child's equilibrium. The most apparently insignificant incident may cause adolescents to lose their self-confidence, to retreat into silence, to become touchy or aggressive. Adolescents need support and encouragement. Parents must ensure that they avoid uttering damaging reproaches.

Respect your teenagers' privacy: don't listen to their phone conversations or open their mail, read their journal, emails or diaries. Don't search their wardrobe or their pockets unless their behaviours give you cause for serious concern. If things become too difficult, don't hesitate to seek the help of a psychologist.

There is little point in getting stuck on minor problems such as dress styles; if your daughter or son dresses outrageously, it is not worth taking offense and turning the issue into an opportunity for conflict: teenagers are convinced that they are affirming their identity even if, in actual fact, they are only conforming to the rules of their tribe. So never mind all of that, the most important thing is that they should not be filthy!

If you refrain from criticizing their crazy clothes, if you pretend not to be shocked, they may grow tired of them more rapidly. On the other hand, if they shave their heads or die their hair pink or green or if they dress impeccably and display militaristic behaviour or acquire extremist views, then you must become very vigilant. You and your husband should take every opportunity to discuss current politics with them. You will need patience and perseverance. Ponder what may have caused your child to go down that path. Is he simply enjoying the provocation or are there more profound and serious reasons at work?

Teenagers and language

Young people's language can be shocking: slang and more slang, abbreviations, swear words. It is fine to tolerate everything except swearing and obscene language, because verbal crassness can lead to a general state of crassness and vulgarity. As you well know, it is enough to hear a person utter two or three sentences to reach a verdict on their standard of education and civility. Vulgar diction, a poor vocabulary and lame grammar will eventually meet with irrevocable social condemnation. Be attentive to your children's language and don't hesitate to correct their flaws and their mistakes.

Respect

Respect goes both ways. If you respect your children's needs, aspirations and dispositions, they will respect yours. Respect and affection are the foundations of any successful relationship. It is now quite common to hear children address their parents by their first names. It seems to me that this familiarity leads to a camaraderie that blurs parental relations.

Savoir-vivre with our spouse's children

In Bordeaux, two children meet for the first time on the first day of school. They are chatting:
"Where do you live?"
'With my new father, Daniel Delarue."
"Ah, that's funny, I lived with him three years ago."
People marry, divorce, remarry, divorce again, and remarry again. In the past, a woman brought a dowry to her husband, today, she brings him her children.

How do we live with other people's children?

Badly. We have for our own children an animal instinct: we love our children, and while we will draw our claws if someone dares throw a critical word or even a glance in their direction, we will reject the progeny of a rival female.

Culture teaches us to suppress our instinctive cruelty, and to tolerate other people: "You will love others as yourself!" says the Bible.

And so, if there is an answer to the problems of living with a spouse's children, culture and *savoir-vivre* must provide it. All women in such circumstances need to exert themselves to accept and to live in good understanding with the children of the man they love. If a woman is not prepared to do this, her married life is immediately compromised, and a second divorce, another failure, is looming.

Should your husband ever reassure you that he loves you more than his children, that only your love truly matters to him, do not ever believe him. He is trying to mask a truth which in the long term will impose itself on reality, along with a litany of reproaches. So, what should one do?

- Charm his children, gradually, to break down the natural hostility they feel towards you.
- Never criticise their mothers, they would hate you immediately; a mother is sacred. Stay neutral.
- Build your own individual relationship with them, get involved in their sporting or cultural activities.
- Be available and a good listener.
- Slip away when they feel like spending time alone with their father.
- Don't compete with your step-daughter. Remember that she may be truly hurting on account of the love her father has for you.
- If you live with your children and your step-children, you should be careful not to show any preference towards your own; be absolutely fair to all. But, alone with your children, let your heart speak.
- Every time you find yourself failing, when one of your step-children irritates or hurts you, tell yourself two things. The first is that they are children and you are an adult; you are the one who is expected to show maturity, intelligence, and understanding. The second is that when you married their father, you caused them a pain they did not ask for, and it is up to you to bridge the gap.

Savoir-vivre and our children's friends

Your children are fifteen and they have many friends. From when they were at primary school, they have been allowed to invite their friends over; for afternoon snacks on Wednesdays [18] and for birthday celebrations. You have organised hundreds of parties. Your neighbours' children, your children's cousins have had sleepovers at your home, and you have always had a spare bed ready.

To invite children to your home is exhausting, but easy.

But how do we cope with our children's friends as they approach adult age? How do we deal with the late night music, with the ashtrays filled with cigarette butts, the fridge ransacked, chaos in the house, and stains on the wall-to-wall carpet.

Teenagers must learn to be responsible and to return your kitchen and your living room in almost the same state as they found them in the first place.

Teenagers who invite friends over need to appoint someone to be responsible for the dishes, for the vacuuming, and the tidying up. Your house is theirs as well as yours, they can enjoy it and they can also take responsibility for it. Since

---

[18] Up until 2013, Wednesdays were school-free days in France, for all primary school children and for many secondary school students. This day off was compensated by longer school days during the rest of the week and for some children with Saturday morning at school. The current government reformed the four day and Saturday morning school week, to a four day week with shorter school hours and Wednesday morning attendance. The reform has faced strong opposition and resistance from teachers and parents in part due to cultural attachment. Since the 1880s, French children have always had a school-free day during the week. Before 1972, the school-free day was on Thursday. [Translator's note]

they already know how to enjoy it, their parents have nothing to teach them in this domain. A sense of responsibility, however, is something else altogether and something that is learned and taught from early childhood, from the first days and the first experiences of life. One can evaluate a child's education from the degree of responsibility he demonstrates.

On the other hand, parents need to remember that if their children don't feel at home in their own house, then they will make their friend's home theirs, or worse, the street. And you know what the street means: loneliness, drugs, tragedy.

SAVOIR-VIVRE AND OUR CHILDREN'S LOVE AFFAIRS

Childhood sweethearts

Co-educational schools have made it normal for boys and girls to live side by side from their most tender age. But what happens when friendship turns into another sentiment? When the girl friend becomes the girlfriend?

Mothers immediately worry:

"That boy is not good enough for my daughter."

Or

"My son is mad to fall for this girl."

They interfere and cause troubles where there is nothing but innocence. To upset first love, now that is a serious mistake! To interfere with your children's nascent sentimental life may have very negative consequences for your own relationships with them.

Mothers need to think back on their first love, their first emotions, and remember the innocence of their own youth, and they will see their daughters in a different light. During this difficult transition, when she is no longer a child, and as yet not an adult, a daughter has no need for either parental criticism or misgivings, she needs affection, understanding, advice and protection.

Also, remember that your first love lasted some time, and that many others followed. Things will be no different for your children. If you don't approve the current boyfriend or girlfriend, keep smiling, you will no doubt get to meet a few others.

Teenage lovers

Children whose parents are divorced often need to have relationships earlier than others. Affected by their parents' separation, the breaking up of the family unit, and its reconstruction through de facto relationships or second marriages, teenagers who are tossed between two families have an unconscious desire for a union which allows them to either bear or repair the parental split. He or she enters into a love affair with a partner of the same age or a little older. They share the same bed, at either of their homes, often to escape from the anxiety of the separation that has wounded them. Often both have the same emotional background.

Meanwhile, research has shown the significance of the first sexual experience: it is a symbolic stage, marking a transition and which at times announces a destiny.

Should parents tolerate their teenagers' sexual affairs? Certainly, it is rare for such relationships not to have some negative consequences. To begin with, school grades and attention might drop noticeably. After some time, the progress reports may improve but the school term is done for. Parents might retaliate by showering their children with reproaches, reducing their pocket money, and reneging on the bike or the holidays they had promised. They demand that their children return to a state of celibacy, and forbid them to play a role that is neither suitable for their age, nor within their means. They then presume that their fifteen or sixteen year olds are incapable of taking responsibility for their failure at school, and to mend their ways. They finally infantilise their children by making decisions on their behalf, without consulting them and without their consent; but their nagging only risks further destabilising the children.

By entering into love affairs before they have reached adulthood, your children may make you feel that they are already leaving you for a world where you are no longer at the centre. But only your disapproval can establish a distance between you. If you accept their first relationship, they will remain close to you. If you reject them, or if you reproach them for their behaviour, they will drift away and God only knows how far.

Fathers may be reluctant to admit that they are pained to see another male stealing their darling daughters. Mothers have little appreciation of the girls hovering around their sons.

And then of course, these young people who taunt us with their winged feet, with their insolent beauty and their insufferable vitality, commit the immense fault of reminding us of our age, taking our place, for we have been chased for ever out of the verdant paradise of adolescent love.

How should parents behave?

If parents are convinced that their children are too young to be in a committed romantic relationship, they must have the courage to say so. However, they should give their reasons for their objections and not impose a dictatorial veto. If one of your children invites a girlfriend or boyfriend who is a legal minor to your house to stay overnight, make a rule of calling the parents to ensure that they have been informed and that they agreed to the arrangement.

Do not be afraid to make a show either of authority or hypocrisy by offering the 'couple' two separate bedrooms. If they meet up during the night, it is best that they do so without your blessing. In the same vein, do not feel obligated to tolerate open displays of affection if this bothers you.

Many parents today no longer feel entitled to show their disapproval, and are incapable of confronting their children. Hence, they remain silent and fail their responsibilities, accepting to live in a permanent state of discomfort, repressing their hostility and in the process losing their children's respect.

While it is true that teenagers will laugh at anyone brandishing the flag of virtue and morality, they nonetheless recognize the necessity and importance of politeness. What they are missing is the fact that politeness and morality overlap.

For teenagers: how to exercise tolerance

If your parents do not share all of your opinions, does this really give you the green light to judge them and assume that they are stupid or old school? If they taught you to accept others, whoever they may be and whatever their differences, you can hardly pass judgement on them for having opinions contrary to your own. To be open-minded and to act democratically in a large assembly or in the public arena is not a great achievement. Tolerance in a relationship of two requires a greater show of virtue.

You cannot impose your own law at home just because you are right. If your parents refuse to celebrate your romantic relationship in their own home, think of their reasons and motivations, and respect their position even if you believe them to be irrational.

If you spend a weekend at home with your boyfriend or your girlfriend, behave as though you are with a friend. Keep your frolicking or the tender expression of your feelings private.

115

You discover that your daughter is on the pill

Let's imagine that one house-cleaning day, you happen to be in your daughter's bedroom, and you discover a box of pills inside a book that dropped at the foot of the bed. Emotion, shock, surprise and indignation leave you speechless. You panic! What! My own daughter, on the pill, and all this behind my back! Who has she fallen in love with? Why did she make such a grave decision without consulting me?

Did she say nothing to you because she feared you would disapprove? Did she want to avoid a confrontation? Does she believe that taking the pill – an adult thing to do – is her decision to make, and hers alone?

What then should you do?

Remove the box of pills from inside the book and place it on the bedside table, in full view – so that your daughter knows that you know.

In the evening (or the next day if you do not feel quite ready to speak calmly about the issue), have a private talk with her and ask her for her reasons. "I found this in one of your books" is a good start.

You should neither beat about the bush nor act like a policeman. If you have a close relationship with your daughter, she will trust in you. You are in your right to ask her questions about the boy with whom she has decided to take "the step". Hopefully, you do know the boy who has set her heart beating.

Whatever you do, however, don't demand that she cease to see him or that she cease to take contraceptives. Rather tell her you would like to get to know him better, and that she should invite him over for dinner, and then make sure that the moment is pleasant for all concerned. Should you throw him dirty looks, or shower him with caustic remarks, your daughter will hate you (only for a few days,

116

but a few days too many). If you are friendly, your daughter is more likely to retain her own critical faculties.

Nonetheless, you may still be worried. Should an adolescent girl decide on her own to embark on this course of action, even as she doesn't entirely grasp the physical or affective consequences? But to get the pill, your daughter had to have consulted a gynaecologist or a medical professional, who no doubt asked her questions, examined her and provided her with information. This same professional will be following up on her health. Three generations of women have now been raised with the pill, and gynaecologists are of the opinion that a sixteen year old adolescent can make love without endangering her physical and emotional health – on the condition, of course, that she is not excommunicated by her parents. Should she live in fear of being discovered, the pill may turn into something sinful which she might find difficult to tolerate physically. If you need reassurance, why not schedule an appointment with your daughter's doctor and discuss the issue with her – or alternatively discuss the issue with your own doctor

Sometimes, girls think that in giving themselves over to a boy, they accomplish more than a loving act. They believe that they are emancipating themselves. And either they really want to free themselves or they really believe that they are freeing themselves, perhaps from a social milieu, perhaps from traditions or from the confines of narrow morality.

IV

SAVOIR VIVRE WITH OTHERS

SAVOIR-VIVRE AND DOMESTIC STAFF

In Paris, I once became attached to a Portuguese woman whom I employed as a housekeeper. Monica was vivacious, intelligent, with a quick and subtle wit. She had a ravishingly lovely face save for a nose, unfortunately impossible to wear. One day, I suggested to send her to a surgeon friend of mine, and she immediately accepted. A few weeks later, she had no reason to envy Queen Nefertiti. She had become a new and superbly beautiful woman. But we were not alone in marvelling at her transformation.

When she returned from her leave, Monica came into my bedroom, her eyes bright with joy and mischief.

"I am sorry to let Madame the Baroness know that I will be leaving her service. I am getting married"

She held out her hand, showing me a huge shining diamond, and added:

"And just as Madame is Madame the Baroness, I too am about to become Madame the Baroness."

Indeed, the person who cleans your house, the person who serves you at table, is no longer called a servant or a domestic, and even less a housemaid. In the course of several decades, she first became a cleaning lady, and then a domestic employee. Today, she is called a "surfaces technician". This substitution of terms deemed insulting with new labels reflects the profound transformation of the relationships between masters and servants. Submission and tyranny are now entirely excluded from this relationship, as are personal whims and deference. Today, politeness goes both ways and we address one another on an equal footing. Only in very grand houses have domestic employees retained the former titles of footman, chef and chamber maid; and only the most stylish of employees today maintain the former etiquette and address their employers in the third person: "At what time will Madame return?"

The homogenisation of dress styles and fashion has also helped reduce social distance. The young woman who comes to work in your house more often than not wears the same clothes as you do... jeans, and a tee-shirt.

Now, there are still people who maintain that there are good and bad houses, and good and bad servants, but generally speaking servants are in their masters' image.

Some houses retain domestic staff for decades because the working conditions are excellent. In others, personnel comes and goes through a revolving door, because employers do not honour working hours, breaks, weekends or yearly vacations – because employers make belittling remarks in front of others, because they never have a pleasant word to say or show any kindness and appreciation.

Evidently, relationships are not the same when someone is employed six hours a week, or someone is a full-time live-in employee.

Hiring and firing

You are in your right, before hiring a person, to verify that the person is either a citizen, or that all paper work – residence permit and work permit – are in order, and to ask for references. Even better, you may ask for a workplace certificate[19] especially if you intend your employee to look

---

[19] The workplace certificate (*certificat de travail*) is issued by the previous employer and provides the names and addresses of both employer and employee, the nature of the work the employee performed, wages and the duration of employment. This certificate

after your children. You can also call their former employers before making a final decision. In cases of negative feedback, there is no need to give the details to the prospective employee. In any event, they will not be under any illusion.

When you let go of an employee, you are obligated to grant her or him a workplace certificate, but the law forbids you to provide any reason for their dismissal. You only need to provide the dates at which employment began and was terminated, without any comment on the quality of the service provided to you.

Workplace conditions

Evidently, workplace conditions must be very good: include accommodation (heating and with hot water) and food (equal to yours). Work hours and days off must be mutually agreed upon and honoured.

You may ask your staff to work some weekends but don't abuse of their good will. They are entitled to two days off a week and five weeks of vacation per year.

Work clothes

It is your responsibility to provide personnel with work smocks, white aprons, and gloves. Should you hand down some of your clothes, only offer those that are in good state.

This said, it is not because domestic staff is hard to come by that you should tolerate carelessness, a lack of politeness or over-familiarity.

---

cannot stipulate the reason for terminating the work contract. [Translator's note]

Now, what can you do if your personnel breaks your most beautiful Baccarat crystal vase? Nothing. Since you cannot put back together a broken vase, the best course of action is to take up reliable insurance as soon as you have purchased an object of value. Where your staff is concerned, breaking an object is one of the risks of the trade. Since you cannot avert the possibility of breakage, you may as well make sure that you are covered. Alternatively, you can always do the dusting yourself.

Practical advice

If you wish for your staff's loyalty, take care of them. If a person in your service is sick, look after her, either by providing care or arranging that she is cared for; if she is in hospital, go and visit her.

When you organise a *goûter*[20] for your children, invite your staff's children to the little party and treat them as your own. At Christmas time, remember to add a small personal gift (jewellery, perfume, a piece of clothing, a bag) to the sum of money which you offer your staff every year.

If one of your friends employs a real gem in her service, do not under any pretext go and poach her, even if you can offer better work conditions, better accommodation and better pay.

---

[20] The *goûter* is a light afternoon meal. If taken by adults, it is similar the English afternoon tea. However, in France, the goûter is usually taken by children. Many French adults eat only two meals a day (lunch and dinner) and since French people eat between 7:30 and 8:30 pm, children are always given a small and usually delicious afternoon meal when they come home from school. [Translator's note]

If you share a housekeeper with a friend, don't ask her about what is going on in the latter's house.

And finally, whatever complaint you may have about your staff, don't go about discussing these troubles with your friends or intimates. No one deserves that sort of punishment.

Young women au pair

Many young couples enlist the help of a young au pair, especially to help with the care of their children.

When my son was five years old, I had help from a young student. The agency which I had contacted recommended a young Swedish woman, named Ingrid. Her health, her refreshing spontaneity, the excellence of her references quickly dispelled my hesitations and I hired her straight away.

As weeks passed, I noticed that her figure was getting bigger, heavier and rounder. I sought some information indirectly.

She answered me, laughing: "Madame, I am drinking too much orange juice."

The season of oranges passed, and Ingrid's belly still inflated. Two months later, a passion fruit had come into the world. I visited the young woman in hospital, and she welcomed me with usual happiness.

"Madame, I may now tell you the name of the father. When I saw the baby, I recognised its daddy."

Should your young au pair turn out to be an unshackled ingénue, counsel her as though she were your daughter, and take special care of her.

You need to provide your au pair with a comfortable room and to respect her class times. However, you do not have to share every meal with her: she may have breakfast or dine with the children. She can also fulfil a few light domestic duties (tidy up the children's room or do their laundry). But under no circumstance, should you ask an au pair to do house cleaning duties or any other demanding domestic work.

Savoir-vivre and the janitor of your apartment building

We no longer call the caretaker a *concierge* or a *pipelette* (babbler)[21], and she no longer lives in a small dark dank lodge. It has been ages since anyone called out: "Bonsoir! Monsieur Dubois, cord please!"[22]

To live on good terms with one's caretaker or janitor is to have access to repair and breakdown services at home at any hour of the day. The janitor repairs your washing machine, fixes a leaking tap, takes care of a blocked pipe. He doubles up as a secretary, signs registered letters and parcels

---

[21] The *concierge* was once a ubiquitous presence of Parisian life, and janitors or caretakers are still employed in many apartment buildings today. Traditionally, the concierge opened the door (see below), received the mail, and cleaned the common areas, the stairwells in particular. The word *concierge* in French is also used metaphorically to denote a busy-body, a person who knows and speaks of other people's business (since the *concierge* is in the perfect employment to know everyone's business!) – hence also the word *pipelet* which means babbler. [Translator's note]

[22] Before electric door bells and electronic key codes, the phrase *"Cordon, s'il-vous-plaît!"* was a common utterance of Parisian life. Late at night, when the front door of the apartment building was locked and the concierge was in her bed, returning lodgers would ring the front door bell, call out their names, and ask for the "cord" – which the concierge would then pull, without leaving her bed, to unlock the front door. [Translator's note]

on your behalf, and saves you having to take a trip to the post office. He can be depended upon to give the right person the letter or the package you have entrusted to him, and he calls you a taxi when needed. The list of the services rendered by a janitor (and you must reward those) is considerable.

So, what should you do for him in return? At Christmas, you offer him a certain sum of money. This is an uncomplicated gesture and the least you can do. *Savoir-vivre*, however, would encourage you to also offer a personal gift: a few bottles of a good wine or Champagne, or a perfume or a scarf, if your caretaker is a woman. Avoid flowers and chocolate as they are too traditional.

When taking possession of a new home, it is customary to hand over to the janitor a sum proportional to the value of your apartment and about 10% of the monthly rent.

Now, you also need to follow the various instructions which the janitor displays, year round, near the rubbish-chute, in the underground car parks, and in the storeroom where bicycles and prams are locked away, as this greatly facilitates his work.

Also, keep your dog on a leash while you are in the corridors, don't throw your cigarette butts on the floor or in the lift, and last, try not to wake the janitor at night when you come home late: make sure you don't slam the front door of your apartment building.

Tips and annual bonuses

Some people are reluctant to leave tips in restaurants, cafés, and so forth on the grounds that they have already paid a service fee, as indicated on their bills. And others behave like royalty and leave huge tips wherever they go.

A tip is paid above and beyond the service fee to show appreciation. If you are especially satisfied with the young woman who washed your hair at the hairdresser, why would you not thank her for her service?

Waiters, maîtres d'hôtel, cloakroom staff, cinema and theatre ushers, taxi drivers – all expect to be tipped. And you simply cannot deprive them of this revenue since the French state automatically taxes them on a combination of salary and an estimation of their tips.

What then is a fair tip? 10% of the total bill if a service fee has been included, and if not, 15%.

Tips are never given to flight attendants, hairdressers who own their own salons, or public servants.

Bonuses

From November, your neighbourhood firemen, postmen, dustmen, and chimney sweeps, come knocking at your door to offer you a New Year calendar.

How much you should contribute is up to you: according to your means and the services which have been provided for you.

Whatever the time of the day, when the fireman, the postman, or the dustman come knocking, greet them with grace and amiability and remind yourself that it cannot be much fun to go knocking on doors asking for a bonus; it is up to you to ensure that no one feels as though they are asking for charity.

Savoir-vivre with our dogs and cats

The love I have for my dog is selfless: I want nothing from him, except his presence; I am not jealous of his secret inclinations and I have no wish to change him – by contrast I usually find something I would like to change in the people I love.

My dog, I love as he is, without reservation, and he loves me as I am, with my faults and my weaknesses. The love I have for him is entirely voluntary. No one, no family connections force me to love him; and above all of this, it is an ideal love, without conflict or insecurities. "Does he love me? Does he love me as much as I love him?" These questions which have tormented me, I have asked them about men, never about my dog.

The love and affection we feel for our dogs scandalises those who have never had the good fortune of living with such companions. Since I have had my little Tibetan terrier, Eros, who belongs to me exclusively, I have had a different life because we are never apart. His vitality, his energy, his capers are a source of permanent joy; my understanding, my patience towards him are limitless; he knows it and every day he devises a new fancy, and this is our game.

The problems begin when we go out into town. Eros cannot bear to be left in the car, and so he has had to learn to walk on leash, to behave on the footpath; he no longer attacks passing dogs, he relieves himself where he is told to, and when we are visiting, he no longer acts like a mad dog but curls up in a ball and falls asleep with one eye and an ear open. I speak to him and treat him as though he were a human being; a dog should no more be his mummy's little doggy-woggy than a whipping boy.

If you care for your dog's health, as I do, you no doubt take your dog to the vet for regular check-ups. The vet has also tattooed your dog's identification number inside his ear, which will make it easier for you to find your pet, should he ever get lost. It is also good idea to attach a tag on your dog's collar with your telephone number, and the town and country where you live.

Your dog should never be a nuisance to your neighbours, whether in your apartment or in a public park, on account of his barking or his smell. To wash and brush our dogs as often as needed is a rule of *savoir-vivre*; just as holding our dogs on a leash in corridors.

If you do not like animals, what should you do when you find yourself in their presence? Make the effort, not to love them, but to accept them. You don't need to go so far as to pretend to have feelings for them, but you can show a modicum of interest, or at least you can show yourself tolerant. Don't demand that the animals be locked away on the pretext that you are afraid of them, or that you find their presence annoying!

Relationships have been made and unmade on account of a dog. A woman and a man who share a love of animals have a starting point for a relationship, and in the reverse, they have a departure point for breaking up.

To abandon a dog on the eve of a vacation or for any other reason is a highly culpable act that should never be committed. And if we witness a neighbour either in the country or in the city ill-treating an animal, we should not look the other way and become an accomplice, we must report the abuse to the local council or to the SPCA and make sure that action follows.

At the dawn of time, cats were such particular, complex animals that they took a significant place in Egyptian mythology. Today, the cat nourishes a vast literature. Solitary and royal, the cat cultivates mystery, and arouses passions or irrational fears.

Whatever their disposition, cats have practical advantages over dogs insofar as they live in the house and can be left alone for some time. However, cats need the same care and attention as dogs, regular visits to the vet, and training – and beyond their lordly demeanours and apparent detachment, they too need permanent affection.

SAVOIR-VIVRE: TRADES AND SHOPS

Savoir-vivre with your dressmaker

Today, dressmakers rarely make dresses and are mostly employed to alter garments. Nevertheless, there are times when we still require the dressmaker's truest skills and services.

I asked my dressmaker what qualities she hopes to find in her customers. Her answer was delivered in equal measure of speed and precision:

- To arrive at their appointment on time
- To know what they want and not to change their minds at every fitting
- To appreciate the work done for them
- To be polite at all times.

And she added, "A woman who is not happy with herself is unhappy with everything. Dealing with this sort of customer, is not doing dressmaking, it is like wrapping packages."

Savoir vivre with shopkeepers

Not so long ago, the customer was king. And at times, he did abuse his royal power. Nowadays, however, the power relations seem in reverse. The shopkeeper is king. And do you know it! I am speaking of the shopkeepers in the larger cities who so rudely handle their customers as to drive them away and deprive them of the very pleasure of shopping.

Only in the provinces can business mindedness still be found, where one feels welcome when stepping into a shop.

Savoir-vivre requires both parties to make some effort. Without common courtesy and understanding, we risk losing delightful exchanges, such as the relationships which the market gardeners who speak of growing their cauliflowers and their artichokes as though they had been present at their birth when they develop with their regular customers.

Customers need to understand that a shopkeeper does not have four arms and that the most basic politeness requires that they wait their turn to be served. And if the fish from the last catch is not fresh, there is no need to trumpet: "Your sea bream is on the nose". Just go and shop elsewhere. On the other hand, if the fruit and vegetable peddler sold you excellent peaches, tell him, it will make him happy and he will take even better care of you next time.

For their part, merchants need to recover the good humour they once had. Their business will surely benefit. The shoe salesman should not show his irritation, or feel free to utter disobliging remarks when a customer asks to try on several pairs of shoes: She is not overstepping her rights.

Today, many people prefer shopping in malls and supermarkets rather than in the small boutiques where they no longer find the warmth or welcome which once made them such appealing places.

Savoir-vivre and your petrol-station attendant

Once upon a time, when filling up the car, it was all too common to wind down the window, hand over the keys and call out: fill it up! And to forget to add *please*, not to mention bothering to notice whether the service person was a man or a woman. Today, not all petrol pumps are automated machines, if a person is serving at the pump, *savoir-vivre* requires you to get out of your car (here is an opportunity to stretch your legs) and to exchange a few pleasant words with him or her.

Trust the mechanic who services your car, there is no need to question his competence. Cars are this man's profession and he knows better than you the mysteries of engines and the costs involved. If you don't want to experience an unpleasant surprise when the work is done, make a list of what needs to be done and what you are prepared to pay for beforehand. Ask for a cost estimate of the work.

As for you, Messrs Mechanics, should you come across a customer such as myself who does not know the difference between the carburettor and the carburettor jet, have the elegance and the kindness not to replace the gearbox while you are at it. An ignorant customer is not always a guilty one.

Savoir-vivre with taxi drivers

In their miniscule habitat, taxi drivers have transported a sizable portion of humanity. They have seen, and heard everything and anything. And some have understood all of it too.

Taxi drivers, in some ways, are philosophers, and I never fail to start a conversation with a taxi driver as soon as I am in the car. It is very rare when I don't learn something new.

These street professionals have a very poor opinion (and probably rightly so) of the customers who impose a preferred route on them. Taxi drivers spend all day driving and they are more familiar and have a better understanding than anyone else of the flow of traffic. Under certain traffic conditions, it is often the case that the long way turns out to be the shortest. I would advise to refrain from dropping hints to show that you suspect the driver is taking you for a ride, as you may just end up spending more time breathing in petrol fumes.

If the driver smokes, you may ask him to lower his window or if the smoke really bothers you, to put out his cigarette. Indeed, most taxi drivers do not smoke and ask that their customers refrain from smoking. Meanwhile, it is best not to stroke the driver's dog, as the animal may not appreciate your familiarity and could respond with an aggressive growl.

As to you, dear taxi-driving ladies and gentlemen, please do not impose upon your customers, the horrendous litany playing on your radio or mobile phone: please wait until you have deposited your passengers before switching your devices back on. We have a right to peace and quiet. This inconvenience aside, I thank you sincerely and gratefully! What would we do without taxis? Out in a dark evening, standing in the cold rain, the lights of your car are to your customers like the sight of the life-saving lighthouse to the sailor.

Still, I have a small request to make of taxi companies. Sometimes, and unfortunately this happens too often, one spends several long minutes waiting on the telephone to be told: "No cars available!" – a miserly three short words followed by the click of the receiver brutally hung up on its hook. Could you not add a polite formula?

Savoir vivre with lawyers and civil-notaries

Without risking to be over the top, like Americans who live with their lawyer's permanent assistance, it is a wise and in the long term, an economical course of action to seek the advice of a lawyer every time we need to place our signature at the bottom of a document requiring our liability.

All too often, the solution to a problem ends up costing ten times what an initial legal consultation would have.

With a lawyer, we should only broach serious and grave topics and exclude familiarity and humour.

Before visiting a lawyer, whose time is always accounted for, it is advisable to prepare a written document detailing all the points about which you are seeking his counsel.

Before deciding on legal proceeding, it is a good idea to ask your lawyer for an estimate of his fees and of the total cost of the proceedings.

The "*notaire*"[23]

If King Leer had consulted a *notaire* before sharing his kingdom and his fortune between his three daughters, the *notaire* would have prevented him from handing out his wealth during his actual lifetime. A *notaire*, indeed, is a man who will protect you from yourself. With the long-term in sight, he can plan for your future and it is with your future in mind that he manages your present. When you sign your marriage contract, before advising you as to the best type of contract for your circumstances, he will first make inquiries about yours and your spouse's personal fortune, your respective professions, and your families, and he will take

---

[23] The *notaire* is a specifically French civil law notary, a highly specialised lawyer. The *notaire* is appointed by the justice minister; he or she drafts, writes and authenticates contracts, wills and other documents. The *notaire* may engage in company, family and property law. [Translator's note]

into account your mutual interests, presently and in the future. A *notaire* will not sign a conflicting document in which one of the parties is at a disadvantage. When called upon to settle a will, this confessor is more familiar than anyone else with the disagreements and resentments in the family closets: he has heard everything, from the guiltiest of motivations to the blackest of deeds, but he will never betray a word of the secrets entrusted to him.

The *notaire* has an ambivalent reputation because we also resent him after the fact, holding against him the dirty secrets which we had to reveal. Observe the *notaire* at a social gathering: he speaks and drinks little because, as he will explain, he cannot take the risk of letting his guard down and saying too much.

The *notaire* has a dual role. He is the only lawyer allowed to authenticate a will or a common agreement, and therefore to confer on such documents their legal status. But the *notaire* also gives you advice that is in your best interest, and in this capacity, he has a triple role: He is at once a mediator (he brings the protagonists to reason), a time manager (time is of the essence) and an arbitrator. His knowledge of the human heart has made him wise. If you have a capable *notaire*, you can sleep soundly.

SAVOIR-VIVRE AND MONEY

Savoir-vivre and your husband's money

Let us presume that you are at home and do not work, or rather that your work – which is considerable if it includes raising children and taking care of running and managing your household – brings you no financial return. You will therefore spend the money your husband earns, and that is entirely legitimate.

However, too often, money problems, that is to say the power and dependency which money engenders, poison marital relationships. The husband demands that his wife spend less, and the wife that her husband earn more. Both sides are wrong.

The best course of action is to jointly decide on a budget suited to the resources at hand. It is unfair of a woman to reproach her husband for the mediocrity of his salary, or to complain that she has to count her pennies or deprive herself in any way! Do such complaints mask others, of a deeper and more serious nature?

On the other hand, if you have a stellar career and resounding financial resources, don't overdo your economic independence. Don't deprive your husband of the joy (and the pride) of offering you a beautiful dress or jewellery, on the grounds that you can well afford to buy these for yourself. If you earn more than he does, take care not to reverse the relations of power. And believe me, to maintain the equilibrium of your relationship, hurry and open up a joint bank account, if not... your husband may well develop an inferiority complex that could lead him where you do not wish him to go.

Savoir-vivre and the bank manager

I am poorly placed to give advice on this count as I was married to my bank manager for over thirty years and today it is my son who takes care of my accounting.

But what about you? Are you pleased with your banker's services?

For the past fifteen years, you have trusted your banker with your entire salary, your portfolio, your savings, your earnings, keeping nothing in your home. And how grateful is your banker? Your bank prospers at your expense, and does not even have the elegance to treat you with a degree of deference. Only a few months ago, when you enquired about a small loan from the person who hoards your money, she had the effrontery of asking you several personal, indiscreet and unwelcome questions. Meanwhile your portfolio has not performed according to the predictions of the stock market indices. Some of your stock has even dropped substantially and your financial adviser remains as a block of ice. True, some of your shares have increased, but who can assure you that they won't suddenly melt away? Certainly not your financial adviser.

What then should and can you do?

To begin with, establish a trusting relationship. The more your bank manager knows about your resources and your needs, the better he or she will be at managing them. Don't hesitate to hand over a complete evaluation of your situation.

People who approach their bank manager to manage their wealth must establish a thorough inventory, sparing no detail or trifle. Indeed, the money we entrust to the bank, our own money, seems to us to be rich in history while the money that we borrow, the bank's money, is anonymous. Whether you are investing or borrowing, put all your cards on the table.

Perhaps you complain about the way your bank treats you, taking for granted the services it provides for you: depositing and withdrawing your cheques and operating your transfers; placing at your disposal automatic tellers; all of which costs the banking institution a fair deal of money. I know very little about bank management, but I also know that digital information makes it much more difficult to provide individualised services. To a computer, all customers are born and remain equal. As for the stock market, a good financial manager, so I have been told, must be judged over one or two years, rather than on a day to day basis. Hence, it is quite useless to phone your bank manager every time your stock loses value. Best to have regular conversations, and in order to better keep track of your accounting, to check the monthly statements which the bank provides for you.

Money and health are the French's two foremost concerns. And they go together. Indeed, in the French language, we say that health and money prosper and that our finances and our health can be ruined. Evidently, you don't have to worry yourself sick when both your body and your finances are in good health…

Savoir vivre with a lot of money

For generations, money was a taboo subject to the French, and the word was never uttered at the dinner table. In the mouth of an aristocrat it would have sounded obscene and in that of a bourgeois woman, most inappropriate. We just went along as though money did not exist.

Today, however, money rules. It is the most powerful of weapons, and one would stoop to any compromise to obtain it. We have evolved from excessive disapproval to abject exaltation!

How does one live with a lot of money? The answer is that one lives well; indeed, very well. But how should we behave with our money? This is the real issue.

Old money does not display itself, and those who have it spend less than they can, and always spend discriminately because they are anxious to preserve and pass on to the next generations the patrimony they have inherited.

The newly wealthy, on the other hand, may well live in ostentatious, noisy and arrogant luxury. Some appear to want to make their money ring at all times, to let the world know that their coffers are full. It is as though no exterior sign of wealth can be counted as superfluous or excessive.

Last summer, during a small dinner in Cannes, the wife of an important real estate developer arrived at her table covered in emeralds: earrings, necklaces, bracelets, broach, and rings on almost every finger. Only her shoes had escaped the jewellery.

At dessert, with a nonchalant gesture, she removed the enormous cross she was wearing around her neck, placed it on the table and told her husband in a fatigued tone: "Darling, it really is too heavy"

A man, seated at the next table, looked daggers in her direction, his eyes meaning: "What martyrdom Madame! Money is such a burden to bear!"

It is neither forbidden, nor reprehensible to earn and to spend a lot of money, so long as we are respecting the rules of *savoir-vivre* – which are:

- Discretion

- Discrimination: one should not dilapidate one's wealth, or spend money whichever way; one does not spend a fortune at the casino.
- To have a sense of patrimony: to turn to good account the money inherited from parents and to pass it on to children.
- To have a sense of patronage.

Perhaps these thoughts make sense to you as they do to me, and perhaps the reasonableness I see in them is my own, rather than yours. The fact is that I have never been attracted to flamboyance or to people who gamble away their fortunes. But at the same time, I admire artists who spend and share whatever they have in their pocket, and care little for tomorrow.

How do we live with little money?

Badly, very badly. Is *savoir-vivre* useful to those who live in poverty? No, for the very poor, there is only *savoir-survivre*. The very poor survive and only personalities like the Abbé Pierre who elected to help the poorest among the poor are entitled to speak on their behalf.

Compassion and generosity consist in giving to others the means to live by their own work and in conditions fit for human dignity. The greater our wealth and the greater our responsibility towards those who have nothing.

SAVOIR-VIVRE AND THE HOSPITAL

Savoir-vivre and medical doctors

Recently, during a visit to a retirement home, an older lady seated in her armchair stopped me and took hold of my hand. Her sight having failed her, she asked me to help her fill in her lotto ticket. Struggling to think up any numbers, I then chose from those before my eyes: the fire brigade, emergency police and ambulance.

"And what will you do, *chère Madame*, if you win the jackpot?" I asked her as I handed her the ticket.

Without hesitation, she replied: "I will ask the doctor to come to my home every single day."

Perhaps a very real fear of death can explain this older lady's answer. However, there are some people, men and women, who are true hypochondriacs, who believe, at whatever age they happen to be, that they are always sick, and therefore entitled to call on their doctors at any hour of the day or night. They would call from the other end of the world without even thinking that they may be intruding on their doctor's time with another patient. They insist on speaking to the doctor without further delay, as though their malaise has priority over everyone else's.

The first rule of *savoir-vivre*: one does not bother a doctor to demand a private consultation over the telephone; and one does not take advantage of having a medical professional at the dinner table (even if a friend) to grab a free consultation.

A doctor receives patients by appointments in her or his rooms or at the hospital. It is only in those circumstances that we should be discussing health problems.

When addressing a medical doctor, we use the title *"Docteur"* – or, if we are addressing a specialist with a university title: *"Monsieur le Professeur"* or *"Madame le Professeur"* while interns and departmental heads will respectfully address the latter as *"Monsieur"* or *"Madame"*.

Savoir-vivre and patients

To a sick person, a doctor is the messiah. A doctor means everything to the sick; patients place their lives into their doctors' hands with a trust that is almost childlike. Dear Doctors, even if your time is limited and accounted for, have the patience and the kindness to reassure your patients, to explain what is happening to them and the stages of their disease.

As you well know, while some are able to confront their illness with equanimity, the majority sink into depression, abandon the struggle and lose their love of life and their will to live. You are the only person who can infuse them with the necessary fighting strength.

Listen to those who are in your care, and with a smile, give them the promise of healing. I thank you for not refusing anyone the possibility of hope.

Savoir-vivre and nurses

In sickness, all patients are (more or less) equal. Whether they are alone in a private room or several in a public ward, the hospital cares for all patients equally. The nurses who devote themselves to them not only provide care from morning to night, but also dispense encouragement and comfort. Where would we be without nurses?

We call and they come running. We bother them to re-arrange a pillow, to take our blood-pressure one more time, to pour us a glass of water; and nine times out of ten, we call on them for very little, or for nothing. It is easy to abuse of their helpfulness, and to forget that they too have good reasons to feel tired. Illness must not become an excuse for abusing of the kindness of others; even in the hospital, there is a *savoir-vivre*, it is simply consideration.

Above everything else, when hospitalised, we need to forget about our social position, to refrain from requesting inappropriate personal attention or care, and finally we need to keep in mind that we are not alone and that others are sick too. Avoid complaining about the care you are receiving or about the doctor who is in charge of you in front of your nurses, as this puts them in an awkward position. Let's not forget that trust plays a significant role in the healing process.

When conversing with our nurses, or with the other patients in the ward, it is good for everyone's morale to steer clear of sickness related topics. It is important not to imprison ourselves in our illnesses, as to do so is to run the risk of remaining in this prison for life.

When we undertake a new and unwelcome treatment, we should not over-burden the nurses with our feelings. They are only following directives and procedures. Let's keep in mind that if the test we must undergo is painful, it is not the nurse's doing. We just have to accept the pain for the time being.

Finally, we must refrain from over-familiarity, a nurse has the right to be addressed as "Madame" as well as a right to all other polite conventions: "Would you mind" or "Would you be kind enough to...". A polite request is never an order and it is a means of building respectful relationships.

Even when you are in a great hurry to leave the hospital, don't leave without thanking your nurses. Traditionally,

143

patients offer a small gift. Perhaps it is best not to offer chocolate, sweets, or a plant for which they have no use, but something more personal: a book or CD, or a scarf. Even better: give your nurses some money. You can hand in a note (even a small one) in an envelope to the matron who will then distribute yours and other gifts to the nurses on her floor.

Savoir vivre with a person who is ill

When you visit a sick person, put a warm smile on your face as soon as you have passed the threshold of their room. Make sure your lies look truthful, and do not fear to come across as over-optimistic, it is impossible to give too much re-assurance to a sick person.

Even if you believe that your sick friend or relative needs to seek a second opinion, refrain from speaking negatively of the doctors, or to shake the trust your friend has placed in them. Even if you have a lot of experience, spare the patient your diagnostic or your predictions regarding healing time and convalescing, as you may well (and without ever meaning to) inflict upon the sick a cruel disappointment.

If you need information on the state of a sick person's health, don't grab hold of the doctor while he or she is doing their rounds in the corridors; *savoir-vivre* requires you to make an appointment. Finally, don't expect the nurse or the doctor to provide you with explanations regarding your friend's or your relative's state of health either in their presence or outside of it, since the ethics of professional confidentiality restrain them from discussing their patients' health.

When calling a sick person on the telephone, keep the conversation brief, and avoid calling either at dawn or late into the night; when visiting a sick person at home, be brief.

144

The sick room is not a parlour. Whether you are visiting someone in a public or a private hospital, you need to keep to formal visiting hours, and if the person you are visiting is in a shared ward, be kind enough to greet her neighbours, and to ask how they are feeling. Don't ask for special visiting rights on account of your own importance or your lack of time.

Finally, and I will repeat myself here, don't bring or send flowers to a sick person as the scent could incommode them. In fact, most hospitals in France forbid flowers in the wards.

Savoir-vivre when we are sick

Illness should not turn us into tyrants. A sick person cannot command the permanent presence and attention of either relatives, friends or the medical personnel caring for them. Everyone is entitled to some rest and freedom. It is important for our own sake and for the sake of others to discuss other topics besides our illness. Our health problems are not the only problems in the world. We must never lose sight of the relativity of things.

A patient with a sense of humour is a golden patient. I will never forget my cousin's words, as he was being wheeled to the operating block, his face pale as a sheet.

In my confusion, I asked: "How are you Jacques?"

"As you can see, I'm on a roll!"

Try not to worry the people around you who are watching for the smallest sign of recovery. Reassure them, it will also reassure you.

Whether we are in a private or a public hospital, it cannot be over-stressed, we must forget our social rank and think of ourselves as everyone's equal. If you are sharing a room with another patient, include him into the conversations you are having with your visitors, and offer him the sweets they have brought for you.

Savoir vivre with the victim of a road accident

You may remember Claude Sautet's film, with Romy Schneider and Michel Piccoli, *The Things of Life* based on Paul Guimard's beautiful book. There is a car accident on a country road, the car rolls over several times and the driver is ejected. Lying in a field, Michel Piccoli is half conscious. The people and the first-aid workers who surround him express their feelings out loud: "He looks like he's had it", "What a terrible state he's in!" "If he's not dead yet, it won't be long", "Nothing can be done for him now".

Meanwhile, the accident victim hears everything and is going crazy with terror. He wants to scream: "Take me away, I am not dead!" but he cannot speak or even open his eyes.

These things don't just happen in novels. A person I know, in fact, a famous professor of medicine, Jean-Claude Chermann, had this very experience after a scooter accident, when he was only twenty years old.

Moral of the story: when standing next to a road accident victim, let's refrain from alarmist comments, and keep instead to reassuring words, never forgetting that the person may well be hearing us. Let's also ask the curious and the importune to step aside and move along. Above all, let's do everything in our power to get the victim to the nearest hospital as quickly as possible.

SAVOIR VIVRE IN THE COMMUNITY

Savoir-vivre and the physically disabled

Every year road accidents leave ever more people physically disabled. Do we know how to live with the disabled? Not truly. Too many of us, when meeting a disabled person, especially when the disability is severe, turn our heads and look elsewhere. But a disabled person notices this movement of exclusion and feels deeply affected. To exclude disabled persons from our everyday life further narrows the limitations which disability imposes on them.

Our civic sentiments and our sense of solidarity must inspire us to overcome our weaknesses and to break the social isolation and the emotional suffering of our fellowmen and women.

To help a blind person cross a street, to describe what she cannot see, to speak without condescension to a person who is mentally handicapped is sometimes difficult but it is always gratifying. When a disabled child smiles with happiness, we are filled with gratitude.

Savoir-vivre and the elderly

In many places in the world, as for example in Sub-Saharan Africa, older persons enjoy universal respect. Elders are owed particular deference; their advice is sought before decisions are made and their judgement prevails. An "old one" is a wise one.

In our Western societies, we lack even the terms to designate old people. They are placed into brackets: age

147

brackets of the third, fourth and fifth category. They no longer have a place among us, the weight of their years imprisons them in a ghetto and cuts them even from their families.

Old age among us is a sad stage of life; on the eve of summer vacations, the newspapers relate terrible stories of old and infirm persons who are left at home, abandoned without help or resources.

In every town in France, there are agencies that organise for retired people to come to our home during our vacations, to house-sit our apartment, to take care of our pets, our plants, our gardens, and forward our mail. Why can we not organise better services to take care of the elderly?

We all should think about old age and prepare for it. How do we do this? By building ties and relationships with older people, by being close to them and by giving them the respect owed to them: let's stand up when they enter a room, give up our seats for them, help them walk up the stairs, help them get on the bus, cross the street. Let's not smoke in their presence without asking if we may.

Above all let's lighten old people's solitude, by phoning as often as possible, by doing their shopping from time to time; by helping with the laundry or with the various administrative forms they always need to fill in; by giving them a lift to their local association; by listening to them; by bringing them a book on tape if they cannot see very well. There are so many ways to give happiness and emotional closeness to older people.

Savoir-vivre and immigrants

"Love foreigners because you too were foreigners in the land of Egypt" teaches the Bible.

Whatever your opinion about immigrants' presence in France, we owe immigrants the same respect (does one really need to state the obvious?) that is owed to any other citizen. Should it be necessary to remind my compatriots that they should address immigrants with "*Madame*" and "*Monsieur*" and to use the formal "*vous*". In whose name should anyone of us criticize their customs, their religions, their traditions? The first rule of *savoir-vivre* is to respect others and their beliefs.

Savoir-vivre with foreign visitors

A country is loved for its landscape or its cities and monuments, but above all, it is loved for the hospitality of its inhabitants.

The millions of tourists who visit France every year say that France is one of the most beautiful countries in the world. But have you noticed that they speak with less enthusiasm of the manner in which we welcome them?

Remember that hosting a foreign visitor at home rather than at the restaurant almost always turns a formal acquaintance into friendship. To open and welcome someone in our home is a way of opening our arms to them. If we accompany our visitors to visit a museum or a cathedral, their touring experience will be utterly transformed.

In the street, we should kindly explain to visitors how to get to their destination, and if we can walk a little of the way with them to make sure they are heading in the right direction – all the better.

One day, we may very well be foreign visitors in their country

V

SPEAKING, TELEPHONING,

WRITING AND E-COMMUNICATING

THE ART OF SPEAKING

From the dawn of times, storytellers have enjoyed considerable prestige. Villagers once awaited their arrival, crowded around their persons, and when the storytellers were gifted raconteurs and skilful orators, their power was indeed great. Those who have the gift of the tongue have influence over their listeners. The lawyer's eloquence spares the guilty's head.

A man who has a fifty word vocabulary can only express the simplest of ideas. His thought is as good as paralysed. A man who has ten thousand words will extricate himself from the most difficult of all situations. This is why educational inequity is the worst of all injustices. But I do believe that it is never too late to learn and to study.

There is little need to recall the Greek orator Demosthenes, or to further stress the power of influence we acquire over others if we are able to express ourselves with talent. If we want to express ourselves clearly, we need to use correct elocution, to pitch our voice well, to speak neither too slowly nor too rapidly, and to use a tone that is neither too low nor too high. Politicians, like actors, take elocution classes. And a good speech instructor is as precious as a good hairdresser. In the United States, some of the large corporations require that their switchboard operators hold elocutions diplomas. The charm of their voices acts upon their clients as the Sirens'' songs on Ulysses.

151

Accents

An accent may add a touch of originality and charm to a person's expression. An accent is also the designation of the *"terroir"*, the home grown territory. Could we ever imagine our great actors, Raimu or Fernandel, speaking with a Parisian accent, or with a form of affected speech, a touch of the "British"?

Pronunciation

To speak French with elegance, we need to pronounce all the letters in a word, and avoid certain contractions at all cost, as for example: *"T'as été au cinéma?"* or *"T'as vu cet homme?"*. A word should not lose any of its vowels: thus, we should say: *je-ton*, and never *j'ton* [token/coin] Genève and not G'nève; *chemin* and not *ch'min* [path]. By the same token, we should not add a vowel where it does not exist: we say *pneu*, not *peneu* [tyre].

A few words, in French, are not pronounced as they are written. For example: *gageure* is pronounced gajure [wager]. Finally, it is important to respect the pronunciation of accented *es*. In the words *féerie* [fairy tale] and *pélerinage* [pilgrimage] the second *e* has no accent and therefore we should not say *féérie* nor *pélèrinage*.

We should also clearly differentiate between the sounds *on* and *en*: *le thon* [tuna] and *le temps* [time/weather] are confused in some people's mouths.

The liaison – linking words

There are some dangerous liaisons: we say *"un homme et une femme"* not *"un homme et **tune** femme"* [a man and a woman]. The best is to avoid the liaisons altogether outside of a few essential ones, which are necessary because the French language is like other languages linked – words are not sounded in disconnection from each other. Therefore we do say: "*Comment **tallez-vous?*" [24]

When speaking in error either by omitting a liaison or by liaising out of turn, it is better to rephrase than to let the error slip. I find regrettable that radio or television anchors do not always respect the liaisons or other formal rules of our language. After all, they have the same civic duty as teachers and professors since it is up to them to complete our education and the education of our children.

Slang and swearing

There is little more to say on this subject than both are deplorable in an adult person's mouth. Only teenagers should have the privilege of making use of the neologisms, abbreviations and the Anglicisms that emerge seasonally – although swearing should really be out.

In the mouth of a forty year old, hipster vocabulary is simply ridiculous. Let's avoid words like OK, or worse *ouais* (yeah), and the word which made the Vicomte Pierre Jacques Etienne Cambronne famous.[25]

---

24 The *liaison* links two words together so as to maintain phonetic fluidity. The liaison in French carries the last consonnant sound of a word over and onto the first syllable of a following vowel-initialised word. Making the liaison: *mon ami* is pronounced *mon* **n**ami, *mes amis* is pronounced *mes* **z**amis. Making the wrong liaison in French has the same socio-cultural value as dropping or adding heches inappropriately in English. [Translator's note]

[25] Cambronne (1770-1842) was a Major in the Napoleonic guard. He is alleged to have sworn at the British request for surrender. To refer to Cambronne's word (*le mot de Cambronne*) is to use a

The art of conversation

One should not speak about just anything and anyhow, cut another's words, interrupt or contradict another speaker; interpret their ideas before they have finished expressing them; by the same token, we owe it to our interlocutors to end our own sentences and not leave them guessing what we mean: "You know what I mean"…

Not all topics are suitable for conversation. There are even some topics which should never be broached: health problems, money problems, family or domestic problems. We should not crow about our successes, or those of our spouses or children or about our dog's prowess. Consideration for others requires us not to avoid speaking about ourselves. We should enquire about the person we are conversing with, their work, their family, or current affairs. We should also try to forget our petty problems and our daily routine, so as to raise the level of the conversation. We banish proverbs and clichés and ready-made verbal expressions, in other words, we avoid anything that hints of impersonality and facility.

Finally, we avoid bad news and catastrophes and focus on pleasant subjects.

Women should abstain from telling off-colour jokes or salacious stories especially in the presence of children or older people. My husband who loved stories could not bear to hear women sinking into vulgarity. It is also in very poor taste for men to boast about their sexual conquests and of their powers of seduction.

---

euphemism for "*merde*". As shoot or sugar is to sh... in English [Translator's note]

154

And when a political or religious difference risks leading to conflict, it is also best to drop the topic.

Keeping a measured tone, one that is neither high-handed nor insulting, grants you a double advantage: it makes you more credible, since you know how to control your emotions, and unfailingly courteous since you are able to respect an opinion that appears to you to be reprehensible or even guilty. The talented hostess distinguishes herself through the art of diverting a conversation that is heading down a perilous path, the art of giving each one of her guests the opportunity, if not to shine, at the very least to express themselves. Unless, of course, she is hosting an extraordinary personality whose words fascinate everyone present.

Knowing when not to speak

"It is a great pity to possess neither enough wit to speak with talent, nor sufficient common sense not to speak at all", noted La Bruyère, who certainly knew something of the human character. Unless a person is in possession of a superior mind, and his or her opinions are expressly sought after, it is a lack of civility to monopolise a conversation. Let's listen to others, let's be courteous and pay attention to their words. Let others express their opinion and allow them to unwind. To be able to listen, to know how to re-kindle a conversation with an appropriate question is as vital to the art of conversation as the gift of speech.

A woman who lends an interested ear to others' talk without showing either impatience or boredom is more likely to charm than an unrepentant chatter-box. Not only is she escaping an incurable disease (egocentrism), but she is acquiring a knowledge of the human heart which makes her a subtle psychologist.

It is never a good sign when someone begins a sentence with "I think", and uses only the negative or the affirmative without caring for grey areas. It is safe to presume that those afflicted by an inflammation of their "I" are about to boast of their relations, their wealth, their personal interests, and show off their position or their titles. A person of quality acts to the contrary. She takes shelter behind an "it seems to me that" or the conditional mood. We are likely to learn nothing of her private life, especially if the latter is brilliant.

Knowing how to end a conversation

I once asked the Chief of Protocol of a European sovereign who was hosting me: "How will I know when the queen wishes to end the conversation?"

"Don't worry about it," he answered, "when Her Majesty turns her hand with her palm upward, her lady in waiting will walk up to you, and walk you out."

No matter the person with whom we begin a conversation, it is important to recognise the right moment to end it. If you are paying attention, you should be able to detect the onset of impatience in your interlocutor: a foot tapping, fingers playing an invisible piano, an eye turning to a wristwatch. These are the signs we need to take immediate notice of, for they are telling us that it is time to end the conversation.

Knowing how to deliver a speech or an address

On occasions, we are called to deliver a speech – as for example, at a birthday party, or when a colleague is taking leave of her position, or at a charity event. The only good improvisations are those we have prepared and written out ahead of time. Indeed, unless one is a born orator or is very

156

experienced in public speaking, a genuinely spontaneous speech will more than likely end up as a sounding like a series of disjointed thoughts. A good speech makes a good effect not as a result of good luck but as a result of sound reflection.

Whatever the audience, public speaking should be:

- Very brief
- Clear
- Simple.

To be interesting, an address must be personal, original, never trivial and never pompous. Politeness demands that we do not inflict on our listeners interminable sermons stuffed with citations.

An address begins with the traditional: "*Mesdames, Mesdemoiselles, Messieurs*", but if an Important Person is in the room, then this person takes precedence: "*Monsieur le Ministre,* or *Monsieur* the Ambassador, or *Monsieur* the Grand Rabbi, *Mesdames, Mesdemoiselles, Messieurs*".

While we cannot always hope to avoid stage fright, we can hope to bring it under control if we have confidence in our text – both content and form – and if we have already read through it aloud several times over. Model on Flaubert: lock yourself up in a room and read to yourself in a full and clear voice, so that you can learn to speak your words with ease.

Another piece of advice: record yourself, in audio or better in video. You will find it easier to correct your diction and your text and also to measure your actual speaking time. When you have completed this exercise, you will feel far more confident. And before you take the microphone, drink a very good (small) glass of Bordeaux. It will act as a pick me up! Even if you know your speech by heart (which is highly recommended), it is best to read the first lines when you start, to give yourself a chance to get your confidence up and find your breathing pace. Then, detach yourself from your written speech and make eye contact with the people in the audience. Avoid speaking too fast or too slowly, keep to an *allegro vivace*. Whether you are sitting or standing, make sure that you stay erect, and that you keep your hands flat on the surface of either table or pulpit: don't grasp at the microphone. If sitting, keep one leg slightly higher than the other.

As for you, Messieurs, remember to button up your jacket and to take your hand out of your pocket.

How to live as a European

How can we construct Europe if we remain locked into our own languages, cultures and customs? To learn at least one second language has become a necessity and the foundation of a European *savoir-vivre*.

Our national education system correctly expects all our children to be fluent in at least one second language. Could we not demand the same of our politicians, even if it meant organizing evening classes for them to catch up to history? I find it depressing to see our leaders using interpreters when they speak with our neighbours. It is high time we came to terms with the fact that French has long ceased to be the language of diplomacy.

SAVOIR-VIVRE AND THE TELEPHONE

The telephone, especially the mobile telephone, has transformed lovers' relationships. It has become the barometer of love – if the telephone is silent, the weather is stormy: if it is permanently engaged, hearts are beating in eternal sunshine. Why say he loves me, when all that is needed is, he called! For people in love, the telephone is a magical machine, a sorcerer, a shaman. The telephone nullifies absence and abolishes time and distance. No matter how far our loved one may be, the telephone will spirit her or him from the depths, and in an instant, dissolve the pain of separation. Words, sighs, secrets and confessions, silences flow from one ear to the other like celestial music.

However, where ordinary mortals are concerned, the ringing of a telephone has something in common with breaking and entering; our time may be casually stolen from us and interrupted during breakfast or a conversation, or during the movie we are watching. And often in order to relate... what exactly? Not much of interest. It is indeed important to know the "when and how" of telephone calling.

To begin: unless we are calling a relative or a close friend who wishes to speak to us, we should not call before 9:00 am or later than 10:00 pm. We should also refrain from calling at meal times, or at news time. When phoning on a Sunday, it is best to be brief and to begin with an apology.

Once you have dialled the number, be patient and let the phone ring long enough for the person you are calling to reach it, to get out of her bath or come out of the kitchen. It is rather annoying to run for the phone and find that the caller has already dropped the call. And when calling overseas, first make sure to check the time difference before dialling.

159

How should we introduce ourselves on the phone?

"*Allô? Bonjour Madame* (or *Monsieur*). *Ici Madame Edmond de Rothschild,* may I speak to *Maître* Jean Dufaure?"

Always begin by introducing yourself: "This is … speaking." A man, however, never refers to himself as Monsieur Buisson but simply as Paul Buisson.

As soon as the person you wish to speak with is on the line, ask: "Am I bothering you? Would you prefer I called back?"

In a professional situation, should you need to telephone either Monsieur or Madame Masson, don't request your secretary to initiate the call and then leave your interlocutors hanging at the end of the line, waiting for you to speak to them. We should never expect those whom we are calling to wait. If we do, they are in their right to hang up.

Phone conversations should be short and to the point. It is inappropriate to use the telephone to make small talk, even when calling a very close friend or relative. Remember too, that it is the person who calls who should end the conversation.

I know women and some men, who spend their lives hanging on the telephone as others would an oxygen mask. These telephomaniacs have several lines and several phones and move from their living room to their bathroom with a phone constantly at their ear. They speak for hours on end, to several persons at once and thus inflict their conversations on all present and absent, from one city to the next, from one friend to another. By the afternoon, they are on several continents, weaving a network of relationships worthy of a network of spies (their taste for intrigue naturally adding to their curiosity). These people will call you at any time of the day or night. They will hold you up for an hour or a second, depending on their whims or their needs, and let you know that they will call back in a moment, because they have been interrupted by the arrival of their breakfast or their masseuse, or because their little dog has just jumped on the bed. And of course, they forget all about you as soon as they have hung up the receiver.

Others (and I know a number of them) only call when they need your help.

What can possibly be the cause of such impertinence? Is it boredom? Or the lack of *savoir-vivre*...

If your domestic staff answer telephone calls in your absence, they should begin with: "Madame (or Monsieur) is absent. Who wishes to speak to her?" and not with: "Who wishes to speak to her? Madame has gone out." Which could induce your caller to think that you do not actually wish to speak to him or her.

Note that a receptionist, a secretary, or domestic staff should never say "Speaking?" but "Who may I say is calling?"

It is hardly necessary to stress the role of the telephone in the success or the failure of a business enterprise. A receptionist or an employee who answer callers with amiability, who is quick to respond and who is efficient and cooperative, increases a company's customer base. By contrast, employees who use a stark tone and a discourteous manner put the company at risk.

When I call a friend, a doctor, a lawyer, or a hairdresser, I first introduce myself: Madame Edmond de Rothschild. On the other hand, if I am calling a publisher or a journalist, I identify myself as Nadine de Rothschild. And if I call a friend at home, I ask to speak to Madame Joseph Couturier, but if I call her at work, I ask to speak to Madame Valentine Couturier.

If I wish to speak to a man, even a famous man, I will always ask for "Monsieur Thierry Ardisson" and never "Thierry Ardisson", as do too many persons. Even if someone is famous, this does not grant others the right to use familiarity towards them.

And when speaking to a receptionist, remember that at the end of the line you have dialled, there is a human being, not a robot. Be pleasant, whether this person's job is to answer your questions or to put you through to another line, she or he deserves to be thanked for their work.

When you are being called

Answer with some deference and cordiality, and show by the tone of your voice that you are happy to hear your caller. If someone calls at the wrong time, ask him or her as soon as you pick up the call, to phone you back and when. There is no reason to chat under duress, if for example you are about to leave the house, or you are in the middle of some work or already engaged in a conversation.

Communicating on behalf of a third person

If you receive a call for a friend who lives in your home, don't ask of the caller: "Who may I say is calling please? Simply say: "If you do not mind waiting, I will fetch him/her".

You then pass the telephone to your friend without giving details such as "It's a man" or "A woman is asking for you."

While your friend responds (politeness here requires the reply to be as brief as possible), you may think of leaving the room so that she or he may speak freely. When returning to the room, do not ask any questions, not even those of the solicitous kind: "Good news, I hope." Nothing should give

162

the impression that you have heard even unintentionally what passed in the conversation. You should act as though nothing ever happened.

Speaker-phones

When you are in the presence of a third person, don't ever place your caller on the speakerphone. A conversation always has the potential for unpredictable developments, and it is possible (and believe me it happens) to let slip a disobliging comment about the caller or one of their close acquaintances.

In what circumstances should we write and never use the telephone?

- In principle, when thanking our hosts for a weekend away or a grand evening party.
- It is mandatory to write in order to congratulate people on the birth of a child, a baptism or a communion, engagement, marriage, the presentation of an award or to address your condolences.

The merits of the telephone

They are so numerous that it is impossible to draw a complete list.

The telephone, beyond its technical prowesses, has the power of nullifying inhibitions and even modesty. On the telephone, in the silence of the night, we may share confidences which we would never broach in the daylight or in a face to face encounter. With their telephones in hand, the timid lose their timidity and the chatterboxes become inexhaustible, which has led me to believe that if psychoanalysis took place at night and over the phone, the conversation would gain in intensity and the cure would progress more rapidly.

Voice mail

A voice mail greeting should seek neither originality nor humour. A simple, clear and short greeting is always best. *"Bonjour, je suis absent mais laissez moi un message. Je vous rappellerai dès mon retour. Après le signal sonore, c'est à vous. Merci et au revoir."* This translates into English as: "Hello. I am absent, but leave me a message. I will call you back as soon as I return. After the beep, it is up to you. Thank you and good-bye." [26]

When making a call, politeness requires us to leave a message before hanging up. Unless the person you called has installed Caller ID on their phone, and they are able to recognise your number, why would you not leave your name and the reason for your call? Leave a message and spare the person you have called the disappointment of listening to an anonymous ring.

Mobile phones

Over the last decade, the "mobilophobes" have dwindled to a handful of inflexible die-hards. Almost all of us work, walk, drive, eat, play sports, and sleep with our mobile phones just

---

[26] Note the cross-cultural difference: In Australia, we would tend not to say "thank you and goodbye" because it sounds dismissive.

as cowboys with their guns. We have fallen into a state of dependency and addiction that is at times frankly worrying. Evidently, the merits of the mobile phone are immeasurable. If you happen to be on the top of the Mont-Blanc and you have just been buried by an avalanche; or you are stranded on a dismasted yacht, your mobile phone can save your life. However, a mobile phone can be as annoying to your neighbours as it can be precious to its owner.

Savoir-vivre and the mobile phone

When you are invited for a weekend at a friend's place, your mobile allows you to make calls without making use of your hosts' landline, without transferring calls to their phone or having to use a phone card. That is fantastic for you and for your hosts, so long as you respect the following rules:

- Make your calls in private: no one, not even your spouse, is interested in hearing your conversation with a third person.
- When you are in the company of others: at the dinner table, in the living room, at the restaurant, in the train or any other public space, either turn off your mobile or set it to vibrating mode. People who keep their telephones on the table lack all *savoir-vivre*.
- Leave your mobile in your bag or in your pocket so that it will not disturb your neighbour if it rings.
- If the screen does not indicate your caller's number, you are not under obligation to answer immediately. Wait until you have listened to the message on the answering service. People who choose to keep their mobile numbers secret should expect this much in return.

- Nothing stops you from deciding which calls to take and which calls to default to the answering system.
- Your spouse is right to feel irritated when you are together at home, and you answer multiple calls. Take the habit (and especially if you are a telephomaniac) of turning off your phone when you open the door of your apartment. The peace of a marriage is well worth this small sacrifice.
- There is no reason to give a mobile phone to a small child. Wait until children are at least ten years old and, more significantly, until there are good reasons for them to own a phone, as for example, if they are going on vacation or exchange in another country.

Last summer, on the plane between Rome and Catania, I witnessed a scene worthy of a Nanni Moretty movie. It was a Friday night, and there was only one seat available, and strangely, I ended up being the only woman on board. We had already fastened our seat belts when the captain announced that, due to traffic congestion, our departure would be delayed by fifteen minutes. As soon as the announcement was made, the plane began to hum like a bird house: "*Pronto! Abbiamo quindici minuti di ritardo. Avvisa Paola, avvisa la mamma, avvisa Alberto. Ciao! Ciao! Ciao!*"

I released my seatbelt and stood up from my seat. From the first to the last row, every single passenger without a single exception was on his mobile phone. I could not help but burst out laughing.

That same morning, I had been sitting at the terrace of a café in the Piazza del Popolo, when a man came to sit at the table besides me. His demeanour and especially the intensity in his eyes reminded me of Vittorio Gassman. As soon as he was seated, he took out his *telefonino* and began a short and

166

firm conversation. He then placed his mobile on the table and took out another from his briefcase. His voice was different, filled with affection, "*Tesoro mio*" the handsome Roman repeated several times.

We started to talk. He explained to me that his first *cellulare* was for his office, the second for his family.

I asked him, "And the third one sticking out of your pocket is for ....?"

With a gleam in his eye, he replied: "Shhh, this is for the one who cannot be named..."

I would not be surprised if of all the countries in the world, Italy has the greatest number of mobile phones per inhabitant.

But as amused as I may have been by these Italian demonstrations of conviviality, I was appalled by the scene I witnessed in a Chinese restaurant of the rue Pierre-Charron in Paris. The couple facing me, in their forties, had their heads turned away from one another, each absorbed in a separate conversation that lasted almost as long as their dinner. This has to be a modern version of purgatory.

The capacities of the third generation of mobile phones appear limitless. The smartphone allows you to connect to the Internet, to find the closest restaurant, to receive images, to take photographs and I know not what else. And then, there are the mobile phones hidden in the tummy of children's teddy bears that connect them to their parents!

The innovation which appears to me most suited to *savoir-vivre* is the SMS. Send your guests a text with your address and the code of your apartment on the morning they are coming to visit.

Can you believe that during the first trimester of 2001, French people sent eight hundred million SMS, and that at the start of 2014, the number of SMS sent on New Year's Eve alone reached five hundred million?

ETIQUETTE AND
THE ART OF LETTER WRITING

I get up very early in the morning, and while listening to the radio, I make a list of the tasks ahead, of the things I will have to do during the day: errands, appointments, letters to write, invitations to send... The list of the phone calls I must make keeps on growing while that of the letters I have to write is shrinking. It is truly a pity!

When, in the midst of looking for something, I come across a friend's letter (and I have kept letters written more than thirty years ago), I will read it, and on reading a word, a memory, an emotion suddenly springs within me, as fresh as on the first day – and yet, I had thought it all forgotten.

When we no longer take the time to write, either to narrate an event or relate a thought, when we stop making the effort to reflect and look for the right word and for the precise nuance, we impoverish our memory.

Is it because we no longer write, that others' letters seem ever more fascinating? The epistolary genre has returned to literary fashion: we publish and re-publish Diderot's letters or Mozart's, Proust, George Sand (with twenty-five volumes already in print), Louise Colet, Flaubert, Camus, Henry James...

A letter serves the same essential purpose as a photograph. Letters fix events and feelings in time: an emotion, a story, a day in our lives, a sunbeam; the letter is the royal road that leads us, or returns us, to the most intimate part of ourselves.

Letter writing is a difficult exercise that requires both lightness and depth, wit and tact, *finesse* and a degree of matter of fact. In conversation, words are underscored and balanced by our eyes, voices, gestures. On a piece of paper, words are alone. But here lies the power and the endurance of the written language!

We must always be careful when choosing our words, for a word may crush or fill one with joy.

Whenever I write a letter that is leaning towards a complaint, I always hold off sending it for a day or two. I will entrust it to the post office only when, after re-reading it, my wording does not appear excessive or hurtful. More often than not, I tear it up and write another, more measured, which I will not regret writing. We should always be wary of words written in anger and allow time to soften our emotions before sending off a letter. A love letter, even a clumsy one, may age well because love will always retain at its core something moving and tender. The same cannot be said of bitterness.

And then, there is the style.

Ah! The *style*! Paul Valéry, the master of style who believed that style could not be acquired, conceded that a style could be developed. So, there is hope!

Style comes with a striking image, a word, or a nascent emotion. When André Breton lived in New York, he would pass a begging man always posted at the same street corner, not so far from his residence. Passers-by read, absent-mindedly, the words on the sign he wore around his neck: "I am blind" and very few stopped to deposit a coin in his bowl. One morning, moved by the man's sadness, André Breton suggested to write him another sign. A few days later, the man's life had undergone a transformation. Coins were raining around him, and people were showing him sympathy. André Breton had written: "Spring is coming and I will not see it."

While it is impossible to formulate a recipe for the acquisition of a writing style (and there are a variety of styles), it is easy to identify what to avoid if we are to produce good letter writing:

- Good writing is never pompous, precious or emphatic.
- Good writing avoids the excessive use of adverbs, adjectives, clichés, proverbs, complicated metaphors, and overly lengthy sentences. Contemporary taste prefers sobriety, which, however, should not be confused with dry language.
- Good letter writing finally admits neither carelessness nor familiarity.

Writing styles will also vary according to the connections that bind the author of a letter to its addressee. We do not use the same tone when writing to our siblings as when we write to the archbishop of Paris. Hierarchical relationships impose personal distance and a degree of deference. In a letter destined to a superior, erroneous language, errors of grammar or spelling, or a correction on the page are unacceptable and they may not be forgiven.

We can write a "good" letter, when calm, alone in a room and with plenty of time; a good comfortable chair, beautiful paper and a pen that moves easily on the page. Under these conditions, words come effortlessly.

Answering a letter

It is always better to write a very short letter (and to apologise for it) than to write six pages after several weeks of silence. At the very least, courtesy demands that we reply to any and all the letters we receive.

If you receive an invitation to lunch or dinner, you need to reply within two or three days so that the person who is inviting you to her table knows that she can count on your presence. And if you cannot attend, she needs to have enough time to invite another guest.

A death notice or a request for information likewise requires prompt responses.

If a letter contains nothing pressing, it may be answered within ten days of its reception.

Since we tend to forget to answer letters (even to friends), I advise keeping two folders – in one, go all the letters that require a rapid response, and in the other the mail that can wait a few days. Each folder has another two sections: one is for private correspondence, the other is for administrative, commercial or professional mail.

I also believe that it is helpful to keep an address book with all useful addresses, and to organise those according to professional categories: restaurants, hotels, cafés, dentists, doctors, masseurs, florists, taxis... In this manner, you can avoid wasting hours trying to find the name of that wonderful bistro or that charming hotel...

For security and easy access, enter these data into your computer or your smart phone, and write them into your address book.

When handwriting is a must

There are circumstances when using the telephone is simply inappropriate. A letter is required whenever you must express:
- Your congratulations on the occasion of
  a wedding
  a baptism
  a circumcision
  a communion or a bar-mitzvah
  an award ceremony.

- Your good wishes in the event of a sickness
- Your condolences on the occasion of a person's death.

Writing paper

The colour

Your personal writing paper may be light grey or slightly blue; only a very young woman gets away with green or shocking pink!

A white, either matt, smooth or slightly grainy paper (of course without lines or squares) is most elegant. Love letters and official letters are always written on virgin paper.

At any rate, the paper and the envelope must be of the same colour. It is best to choose envelopes with an interior lining and a paper that is neither too transparent nor too absorbent.

Paper dimensions and format

You may use a single or folio sheet (double sheet of paper folded in the middle). What matters is that the width of the paper should correspond to that of the envelope. If by chance, you have to use an envelope that does not match the paper (colour or size), apologise to your addressee and add a few words explaining that you wished to write without further delay – especially if you are in the country and the local grocery store does not sell writing paper.

Remember to use a glue stick to close an envelope that lacks adhesion, and never sticky tape.

If you are of a laconic disposition, use a small format writing paper and leave the larger sheets to the heirs of Madame de Sévigné.

Etched or printed paper

A personalised writing paper indicates, in print and at the top left corner, the address and – at a pinch – a telephone number. Family and personal names, however, are not indicated. The name of a house, a villa, or a chalet can be printed at the right hand corner.

Etched paper is the more elegant choice though it is a little more expensive than printed paper; the address is printed in a dark blue or black ink, and in green for a country house. When a letter requires several sheets, the address only appears on the first sheet. Therefore, when you order your personalised writing paper from the printer, you need to remember to order blank matching paper with it.

Envelopes must remain blank. Addresses are printed only on envelops that are used for commercial purposes.

The traditional obituary paper and envelop, with matching thick black borders, have now been replaced by a card bordered with a thin black line and a white envelope.

Ink

Ink should be blue, black or dark blue. Coloured inks, even purple are definitely out. An official letter is written in black ink.

The era of the goose quill and the rounded nib is long gone. The fountain pen has also been replaced, by the ballpoint or felt pen. It is a pity as only a metallic nib can do justice to the full outline of a letter – of up and down strokes. "A good pen is one of the pleasures I find in writing" André Gide used to say. And indeed, it is well worth having a pen that suits our handwriting.

A letter written to an intimate, a significant person, a superior or an older person should be handwritten. Or at least, this used to be the rule. Today, we have come to accept that those whose hand-writing is unreadable should type their personal letters on their computers.

In the course of thirty-seven years, I expanded a great deal of effort deciphering my husband's handwriting whenever he wrote to me. I remember that during our engagement, I had to ask his secretary at the bank to help me understand, and how this discreet woman would maintain an utterly professional tone while reading these letters, which were far removed from bank account statements.

We should at least hand-write when we address our recipient – whether we begin with "*Chère Jeanne*" or "*Cher Monsieur*"; when taking leave with the polite formula: "*Croyez, chère Jeanne, à toute mon amitié*" (Be assured, dear Jeanne, of my friendship) and of course when we are signing the letter – as legibly as possible.

On the other hand, when writing to a non-French speaking friend, and even if your writing flows as clearly as spring water, it is best to write on a computer with the caution: "I am writing to you from my computer so that you may read me more easily."

Letters of congratulations or condolences should always be handwritten. Circumstances demand it.

And of course, with a little time and patience, we can apply ourselves to improve the form of our vowels and consonants, to dot our i's and to cross our t's.

The presentation of a letter

The presentation of a letter should be light and breezy: leave blanks between the date and the salutation, the last line and your signature. The text of a letter written to an intimate friend or kin begins at one third of the page. Remember that a tight text or an overfilled page will put off your reader.

Margins

The left-hand margin is mandatory; although its dimensions may vary with the format of the paper, it cannot be less than two centimetres in width; when using a large sheet of paper, the left-hand margin may be as wide as five centimetres. A letter that is handwritten may dispense with the right hand margin; when using word processing on the computer, the right hand margin should be set at one or two centimetres.

Margins should not be squiggly. Even in a handwritten letter, margins should be plumbed and written lines should be as horizontal as possible. Margins must also remain free of any writing or annotation. The same goes for the space between the date and the salutation.

Finally, and especially when writing an official letter, paragraphs should be indented at a centimetre. Paragraphs can also be separated by a blank line.

The date

A letter should always be dated, either in the right hand top corner of the first page, starting at five centimetres or so, from the edge of the paper – or at the end of the letter, before or after the signature. There are several dating styles. In French, a date may be written as:

- Vendredi 28 juin 2014
- 28 juin 2014
- Le 28 juin 2014 , or
- Londres [London], 28 juin 2014.

Personally, I like to see the place alongside the date, because we all travel so frequently.

Never write: *Ce vendredi 28 juin 2014* (On this Friday 28 June 2014) even if you believe that this day is particularly significant. And only a love letter indicates *"Vendredi soir, 23h16"* (Friday evening, 11:23 pm). Indeed, this not only suggests daily correspondence but that, when in love, every detail is meaningful.

Polite formulas

The manner of beginning and ending a letter often plunges us into profound confusion: How should we address a letter to a bailiff, a lieutenant commander, the wife of a general, an ambassador, a senator?

Specific salutations are required for specific purposes: if they are overly respectful, they become ridiculous, if they are too casual, they become disrespectful or plainly rude.

The diversity and nuances inherent in salutations are daunting. They leave no room for improvisation – these polite formulas obey strict traditions and rules, and these rules must be observed.

The bearers of political, judicial, administrative, military and religious positions are entitled to specific forms of address.

The reader will find a list of these prescriptions at the end of this section.

Salutations – addressing formulas[27]

"*Chère Joséphine*" will be written on the left hand side, a few centimetres below the date. In relation to the rest of the text, this formula is indented, and begins at a centimetre or two to the right of the left-hand margin.

Le 28 juin 2014

Chère Sophie,

I received the news of your wedding with great joy............

The type of salutation varies in accordance with the social position, the age, and gender of the person you are writing to, as well as the degree of personal or professional connection.

The simplest salutations are: Monsieur, Madame, Mademoiselle. They apply to persons we do not know very well.

After this, we may write: *Cher Monsieur et ami* [Dear Sir and Friend] or *Cher collègue et ami* [Dear Colleague and Friend], or *Chère confrère et ami* [Dear Fellow Member and Friend].

---

[27] In this section of the book, all formulas are given in both French and in English translation, with added explanations, for the use of readers who wish to extend their French language and cultural skills. [Translator's note]

The same formulas are used when addressing women but they are given in feminine form: *Chère collègue et amie,* or *Chère collègue et confrère* (avoid the word *consoeur* and the irony inherent in its use).[28]

You should always write Monsieur or Madame in full, and never in abbreviated form, as for example: *M. et cher ami.*

It is also inappropriate to write: *Mon cher Monsieur* or *Ma chère Madame,* since the possessive adjectives *mon* and *ma* are already stated in the words *Mon*sieur et *Ma*dame.[29]

As a general rule, the family name must not be included in the salutation: you should not write *Cher Monsieur Moulin* or *Chère Madame Detournelle,* unless you are writing to a former school friend or fellow university student you used to address by his or her family name.

Valedictions – ending formulas

Valedictions may appear old-fashion, ridiculous and meaningless but an official letter obliges its author to make

---

[28] Strictly speaking the word *consoeur* which means literally co-sister, designates the female members of a female only association, social club or religious order, as well as the female fellow members within a mixed association, but the word *consoeur* is a suitable form of address among women only. A man should address a female fellow member as: *ma* confrère since the use of *ma consoeur* presumes that the person doing the addressing and the person being addressed are both women, i.e. co-sisters. Note that something similar attaches to the word *fellow* in English, which is a masculine term, but nevertheless designates male persons as well as female co-members of an organization. [Translator's note]

[29] Literally, Monsieur and Madame mean My Sir (My Lord) and My Lady. [Translator's note]

an appropriate choice between a set of statements that take into account the recipient's position and social status.

When writing to a head of state or other high-ranking person, you may select from the following:

The first half of your statement will consist of:

"*Daignez agréer l'expression de...*
Je vous prie d'agréer or de bien vouloir agréer...
Je vous serais obligé d'agréer...
Je vous serais reconnaissant d'agréer..."

And the second half of:

"*l'expression de ma très haute considération...*
l'expression de mes sentiments déférents...
l'expression de mes sentiments dévoués...
l'expression de mes sentiments respectueusement dévoués...
l'expression de mes sentiments fidèlement dévoués..."

The first part of the above statements means: "Deign to accept the expression of... Please accept the expression of ... I would be obliged to you for accepting the expression of ... I would be grateful to you for accepting the expression of ..." as to the second half: "my highest consideration ... my devoted sentiments... my respectfully devoted sentiments ... my faithfully devoted sentiments."

These formal French valedictions resemble such English forms as, *I am Sir your most humble and faithful servant...* which in contemporary English usage is simply *Yours faithfully*.

An official letter addressed to a lawyer, an attorney, or a public servant should end with one of the following formulas: "*Veuillez agréer, Monsieur (Madame), l'assurance*

179

de ma parfaite considération – or *l'assurance de mes sentiments distingués"* These translate into English as "Please accept the assurance of my perfect consideration ... or ... the assurance of my distinguished sentiments". In contemporary English usage, the formula will be rendered appropriately with *Yours faithfully* when the addressee has not been named (*Dear Sir or Dear Madam*); or as *Yours truly* when addressing someone in a higher social position; or *Yours sincerely,* for social correspondence.

In a letter written to someone with whom we are already acquainted, the valediction is infused with a more personal feeling: *"l'assurance de mes sentiments les plus cordiaux… l'assurance de mon très fidèle souvenir… l'assurance de mes sentiments les meilleurs"*, which translate literally as "the assurance of my most cordial sentiments… the assurance of my most faithful thoughts… the assurance of my best sentiments" and may be given in contemporary English usage by "With best regards" or if well acquainted with the recipient, "With warm regards".

When a man writes to a woman he is acquainted with, he may end his letter with any of the following statements: *"Veuillez agréer"* or *"Daignez agréer, Madame, l'expression or l'assurance de*:
- *mon très profond respect* [my most profound respect]
- *mes respectueux hommages* [respectful respects]
- *ma sincère amitié* [sincere friendship]
- *mon fidèle souvenir* [faithful regards]
- *mon respecteux dévouement* [respectful devotion]
- *l'hommage de mon respect* [the hommage of my respect]
- *ma respectueuse sympathie* [my respectful feelings]

or

180

- *"Croyez Madame, à mes plus fidèles penséees"* [Trust, Madam, in my most faithful thoughts].

When a woman writes to a man, she may end her letter with: *"Je vous prie de me croire, cher Monsieur, bien fidèlement vôtre"* [I pray, dear Sir, that you will believe me most faithfully yours].

Nevertheless, there is a trend today to adopt the shortened Anglo-Saxon style of valedictions:
- *Sentiments distingués* [with distinguished sentiments]
- *Sentiments dévoués* [with devoted sentiments]
- *Sentiments amicaux* [cordially]
- *Bien à vous* [yours]
- *Bien sincèrement à vous* or *Bien sincèrement à toi* [yours sincerely/ truly]
- *Cordialement vôtre* [cordially yours]
- *Bien amicalement à vous* [cordially yours]

Salutations and valedictions

The salutation and the valediction should match in tone and in register. Therefore, if your letter begins with: *Monsieur et cher collègue*, the rule demands that it should end with: *Croyez, Monsieur et cher collègue, à mes sentiments les meilleurs*. There are no exceptions to this rule!

Many French speakers write: *Croyez, Monsieur, **en** mes sentiments* but this is a grammatical error. The preposition *en* applies to the notion of believing in something, as for example, in God, one's friends, oneself while the preposition *à* is used to express that one thinks something.

Writing a letter

The text

The first line of text begins one or several lines below the salutation. However, the space between the salutation and the text is relative to the importance of the addressee – the more "important" the person addressed, the larger the space.

When we write to intimates, as for example, our mother, we can include the salutation in the first line of text. "How can I thank you, dear *Maman*, for agreeing to...". But if we are writing to the Prime Minister, we must leave between the title, *Monsieur le Premier ministre,* and the first line of text, a large blank, with the text beginning just above the bottom half of the page.

Unless you are using a highly respectful statement such as "*I* have the honour to solicit...", it is advisable not to start a letter with an "I" statement. In every language, self-reference is despicable because consideration for others is the rule. It is easy to find ways of avoiding this all too personal pronoun. For example, whereas we could write: "I was delighted to receive your letter", we can write: "Your letter gave me much pleasure".

Before speaking about ourselves, let us inquire about others. I have found myself counting the number of "I" in some letters, and awarding a first prize for egotism to their authors.

Spelling

Orthography with its two h's, its rules, its difficulties and its traps has set many tongues wagging. Should spelling be

182

simplified or not? Well, until reforms are enacted, we better respect the norms of spelling. There is only one way to achieve good spelling, and it is to keep company with that irreplaceable tool – the dictionary.

We should never write without having at hand the possibility of checking the exact meaning of a word, the conjugation of a verb, the doubling of a consonant. The use of a thesaurus is equally indispensable: the thesaurus avoids repetitions, enriches our vocabulary, and allows us to choose the exact word and the appropriate nuance.

Treating accented vowels casually shows a lack of discipline. Too many people do not differentiate between: *une vilaine **tache*** [an ugly stain] and *une lourde **tâche*** [a heavy burden]; *pêcher* [to fish] and *pécher* [to sin].

I know an old gentleman whose life interests are defined by taxes and retirement. With indestructible faith, he has written, his all life long, the word *retraite* [retirement] as *retraîte* [retreat] and the word *impôt* [tax] erroneously as impot, thus granting to the first what he subtracted from the second.

Punctuation

An ill-placed comma or full stop can change the very meaning of a sentence! Lawyers know the full significance of punctuation. Punctuation allows a text to breathe, and to acquire its full meaning. Not surprisingly the unpunctuated novel was only very briefly applauded as a prowess! When in doubt about the punctuation of a sentence, read it out loud and you will soon find its rhythm. On the subject of punctuation, I recommend the delectable book by Jacques Drillon, *Traité de la ponctuation française.*

Pagination

When using single sheets of paper or a relatively thick stock (opaque), you can write a personal letter on both sides of the paper. However, an official letter should always be written on the recto (front side), and a new sheet must be used to continue the text.

When using a folio of paper (a double sheet folded in the middle), I always write in the traditional manner, on page 1 and page 3, then on page 2 and page 4. However, today, the rule is that letters be written in the order of page 1, 2, 3, 4.

Signature

A signature is placed in the bottom half of the page, on the right, and two to three centimetres below the last line of text. A signature should be legible and not overly flamboyant. On many occasions, I have been unable to reply to a reader or an acquaintance as I could not decipher their signature. If the person you are writing to is not a close acquaintance, I recommend that you write your full name and even your address in capital letters below your signature.

Legible and therefore reasonably sober, a signature should not spread across the whole width of the page; a signature should not be adorned with pretentious flourishes or rise as a conquering arrow; and it should not be underlined. Indeed, some signatures show up the character traits or the level of education of their authors.

How then should we sign off? A first name is of course enough when writing to family or friends who will know straight away that "Florence" is you. To ensure that there is no possible confusion, however, you may also want to add the first initial of your family name to your signature: Florence R.

Any official letter must be signed with your first name and surname or with the initial of your first name followed by your family name: F. Rainaud.

When signing a typed and therefore a relatively formal letter, type your name and surname below your signature.

It is best not to change signatures every three months, but instead to settle on a style which you have selected because it best represents you.

When placing a letter in an envelope, your signature should always be on the same side as the closed top flap so that your addressee is able to identify the writer as soon as he unfolds the letter. [30]

Reading over a letter

Before sending a letter it is absolutely indispensable to re-read it, even if it adds up to only a few lines and even when it is addressed to your mother. Perhaps you have left out a word or the sentence is incomprehensible, perhaps you have misspelt a word... Re-reading a letter spares us doubts and uncomfortable questions down the track: "Did I tell him that...? Did I include the date?" Re-reading an official or a business letter is even more important as even the slightest error can have unfortunate consequences.

An important letter requires a draft and cannot be written according to the flow of your thoughts. A letter

---

[30] The name and address of the sender does not figure on the envelope in personal correspondence. See later in this chapter. [Translator's note]

demands thought and reflection and its presentation cannot include either crossing-out or approximation.

Post-scriptum

When you are reading over a personal letter, if you notice that you have forgotten to clarify a detail, do not write in the margin but add a note in post-scriptum. If you have omitted a detail in an official letter, however, you will need to start the letter over again, to remedy the oversight. The post-scriptum has no place in formal correspondence.

Writing multiple letters

If you happen to write to several persons in the course of a single day, don't forget to double-check before you seal the envelope that you are not about to send to your mother-in-law the letter you wrote to your best friend, as this could have very unpleasant consequences. Beware of your unconscious playing nasty tricks on you!

Let me tell you a story which happened a few years ago. I had invited twelve persons for dinner. Two days later, I discovered the following letter in the morning post:

"I had no desire to go to Nadine's. Several times, I was on the verge of calling her to let her know that I would not come, and every time, I could not go through with it. Did I have a premonition? Did I know that we were to meet? The words you whispered to me at the table in the salon are still resonating in my head. I feel dizzy. Your entreaties have won over my hesitations. I bow to your reasons, I surrender to your folly. Yes, I will be at the *Bar des Theâtres* tomorrow at 7:00." The letter was signed: L.

"That's interesting," I thought. Who is the intended recipient of this letter? Certainly, it had not been written for me. Who was sitting next to L.?

Since our butler always keeps a record of the sitting plans and menus of our dinners, a quick glance at the sitting plan allowed me to identify where the author of this extremely sweet *billet* had been seated – on the right of... Heavens! My husband![31] Impossible!

How could this love letter be addressed to my husband, in my own home! Of course, it had to be addressed to another man, to the gentleman seated to L's left. But this was even more astonishing! The said gentleman was handsome but his demeanour was more serious than the pope's! I could not imagine him as a playboy, a Don Giovanni!

What was I to do? What rules of the art of living applied in this situation? Should I contact L. to inform her that she had placed her letter into the wrong envelope? Perhaps... this could be of some help but it would also plunge her into the greatest embarrassment.

Should I then say and do nothing and thus end the budding romance? Since L. had send me the letter destined to the gentleman, she had most likely mixed up two envelopes,

---

[31] The author is being humorous: the expression Heavens! my husband! [*Ciel, mon mari!*] appeared in the light theatrical works of the Belle Epoque (the French version of the Edwardian period – the Beautiful Epoch), with playwrights such as Georges Feydeau. This stock exclamation is always uttered by a married woman when she discovers her husband together with his mistress, or when her husband is about to discover her with her lover. The exclamation is immediately recognized in France as a playful nod to the eternal triangle and the histrionics of stage melodrama. [Translator's note].

and sent the customary thank-you letter destined for me to the object of her interest...

So, should I wait until the handsome suitor called me – to inform me that he had received a thank you note addressed to me?

Having pondered the matter, I decided to have the pretty lady's letter delivered to its intended recipient, without adding any explanation. Then, I waited for what came next.

I did not wait very long.

The following day, when I came home towards the end of the afternoon, I found a box awaiting me. Inside it, there was a beautiful Vieux Paris porcelain figurine featuring three monkeys. The first covering his eyes, the second his ears, the third his mouth. And, there was L's thank-you letter to me, sent together with the gift.

There was no other written note but the message was clear: "See nothing, hear nothing, say nothing". I was delighted and filled with admiration.

What a man! Handsome, charming, *and* a true gentleman. L. was blessed with all the luck and good fortune!

Attachments

Should you attach a document to a letter, either a photograph or an invoice, staple it, do not use a paper clip or even worse a pin (which, in any case, the French postal services prohibit).

If your daughter lives some distance away, don't mail her a bank note on her birthday: on the one hand, you would be breaking the law since money must be sent by postal money order or by bank transfer only, and on the other you would risk losing the money without recourse.

188

The envelope

Until the 1850s, a letter (which women always perfumed) was posted after being folded in three: first lengthways and then again along the short grain of the paper after which it was sealed with wax. The envelope did not exist and in any case only aristocrats and members of the high bourgeoisie dedicated time to letter writing. An Englishman, Brewer, a stationer and bookseller at Brighton, invented the envelope.

The address

At the top is the first name and the family name of the person the letter is addressed to, with either Monsieur, Madame, Mademoiselle written in full. When writing to a couple, you use Monsieur *et* Madame followed by a single first name and family name: both are the husband's. No one writes: *Monsieur Jean et Madame Antoinette Duchamps.*

When writing to a relative of the same generation as yourself or to a close friend, I advise you to resist the contemporary usage which does away with formality and dispenses with Monsieur and Madame, and to stick to the traditional usage: Madame Antoinette Duchamps.

If your godmother is still single at sixty-two, should you write: "*Mademoiselle Letellier*" ? Yes, if she is known as such in her social circle. If she is not, then you should write: "*Madame Letellier*".

Some rare individuals still address their mail as it was done during the *Grand Siècle.*[32]

---

[32] The term *Grand Siècle* (great century) refers to the XVII century and the classical period, with at its centre, the reign of Louis XIV. [Translator's note]

A Madame
Madame Jean Delamotte
Contemporary usage has settled on a different form but I personally recommend a compromise: *A Madame Jean Delamotte.*

The first name and the family name are followed by:

- The position – i.e.:
  Monsieur Jean Larguery
  Député des Bouches-du-Rhône
  [Bouches-du-Rhônes representative]
- Or the profession – i.e.:
  Monsieur Jean-Pierre Bouvier
  Antiquaire [antiquarian]

After which come the street number and name, separated by a comma: *16, rue du Parc-Montsouris.* Next:

- The identification of the post office (*bureau distributeur*) preceded by the five-digit postcode. The name of the town is written in capital letters and should not be underlined:

  14, Place Huche
  56170 QUIBERON

If the addressee lives in a villa or a chalet near a village, the name of the residence is written as follows:

Chalet "Les Chardonnerets
74120 MEGEVE

The address is always left-aligned:

Monsieur André Bonan
114, avenue Mozart
75016 PARIS

And never right-aligned

Monsieur André Bonan
114, avenue Mozart
75016 PARIS

Nor centred.

The words for street, avenue, and so forth are written in lower case. They can be abbreviated: av. (avenue), bd. (boulevard), fbg. (faubourg), sq. (square), pl. (place), and so forth. Do not omit the dot point completing the abbreviation.

In the same vein, you may abbreviate Saint-Honoré to St-Honoré. Remember the hyphen. Generally hyphens are used for all street names: avenue Victor-Hugo, rue Vieille-du-Temple, rue Gaston-Tissandier, rue du Générale-Appert.

However, there is no hyphen with:

- an apostrophe as for example in: rue de l'Abbé-de-l'Epée.
- or when the name begins with the articles Le, La or Les, including when these articles are used as patronymic particles, as for example in: avenue La Fontaine, rue Le Goff.

When writing to a person living abroad:

Respect the rules of the country of destination; thus in Germany the name of the town precedes the street name and number:

> *1004 HAMBOURG (or HAMBURG)*
> *Jesselstrass, 9*

Note that the name of the country should always be written in French, we do not write United Kingdom, Denmark, Italia or U.S.A. but Royaume-Uni, Danemark, Italie, Etats-Unis (but no need to add d'Amérique).

The French postal services have also decided on the correct layout of the envelope.

If your recipient lives at a third person's, the formula is not:
> *Monsieur Jean Larguery*
> *chez Madame Dardonville*

but
> *Monsieur Jean Larguery*
> *Aux bons soins de Madame Dardonville*
> *[literally: in the good care of Madame Dardonville]*

or even better use the English expression
> *C/o Madame Dardonville*

On the back of the envelope

If your letter is personal, the rules of privacy require that you omit your name or address from the back of the envelope. However, if you are unsure of your recipient's address, then include your own, so that your letter can be returned to you if need be.

The stamp

The postage stamp is placed on the right-hand corner of the envelope; stickers such as *Avion* (airmail) or *Express* are affixed on the left. If the mail you are sending weighs more than twenty grams, you will need to have it weighed and stamped correctly so as to save your recipient the cost of the excess postage.

When should you attach a stamp for return mail? Never, if you are writing to either a relative or a friend – who would find it offensive and be under the impression that you are forcing a reply. But if you are requesting a reply from an organization, a local council, an institution, or even an actor, you should attach not only a stamp but also a self-addressed envelope.

Only the registrar's office in Nantes, where the records of all foreign-born French citizens are kept, does not require you to attach a stamp when requesting a birth, marriage or divorce certificate.

Finally: it is highly impolite to misspell the name of your recipient, so make the effort to check the correct spelling. There is a story that one of the Rothschilds, at the end of the 19th century, received a letter addressed to: Le Roi de Chine [the King of China].[33] Indeed, in this instance, there was no reason to take offence!

---

[33] Rothschild in French is pronounced: Ro-t-cheeld, hence the phonetic correspondence with - le roi de Chine: le rwa de sheen. [Translator's note]

Posting a letter

If you ask a third person to deliver or post a letter on your behalf, politeness requires you to leave the envelope open so that he or she may seal it in your presence.

Letter marked "private" (*Personnel*)

When you send a letter to a friend at their workplace, you will need to write *Personnel*, i.e. private on the left-hand top corner of the letter to prevent your correspondence being open by a secretary along with the rest of the mail addressed to the company. Do not, however, send a letter marked private to a private address if the person is married. Their spouse is bound to take offence at the mistrust they are being so obviously shown.

As a general rule, we never open a letter that is not addressed to us personally, no matter how close our relationship to the recipient. Even a mother should not open a letter addressed to one of her young children. Respect for others' privacy does not bear exceptions and begins in childhood.

Forwarded mail

When you go on holidays, you can ask the caretaker of your apartment block to forward your mail, which he will do without charging a fee. There are also specific envelopes for forwarding mail. If there is no caretaker, you can arrange, for a minimal fee, for the post office to forward your mail.

Poste Restante

If you address a letter to Poste Restante, you will need to use the postal code of the post office (*bureau distributeur*) servicing your addressee. Thus, if your recipient lives in Paris in the 16th arrondissement, you will write:

> *Monsieur Louis Portal*
> *Poste restante Paris 53*
> *75016 Paris*

If you do not want the recipient of your letter to pay the modest contribution required for him or her to collect the letter, you can pay the excess yourself at the post office of origin, a gesture which the person receiving the letter will no doubt appreciate. Note that a letter can only be retrieved from the Poste Restante by providing a piece of identification. For a French citizen, this is the national identity card.

Express mail

If you wish to thank someone for a thoughtful gesture or for a favour and you do not want to wait, it is best not to entrust your letter to the postal services and to deliver it yourself – given, of course, that your addressee lives in the same city as you do. You may otherwise have the letter delivered by a special service run by the Post Office (*service spécial de la Poste*) so long as the recipient of the letter lives in France, Monaco or Andorra.

Visiting cards

In the times when people still paid personal visits, a man would always deposit a visiting card, with the left-hand corner folded over, at the residence of the person to whom he had come to present his compliments. Today, this small rectangular piece of Bristol card has become an ever more common mode of communication, both in our private and professional lives. A visiting card is made of a high quality white stock, either printed or engraved and of varying format and size. The smallest measure 60mm x 30mm, the largest: 155mm x 110 mm. The envelopes containing the visiting cards are in matching stock and size. One should refrain from eccentricities regarding the choice of paper: we shall leave out cork and wood, as to the choice of colour, none is better than white. The only permissible originality lies with the size and format which you can choose according to the use you intend to make of the cards. If your cards are simply intended to provide your name, address and profession, they can be very small (60 x 30) like American business cards. But if you use your visiting cards to communicate in writing, then choose the large format.

Cards on which your details are etched rather than printed are more expensive, but the copper plate can be used and re-used indefinitely until you change residential address. Block fonts or English style fonts[34] are the simplest and most elegant.

What details should be included on a visiting card?

---

[34] As for example Baskerville or Bell. [Translator's note]

For a couple

A married couple's visiting cards provide a first name and surname preceded by M. et Mme written in abbreviation. This is followed by either the husband's professional title or rank, in which case the title of Madame is written in full.

> *M. et Mme Serge Brandy*

And:

> *Le professeur et Madame Serge Brandy*

Titles of nobility are never preceded by Monsieur or Madame.

> *Le Baron et la Baronne de Brandy*
> *Le Comte et la Comtesse de Brandy*

However, it is in good taste not to mention one's titles or decorations on visiting cards. Other than their names and surname, a couple's visiting card may include their address and telephone number.

The telephone number is placed on the bottom left corner and the address on the right hand corner. Only the name, surname (without Monsieur or Madame), the address and the telephone number are indicated on a visiting card intended for personal use. The profession is optional. Title, position, address and telephone numbers must all be included on a professional or business card.

A married woman's visiting cards

On her personal cards, a woman identifies herself as Madame Serge Brandy. On her professional card, however, a woman

197

provides her first name and not her husband's: Madame Marine Brandy.

A divorced woman's visiting cards

They may indicate the name of her former husband hyphenated to her maiden name: Marine Brandy-Galt.

A widow's visiting cards

A widow's visiting cards are the same as a married woman's cards and never indicate her widowed status. Hence, Madame Anatole Froissard will be printed on her personal cards, and Madame Sabine Froissard on her professional cards.

A child's visiting cards

It is in very poor taste to print visiting cards for a child or a teenager. It is only after one has reached eighteen years of age that it is appropriate to have visiting cards.

Using visiting cards

- When thanking a person:
  for a present (or when we give a present)
  for an invitation
  for a lunch or dinner
- To congratulate a person:
  on the occasion of a happy event

for an academic achievement (school or
university)
for receiving an award
- To join to a cheque addressed to: a doctor, a lawyer or
a notary
- To announce a change of address
- To say good-bye when we are going abroad, in which
case it is customary to write in the left-hand corner
the initials P.P.C., meaning: *Pour Prendre Congé* –
on vacation.

How should we write on a visiting card?

A formal note written on a visiting card is always composed
in the third person and does not include a signature.

Anatole Froissard
*Sincerely thanks Madame Brandy for her kind
invitation to dinner, which he accepts with pleasure, and
sends his faithful respects.*

But when sending a card to a friend or relative, it is enough
to strike the name printed on the card, write a few lines in the
first person and sign with our first names.

Postcards

Not so long ago, it was mandatory to send postcards to
relatives, friends, colleagues and workmates whenever we
went on holidays. Today, we leave the city so frequently –
Christmas, Easter, all summer vacations, and every long

weekend – we prefer to send postcards from more remote destinations: Bali, Honk Kong, or Easter Island.

Writing a postcard requires true talent and imagination. It is too easy otherwise to resort to the usual clichés: "Wonderful weather, dream holidays – we're all well, and thinking of you" scribbled at the beach or at the restaurant while we are waiting to be served.

If we choose to send postcards, it is worth making the effort to choose a landscape or a cultural landmark that will resonate with the person we intend the postcard for. Avoid caricatures or humorous cards that are not funny. On the other hand, people who collect vintage and antique postcards will no doubt appreciate you finding a few for them during your travels.

Also, it is preferable to write a single well composed sentence rather than words in telegraphic style. No need to discuss your holidays which are bound to be "wonderful" and "unforgettable". A small personal word addressed to your correspondent will bring greater joy. Remember to sign your name legibly, and if you are not writing to a close friend, add your family name to your first name so the person receiving the postcard will not have to wonder which of the Françoises he is acquainted with, is vacationing in Barcelona. It is also a good idea to place the postcard in an envelope, so that it will not be read by third persons and, not least, so that it will arrive at its destination faster.

Finally, avoid sending your postcard on the eve of your return home.

Having said as much, may I now confess to you that I never send postcards? I prefer to return with small souvenirs as gifts or to phone my friends to inquire of their news and assure them of my loyal friendship.

I have over a hundred telephone numbers stored in my mobile phone, and nothing is simpler or more pleasant than to call those whose voice I long to hear.

Greeting cards

So, I never send postcards. However, I do send hundreds of greeting cards, and every year I send more than I did the previous year. I have great pleasure and even a need to reconnect, at least once a year, with foreign friends or others whom I see little of because they live in the provinces. A new year must be celebrated with all those we love, know, and appreciate and I find it very comforting to experience the solidarity of this long chain of friendships and relationships across the world.

I display on the mantle-piece of my fireplace, in Megève where I always spend Christmas, all the cards which I have received. And the more I receive and the better the start of the year!

When writing a card, I always try to add to the usual greetings a small word of affection, and to do my best to personalise my good wishes.

We should send greetings to:

- All those who sent us greetings
- Our family, friends, intimates and professional relations
- Those to whom we wish to express our affection, friendship, thoughts, and gratitude.

Special formulas used in the composition of a letter

The salutations

– To the Pope: *Votre Sainteté* [Your Holiness]
– To a sovereign (king or queen): *Votre Majesté.*
– To a sovereign prince: *Votre Altesse Impériale, Votre Altesse Royale, Votre Altesse Senissime, Votre Altesse* [Your Imperial Highness, Your Royal Highness, Your Most Serene Highness, Your Highness].
– To an orthodox patriarch: *Votre Béatitude* [Your Beatitude]
– To a Cardinal: *Votre Eminence* [Your Eminence]
– To a foreign ambassador, nuncio, archbishop, bishop, mufti: *Votre Excellence* [Your Excellency].

However, when addressing the Pope, a sovereign head of state, the princes of a royal house, an ambassador, or a cardinal, you must use the third person in the actual text of the letter. In text, therefore, we will write as follows: *Sire , Votre Majesté* has deigned to…
– To the queen: *Madame, Votre Majestée* has deigned to …
– To the Pope: *Très Saint-Père*, [Holiest Father] *Votre Sainteté* has deigned …

List of all Salutations

– The president of the Republic: *Monsieur le Président de la République* (not *Monsieur le Président*)
– The Pope: *Très Saint-Père*
– The Prince of Monaco: *Monseigneur*
– The heirs to the throne: *Monseigneur*
– The members of the diplomatic corps:
1) Ambassadors: only foreign ambassadors are addressed as *Votre Excellence*. French ambassadors are addressed as "*Monsieur l'Ambassadeur*", but *Votre Excellence* is used in text: i.e.: *Monsieur l'Ambassadeur, Je remercie Votre Excellence d'avoir bien voulu* [Monsieur l'Ambassadeur, I thank Your Excellency to have agreed…]. Note that when we write to a woman ambassador the correct salutation is *Madame l'Ambassadeur*. It is the wife of an ambassador who is saluted as *Madame l'Ambassadrice*.
2) Plenipotentiary ministers: *Monsieur le Ministre, Madame la Ministre.*
3) Chargé d'affaires: *Monsieur le Chargé d'Affaires, Madame la Chargé d'Affaires, Monsieur le Conseiller, Madame la Conseillère.*
4) Embassy secretaries: *Monsieur le Premier Secrétaire, Madame la Première Secrétaire.*
5) Consuls and vice-consuls: *Monsieur le Consul Général, Monsieur le Consul, Madame la Consul …*

NOTE: Former ambassadors and former prefects keep their titles for life.

Politicians

The head of government: *Monsieur le Premier ministre, Madame la Première ministre.*

Ministers, secretaries and under-secretaries of State: *Monsieur le Ministre, Madame la Ministre.*

The minister of Justice: *Monsieur le Garde des Sceaux, Madame la Garde des Sceaux.* [35]

Chairman/chairwoman and vice-chairs of the National Assembly, Senate, or Conseil Constitutionel [Constitutional Council]: *Monsieur le Président, Madame la Présidente.*

The members of the Conseil Constitutionnel: *Monsieur le Haut Conseiller, Madame la Haute Conseillère.*

The chairpersons of the Economic and Social Council, and parliamentary commissions: *Monsieur le Président, Madame la Présidente.*

The chairpersons of the General Council, special delegations, the chairmen/women of the Parisian regional council: *Monsieur le Président, Madame la Présidente.*

The quaestors of the assemblies: *Monsieur le Questeur, Madame la Questrice.*

The senators: *Monsieur le Sénateur, Madame la Sénatrice.*

The deputies: *Monsieur le Député, Madame la Députée.*

The general councillors: *Monsieur le Conseiller Général, Madame la Conseillère Générale.*

The mayors: *Monsieur le Maire, Madame la Maire.*

The adjuncts: *Monsieur l'Adjoint, Madame l'Adjoint.*

The municipal councillors: *Monsieur le Conseiller, Madame la Conseillère.*

---

[35] Literally the "Keeper of the Seals", in other words the Attorney General in Australia and in the US, and the Lord Chancellor in the United Kingdom. [Translator's note]

Legal Authorities

The vice-chairman/chairwoman of the Conseil d'Etat [Council of State]: *Monsieur le Président, Madame la Présidente.*

The presiding justice of the *Cour de cassation* [Court of Cassation, the court of last resort and final appeal]: *Monsieur le Premier Président, Madame la Première Présidente.*

Other persons are also addressed as *Monsieur le Premier Président, Madame la Première Présidente*:

    – the Chief Baron [*Premier président*] of Court of Audit [*la Cour des comptes*]

    – the Chief Justice [*Président*] of a court of appeal.

The chief prosecutors of the Cour de cassation, of the *Cour des Comptes*, the *Cour de justice*, and a court of appeal: *Monsieur le Procureur Général, Madame la Procureur Générale.*

Public prosecutors [*avocats géneraux*] and deputy public prosecutors [*substituts généraux*]: *Monsieur l'Avocat général, Madame l'Avocate générale.*

Civil Servants

The Grand Chancellor of the Légion d'honneur: *Monsieur le Grand Chancelier, Madame la Grande Chancelière.*

The Chancellor of the Ordre de la Libération: *Monsieur le Chancelier, Madame la Chancelière.*

A High Commissioner: *Monsieur le Haut-Commissaire, Madame La Haut-commissionaire.*

A General Commissioner: *Monsieur le Commissaire général, Madame la Commissaire générale.*

All the general secretaries of the French administration and parliamentary assemblies: *Monsieur le Secrétaire général, Madame la Secrétaire générale.*

Prefects: *Monsieur le Préfet, Madame la Préfète.*

Presiding judges [*présidents du tribunal*]: *Monsieur le Président, Madame la Présidente.*

Public prosecutors [*procureurs de la République*]: *Monsieur le Procureur, Madame la Procureur.*

Deputy public prosecutors [*substituts*]: *Monsieur le Substitut, Madame la Substitut.*

Clerks [*greffiers*]: *Monsieur le Greffier, Madame la Greffière,*

Military

A Maréchal de France [Marshal of France][36] : *Monsieur le Maréchal.*

The wife of a *Maréchal de France*: *Madame la Maréchale.*

Generals: *Mon Général,* when addressed by a man – and *Général,* when addressed by a woman.

Colonels and *lieutenant colonels*: *Mon Colonel, Madame la Colonelle.*

Commandants: *Mon Commandant.*

Subordinate officers: *Monsieur, Madame*

---

[36] The Maréchal de France holds the highest French military distinction. This distinction originated in the 12th century. It is not a rank but an honor granted to a commanding officer who has served in actual conflict. There is no living Maréchal de France today. [Translator's note]

206

Navy

Admirals:[37] *Amiral, Madame l'Amirale.*
Commanders [*Capitaine de frégate*], Lieutenant Commanders [*Capitaine de corvette*], Ship-of-the-line Captain [*capitaine de vaisseau*]: *Commandant, Commandante.*
Ship-of-the-line lieutenant [*lieutenant de vaisseau*]: *Capitaine or Monsieur, Madame.*
Ensigns and lieutenants: *Lieutenant, Lieutenante,* or *Monsieur, Madame.*
Midshipman: *Monsieur, Madame.*
Medical general officers: *Monsieur le médecin général, Madame la médecin générale.*

Religious authorities

Apostolic nuncio: *Monsieur le Nonce, Monseigneur* (for private correspondence).
Cardinals: *Monsieur le Cardinal, Monseigneur* (for private correspondence) for salutations – *Eminence* in text.
Archbishops and bishops: *Monsieur l'Archevêque, Monseigneur* (for private correspondence) – *Excellence* in text.
Apostolic delegates, curates, apostolic administrators: *Monsieur le Délégué apostolique, Monsieur le Vicaire apostolique, Monsieur l'Administrateur apostolique.*
General curates, canons, dean archpriests, priests, vicars and abbots: *Monsieur le Vicaire général – le Chanoine, le Doyen*

---

[37] The equivalent navy distinction to Maréchal de France is Amiral de France. [Translator's note]

207

Archiprêtre, le Curé, le Vicaire, l'Abbé; Madame la Vicaire générale, l'Abbesse.

Superiors of religious orders: *Monsieur le Supérieur, Madame la Supérieure* or better even *Madame.*

Superior, Carthusian order: *Monsieur le Ministre général.*

Prior, Cartusian order: *Très Révérend Père.*

Superior, Trappist order: *Monsieur l'Abbé général.*

Superior, Dominicans (Order of Preachers): *Monsieur le Maître général.*

Superior, Jesuits: *Monsieur le Préposé général*

Superior, Christian Brothers (Lasallian Brothers): *Monsieur le Supérieur.*

Superior, Oratorians: *Mon Révérend Père.*

Superior Benedictines: *Monsieur l'Abbé primat.*

Superior Lazarists: *Monsieur.*

Other members of religious orders are addressed as: *Mon révérend Père, Mon Père, Mon Frère, Très cher frère.*

Other members of women religious orders are addressed as: *Ma Révérende Mère, Ma Mère, Ma Soeur, Madame.*

Military chaplains of all denominations are addressed as: *Monsieur l'Aumônier.*

The Grand Master of the Order of Malta: *Mon Seigneur* – and in text: *Son Altesse éminentissime.*

The Grand Master of the Order of the Holy Sepulchre: *Monseigneur.*

The ministers of the Orthodox Church: *Monsieur l'Archimandrite, Monsieur l'Archiprêtre.*

Ministers of the Protestant churches: *Monsieur le Pasteur.*

The Chief Rabbi of France: *Monsieur le Grand Rabbin.*

The Imam: *Monsieur l'Imam.*

Members of the Academies
University Professors
Artists

We address musicians, painters, sculptors, famous writers and Academicians as *"Maître"*. The salutation and address: *Monsieur, Madame le Professeur* is the preserve of teachers in higher education. Secondary school teachers are addressed as *Monsieur* and *Madame*.[38]

Members of the Nobility

Nobiliary titles are never used in salutations – except in the case of Princes and Princesses, who are addressed as *Prince, Princesse*, and *Monseigneur* and *Madame* if they are reigning princes; Dukes and Duchesses are addressed as *Monsieur le Duc, Madame la Duchesse*.

When writing to the members of sovereign houses, the address on the envelope will indicate: S.A.R (*Son Altesse Royale*), LLAARR (*Leurs Altesses Royales*), LLAAII (*Leurs Altesses Imperiales*).

---

[38] Secondary school teachers, nonetheless, are *professeurs*. A primary school teacher is called *instituteur/ institutrice*. [Translator's note]

Members of the Liberal Professions

Notaries, lawyers, bailiffs, official court auctioneers are all addressed as "*Maître*".

Doctors and veterinary surgeons: *Monsieur le Docteur, Madame le Docteur.* Medical students address their professeurs as: *Monsieur, Madame.*

The director or chief executive officer of a commercial enterprise, industrial enterprise or a school: *Monsieur le Directeur, Madame la Directrice.*

E-COMMUNICATION

Since its origins in the American Military's desire to communicate continuously and instantaneously, the Internet has spread its network across the planet. Even in developing countries, the young crowd in cybercafés to surf the Net and acquire a variety of knowledge – from e-learning offered by virtual universities to searching for the latest hits or movie trailers. The personal computer provides a lot of entertainment, including advertising, animation, and the jokes are sometimes so funny that we must at all cost rush to our email service to forward them to our friends.

E-mail

Le mél or *le courriel* is the joy of Net users. In the morning, before even opening their eyes, some (single people in particular) switch on their computer in haste to read the messages they received during the night. They are in a hurry to respond. The magic of a letter that can be answered and returned as soon as it has been received cannot cease to fascinate.

Whereas scholars have been discussing spelling reforms for over a century, Internet users have already solved the problem and applied the solution in no time at all, creating a new language – which "modern" enterprises have been quick to pick up and to integrate into their internal communications. Beyond the multiple abbreviations, deciphering the languages of various users requires some training as the new codes are permanently enriched with

English, Spanish, Italian words... One expresses joy with the simple sign :) or surprise with O.

An international language is appearing, a form of globalisation which, thankfully, owes nothing to politicians.

Savoir-vivre and internet surfing

- In a first email or web conversation, adopting a formal tone is a must. Before composing a message, we need to find out the age, the profession, and the tastes of our correspondent, as a great many people do not appreciate familiarity or the absence of polite formulas. Furthermore, anonymity and the use of pseudonyms in various forums should not become an excuse for vulgarity and verbally abusive behaviour.
- Avoid impersonal or vulgar group mail.
- Do not post all your baby photos, you can select the best for viewing. Also do not overload your receiver's broadband capacity by sending excessive messages.

To be able to access education, entertainment, shop, visit the New York Metropolitan Museum, rent a house in Sydney, book a theatre or cinema ticket while sitting in one's armchair makes life considerably easy. But is it not also, at times, disconnecting from reality? Surely, buying tomatoes or grapes on the Internet without the possibility of choosing, seeing, smelling as we do at the local market, deprives us both of the sensory pleasures and of personal exchanges with our peers? Indeed, thousands of new acquaintances are made through the Internet, but do we savour those as we savour a chance meeting on the terrace of a café?

The Internet is a place of freedom. And it is a place where everything but also anything goes. There is a dark side to freedom. Swindles, gambling, extremist views, and pornography thrive on the Net. We cannot ignore the high level of Internet traffic dedicated to pornographic sites, which now account for up to seventy per cent of connections. And where is the genial programmer who can delete and permanently erase the paedophiles' images?

VI

ON BEING A HOSTESS

AND

BEING A GUEST

Some women maintain open dinner invitations. They invite easily and generously because they believe that every new guest who enters their home broadens, renews and enriches their universe. Indeed, it is around a dinner table that friendships are made, that ideas are exchanged, and projects are born.

To have guests in my home is a social obligation which I accept with pleasure. To welcome guests and lavish warm smiles upon them is the mark of a charming hostess; and if you present the table setting, the menu, and the service with attention and care, your guests will heap praises on you and they will never refuse your invitations.

After going out to see a performance, I also like to be invited to informal and spontaneous dinners. Improvised dinners can be even more fun that formal dinner parties.

ADVICE TO A YOUNG HOSTESS

Invite your family and intimate friends to your first dinner parties. It will enable you to get up to the firing line without risking being shot at. Begin with dinners for six persons and simple menus.

The day you host your guests for dinner, refrain from experimenting with a new recipe or an exotic dish. Serve those after you have trialled them, and you are sure of your skills.

If you do not have anyone to help you cook or serve at the table, avoid meals that require you to spend more time in the kitchen than with your guests, or force you to run from the table to the oven. Your guests will prefer eating cold cuts in the presence of a calmly seated hostess than succulent scampi brochettes with zucchini flowers fritter, served in agitation while their hostess runs to and fro.

For smooth service, consider preparing two tables on coaster wheels. One table is positioned next to your husband. On it, place the wines, clean plates, the garden salad (the cheese must always wait in the kitchen). On the other table, which you keep next to you, store the plates that you are removing from the table after each course, and the main dish (which you keep on a dish warmer if it is a hot dish).

Hors-d'oeuvres and potages can be placed on the table before the guests are seated. The dishes can also be passed from one guest to another without worrying about the order of service. The important thing is for the service to go smoothly, and for the conversation not to be interrupted by a technical mishap. Rather than waiting to be served by you, your guests will prefer to help themselves – everyone passes and holds the dish to the next person.

Although our society has democratised, do not be surprised if you find that guests who are not of your social or intellectual milieu, refuse your invitation.

If one of your guests cancels at the last minute, there is nothing you can or should do. Don't make yourself sick over it, it is not so serious.

And if one of your guests arrives with a friend without giving you notice ahead of time, just add another table setting, with as little fuss as possible, and keep smiling.

If a guest arrives more than half an hour late, follow my example, don't wait for him or her. Sit the people present and start.

For unforeseen circumstances, keep a reserve of terrines, canned vegetables and fruit compotes.

Never bring your guests a meal served on a plate as is done at the restaurant. Dishes should be placed on the table for everyone to help themselves from.

At the end of a dinner party, ask yourself: did anything go wrong, either in the way I welcomed people, or with the service, the menu, the conversation? Engage in a critical review of the evening. You will certainly have even more success at your next party.

Match your choice of menu to the places where you are giving your party. In the country, serve pot-au-feu or lamb stew; in the mountain, serve fondues, rabbit chasseur, *raclette*. In town, offer classic menus.

If you do not have a lot of time, you can order out: As for example, sushi from an excellent Japanese *traiteur* – the presentation alone will be a delight.

What to serve at lunch

For entrée: Hors d'oeuvres (salads, ham with figs or melon), a soufflé or a quiche. Potage or soup should not be served as an entrée at lunch, even in winter.
Main meal: Fish, meat, poultry or game, accompanied by two or three vegetables.
A dressed green salad
Cheeses – note that the salad and the various cheeses are often served together.
Entremets (sweets)
Fruit or in summer ice-cream and red fruit.

To serve at dinner

Substitute potage, a hot entrée (winter), or cold entrée (summer) for the salads served as entrée at lunchtime.

I have noted that everyone eats less and less and yet gets fatter and fatter. With this in mind, I now offer the entrées to my guests only once, while I only replenish the main dish if there is no cheese on the menu. On the other hand, I always offer the desserts twice, much to everyone's satisfaction and especially my own![39]

---

[39] In France, people usually help themselves to the dishes presented on the table. The second presentation of a dish at a dinner party, therefore, is not a matter of satisfying the appetite but of indulging the guests' love of food – what the French call gourmandise. [Translator's note]

Faux-pas

- Two tarts in the same meal. If you begin with a quiche, do not serve an apricot tart for dessert.
- Two dishes with different sauces. You should not serve asparagus Hollandaise with a tournedos Béarnaise.
- Two dishes with the same foundation, as for example, a fish pâté or seafood croustade, followed by braised salmon.
- Two dishes with salad dressings: If you serve leeks with vinaigrette for entrée, do not serve a dressed green salad with the cheese.

Think of your guests' health and diet choices. Don't offer sweets to diabetics, or salted dishes to people with high blood pressure, or meat to a vegetarian.

Consider their religious convictions: Practicing Jews do not eat shellfish or pork, and pork is also prohibited to Muslims.

INVITATIONS

Extending an invitation

To a casual lunch, a family dinner or a casual dinner party with friends

You may invite your guests in person or by telephone a few days or even the day before an informal lunch or dinner.

To a more formal lunch or a small dinner party

Invitations should be given by telephone eight days prior. This done, it is good form to send to the persons who have accepted your invitation, written details of the time, date and the expected standard of dress on your visiting card. If you write: *"Tenue de ville"* [semi-formal], your guests will understand that they need to wear a dark grey or dark blue suit (men) and a smart dress or dress-suit (women).

If you invite guests to the country, attach a map and directions with the invitation, so that they can find your house without difficulty.

To an official dinner

Invitations must be in writing, and sent ten to fifteen days ahead of time. They are printed or etched on a card. They indicate the time, the date, the expected standard of dress with "RSVP" [*Réponse S'il Vous Plaît*]:

La Baronne Edmond de Rothschild kindly requests
Monsieur and Madame Claude Leylan
To come to dinner
Sunday 6 January at 8:00 pm

Black tie   Château de Pregny
Long dress   1292 Pregny-Genève

RSVP by telephone

If you have written on your card: "Black tie", men will understand that they should wear a smoking jacket, and women, a very dressy short cocktail dress. Therefore, it is best to specify "Black tie, Long dress", if you prefer your women guests not to arrive at your home attired in superbly short dresses. Invitations requesting *Habit* are today extremely rare. In this case, however, a long dress is *de rigueur*.

According to the rules of politeness, guests should answer an invitation within forty-eight hours, either to confirm their presence and address their thanks, or to express their regrets and give their hostess time to send other invitations.

When planning a dinner party, it is wise to keep additional guests in mind in case of cancellations.

To receptions, balls and weddings

You may write on the invitation card: "Reply before 6 August 2015". Your guests should conform to your wishes to allow you to organise your reception in an optimal manner.

Some people have the unfortunate habit of arriving late for dinner, and very often also they have the habit (even more impolite) to reply to an invitation at the last minute. I am always amazed that there are still people willing to invite them!

Choosing the guests

The success of a dinner depends in the larger part on the quality of the guests and of the chemistry they are likely to produce in each other's company. I always draw a guest list according to the type of lunch or dinner I am organising.

At a business dinner

I believe it is best to invite businessmen and their spouses, as well as a few single persons who have similar professional activities, so that the conversation remains accessible to all and at a similar level.

At a sit-down cold buffet

Unlike for the preceding reception, I attempt to invite the greatest diversity of persons; I may invite movie stars, orchestra conductors, painters, fashion designers, ambassadors, scientists, a minister, singers... Add pretty women whose beauty enhances the glamour of my table and everyone will no doubt get on as the best of friends in the best of all worlds.

But it is not necessary to be a minister to be brilliant or an actress to be beautiful and witty. Intelligence and beauty (fortunately!) are qualities granted to a great many persons.

I do avoid bringing together people who risk upsetting one another, including recently divorced couples. I always attempt to invite an equal number of men and women, and if there are last minute cancellations, I can call on a number of single friends willing to play the role of "guest of last resort"! To be a last minute guest could well play in the hand of destiny, and one should never refuse this stroke of good fortune. The number of love affairs that began in my home as a result of such chance encounters is astonishing.

At a society dinner

I will choose in equal numbers, people who are from the same social milieu but from different professions.

223

SETTING THE TABLE

Where should we dress the table?

The dining-room is a 19th century bourgeois invention. In former times, tables were dressed in various places: in a boudoir, on a balcony, under a garden arbour, in the library, in the foyer of the house, in front of a lighted fireplace... One would select the surroundings according to the season or to one's humour.

In Spring or Autumn, why not set your table in front of a window that opens onto the trees, or the opposite, why not make the best of the half-light in a room to dine by candle-light? Power to the Imagination! This rallying call will never become unfashionable!

To give greater comfort to our guests and to protect the wood on our table tops, we can place under the tablecloth a piece of flannel of the same size and shape as the table. When using individual place mats (at lunch only), we place a piece of rubberised mat of the same dimension as a plate, inside fitted white cloth covers.

Tablecloths

The choice of tablecloth varies according to the place and circumstances: a lunch on the coast, in the country or in the mountains... There are all manner of tablecloths in various bright colours and materials, rustic, Indian, embroidered voile or linen to choose from. When I am inviting a few people for lunch or dinner in Paris or Genève, I always use a white damask tablecloth, on which I place a large circular lace table piece. At a lunch for two or three people, I set the table in the salon with a white tablecloth embroidered with coloured flowers.

Plates

Plates are placed one to two centimetres from the edge of the table, and at fifty or sixty centimetres from each other. Never place two dinner plates one on top of the other. For the potage: the soup plate is placed on the dinner plate, but both are removed at the same time when serving the next course.

Cheese and dessert plates do not have to match the dinner set: Gien ware, or porcelains of various origins: Hungarian, Chinese, Japanese, adding a playful touch can be found in small series in second-hand or antique shops.

Some hostesses place a small bread plate to the left of the dinner plate, next to the glasses. In my house, the bread is placed directly on the tablecloth, on the left of the plate. And I place, on the right, a small dish filled with butter, with its own knife.

Cutlery

Knives are arranged in order of use to the right of the plate, with the sharp end turned towards the plate, as is the soup spoon if potage is served, which is turned towards the table, back up. On the left are the forks, with the sharp ends placed on the tablecloth so that the coat of arms or the initials are visible – if, evidently, the cutlery is stamped. In England and the United-States, by contrast, forks and spoons are placed facing up, not down.

There is no need for knife-rests if the cutlery and the plates are removed after each course.

Silver cutlery should shine and glow. I store my cutlery in air-sealed plastic sleeves rolled in black tissue paper to preserve their shine longer. It is possible to find beautiful silver cutlery at auctions, where it is sold by weight at the cost of the silver.

In the country, you can use stainless steel cutlery, with wooden or coloured plastic handles.

Since fish knives and forks are a recent invention, they are not included in the silverware of some very traditional families who continue to ignore a usage which they find too bourgeois for their taste.

If there is a person serving, you should not place the cheese knife, or the dessert spoons and forks on the table. The maître d'hôtel will place them before each guest in due course. If you don't have anyone serving, the dessert fork and spoon are placed between the plate and the glasses.

Glasses

Glasses should be washed by hand, with pure water and no detergent. Well rinsed, they are wiped with a fine, and very clean cloth after which they are stored in furniture, away from dust, and free from odours – either wood, varnish or wax. Before placing the glasses on the table, wipe them with a very fine white cloth so that they are impeccable. Glasses are placed on the table in order of size, decreasing to the right. The larger glass, the water glass is the first, the second is the Bordeaux glass, the third, smaller again, is for white wine if white wine is served. In grand dinner receptions, there may be two Bordeaux glasses, one for the wine that is served with the meat, the other for the wine served with the cheese.

Champagne served in flutes keeps its temperature longer than Champagne served in a coupe. Even at a family dinner, two glasses are necessary: the water glass which may already be filled (not to the brim) and the wine glass.

Manufacturers such as Lalique and Christofle have created glasses of Bohemian crystal or blown glass which are true works of art.

Napkins

At lunch, the napkin is placed on the plates and folded in a triangle; at dinner, it is folded in a rectangle, and placed to the left of the plate over the forks.

If you are serving shellfish, provide large napkins which you will remove along with the plate, at the end of the course.

Finger bowls

Finger bowls may be in silver, glass, copper (in the country). They are brought to the table after serving asparagus or seafood (mussels, oysters, lobster), and placed on the left of the place setting.

Add a few drops of lemon or orange blossom water to the warm water. Finger bowls are removed along with the plates at the end of the course.

Salt and pepper

Salt should be presented in a small dish, along with a tiny spoon and placed between two guests because superstitious people do not want to ask their neighbours to pass them the saltshaker.

In the country, along with the salt, ground pepper and mustard can also be placed on the table.

Cigarettes and ashtrays

Although (in principle) one should not smoke until the cheese or the coffee is served, ashtrays, either in silver, or matching the dinner set can be placed on the table along with cigarettes arranged in tumblers. The person in charge of the service ensures that the ashtrays are emptied regularly.

Candleholders

You may place a single candleholder with several branches on a small round table, two or more, on an oval or rectangular table. The candleholders may be in silver, crystal or a pretty antique porcelain. In the country, the candleholders are made of ceramic, copper, brass, wood, porcelain or faience. Sometimes, my preference goes to small individual candle holders, either in silver or matching the dinner set.

In the city, the candles are lit just before sitting at the table. They are preferably white or ivory (and dripless...). In the mountain, the candles are red, at the seaside, blue or green – according to the tablecloth. Whichever you choose, the candles must be at the height of the faces, or slightly above. A light placed too low is unflattering to women's faces.

228

Flowers

Flowers should match the colour of the tablecloth and the dinner set; their perfume must be very light (avoid wattle, freesia, tuberoses or gardenias, flowers with heady scents). In a dining room, the only perfume should emanate from the dishes you are serving.

If your tablecloth is white damask, choose pastel or white flowers. In the country, we will select wild flowers, anemones, primroses and garden roses; no precious flowers.

And there are so many ways of arranging flowers for a table!

In town

In town, where the dining rooms are usually smaller, flower arrangements should always be quite low so as not to block the faces of the persons seated in front of each other. You can arrange a long table centrepiece, or a circular central piece flanked by two smaller bouquets which can be placed next to the candle holders. For an intimate dinner, you might assemble several Champagne flutes of differing sizes (if you have them), and place a rose in each of them.

Charming, small circular centrepieces of roses, peonies, hydrangeas may be placed in tumblers.

You can also put flowers in glass cups or small flower pots, with moss or small pebbles to stabilise the arrangement.

A pretty soup tureen, either of silver or Saxe porcelain, placed in the centre of the table can be filled with daffodils, gillyflowers, or buttercups along with light foliage.

229

In the country

In winter, a mixture of plants in a basket or flowers in a pot make a table centrepiece. The pot can also be painted in the colours of the tablecloth or the dinner set – pink, turquoise, yellow, or be varnished with linseed oil.

In autumn, I always choose red foliage, ferns, ivy, and have fun with vegetable arrangements – aubergines, radishes, capsicums, dwarf pumpkins, lemons – to which I add anemones and foliage.

At Christmas

So-called Christmas roses, adorned with holly, make ravishing arrangements, as do dried and fresh flowers mixed in bunches.

Table decorations

Along with the candleholders and flowers, the centre of the table can be decorated with small figurines, silver animals, or beautiful porcelain birds. To add a spot of colour, I fill small porcelain or silver dishes with chocolate pastilles or mint chocolate fondants.

PLACE SETTING

In France, the host and hostess sit at the centre of the table, facing each other, unlike in England where they sit each at one end of the table. Where guests are concerned, the places of honour are: for a woman to the right of the host, and for a man to the right of the hostess.

If two couples of equal status are invited, as for example, the Moréchands and the Camoins, Monsieur Moréchand will sit on the right of the hostess and Monsieur Camoins on her left, but Madame Camoins will seat to the right of the host and Madame Moréchand will be at his left. This way, the couples are honoured equally. If your guests are all of equal social importance, then the places of honour go to the persons whom you are inviting for the first time, or to the oldest.

Married couples are never seated together except for couples who have been married for less than a year.

Tables of six, ten, fourteen and eighteen allow the host and hostess to sit face to face across the table. For tables of eight, twelve or sixteen, the hostess will have to shift one place down or up in order to respect the rule of gender alternation.[40]

The same applies at a round table although the shift is less evident.

---

[40] In France, custom requires guests to sit man-woman-man-woman, hence efforts are usually made to invite equal numbers of men and women, as well as to have an even number of guests. [Translator's note]

Sitting arrangements for an unmarried host or hostess

A single woman never sits a single man or a married man directly in front of her (and therefore at the place of honour), but a relative or a woman friend. Conversely, a single man will place directly in front of him the wife of a friend (if the friend is also present), or a superior, or more simply an older woman or and older man.

Place cards

Place cards with the guests' names (handwritten) are used when eight guests and more have been invited. Married women are named by their husband's first name, i.e.: "Madame (written in full) Jean-Claude Lalane". The card is placed atop the water glass.

At embassy receptions and official dinners, the seating plan of each table is usually displayed in the entrance. The Maître d'Hôtel hands each guest a card with either the number or the name of their table – Table with the Red Roses, or Yellow Roses, where they find the place card with their names, on the water glass.

THE MENU

At a dinner for eight, four menus are used, and placed between two settings. The menu should be handwritten on white Bristol board, with a fine gold border. The date should also be indicated on the menu.

In the country, you can use a postcard with an image of your chalet or your house, or one of the local landmarks. At Château-Clarke, I have the menus written inside a greeting card showing the initials of the winery and a photograph of the storehouses. On the back of the card is the list of the wines I will be serving.

For a wedding, a birthday celebration or a baptism, the menu could display a photograph of the couple, the birthday person, or the baby.

For the past thirty years, I have been collecting the menus of the lunches and dinners to which I was invited, some of them signed by my hosts. Today, I have about two thousand menus. And yet, as the years pass, we eat and drink less! What a pity!

Dinner of the 6 January 2002

Saumon à l'oseille
Salmon with sorrel garnish

Selle d'Agneau Richelieu
Saddle of Lamb Richelieu

Coeurs de laitue mimosa
Lettuce hearts with mimosa egg

233

Sablé aux fraises
Strawberry short-bread

Pouilly-Fuissé 1987
Château-Clarke 1995
Lanson Noble Cuvée 1989

I will remind the reader that while green or garden salad is indicated on the menu, the cheeses are not, because there is no such thing as a good meal without cheese. Dishes should be named in the simplest manner: a menu is not a guessing game. At a hunting luncheon given by Madame de V., there was written on the menu: "Croustade Napoleon III". After tasting this dish, I leaned over to my neighbour, a Russian man of the Belle Epoque, and said: "Where I live, this is called Hachis Parmentier [Shepherd's Pie]."[41]

Informing guests of the contents of a menu is a form of politeness. If there is no written menu, the hostess may announce the order of dishes to her guests once they are seated.

---

[41] Hachis Parmentier is the household name given in France to the dish called Shepherd's Pie in English speaking countries. The word *hachis* means "mince". The Hachis Parmentier is named in honour of Antoine-Auguste Parmentier (1737-1813) who, among other brilliant achievements, campaigned with intellectual energy and cunning tricks to gain the recognition of the potato as a food suitable for human consumption. Up until the end of the 18th century, the potato was viewed with extreme distrust. Suspected of causing leprosy, it was cultivated almost exclusively for animal fodder. [Translator's note]

Planning and composing a menu

I discovered a menu, set for twenty, given in 1867 by the Baron James de Rothschild.

Consommé of spring vegetables and barley
Turtle soup *à l'anglaise*

Timbales Woronzoff
Turbot in crayfish sauce and melted butter
Bohemian beef fillet

Pheasant cutlets with mushroom purée
Chicken breast *à la Périgord*
Marquise Ortolan *chaudfroid*
Russian lobster salad

Asparagus Hollandaise sauce
Roasted grouses and woodcocks
Sicilian pistachio bread
Small pineapple ice-cream *soufflés*
Moka *à la Parisienne*.

Reading this menu, we can measure the evolution of our eating habits over the past hundred years or so. Today, the mainstay of our menus consist of an entrée, a main dish, a salad, cheese and dessert, and it would never occur to anyone to serve fish, meat, poultry and game at one sitting, not even at a gala dinner.

A few recipes

The following is an example of a menu with accompanying recipes, which we often serve at home and with guaranteed success.

Menu

Potage Laguipière
Gigot de sept heures et jardinière
[Seven hour leg of lamb and garden vegetables]
Salade printanière [Spring salad]
Cheeses (which you don't write in the menu)
Soufflé glacé aux framboises [raspberry ice-cream soufflé]
Château-Clarke 1982
Champagne Taittinger 1983

Recipe

POTAGE LAGUIPIERE
2 kg of mussels
1.5 litres of fish broth
1 onion
parsley
0.5 litre white wine

- Cook the mussels with the onion and parsley. Shell them and cook them again with the fish broth.
- Strain the cooked mussels.

- Make a roux to which you add the mixture of mussels and fish broth.[42]
- Add cream and saffron.
- Gruyère cheese and croutons.

GIGOT DE SEPT HEURES

1 leg of lamb
1 veal trotter
2 carrots
3 cloves of garlic
2 onions
1 bottle of white wine
1 *bouquet garni*

- Peal the onions, the carrots and the garlic, then dice the onions and the carrots.
- Render the leg of lamb and the veal trotter.
- Remove the lamb and veal and render the onions and the carrots.
- Place the lamb and veal back into the pan, and add the garlic and *bouquet garni*.
- Once the onions are brown, add the white wine. Reduce, then add water to level with the leg of lamb. Add salt and pepper.
- Cook for seven hours at very low heat (let it simmer).
- At the end of the cooking time, reduce the sauce and brown the leg of lamb in the oven under the grill.

---

[42] The roux is the thickening foundation used in many French sauces including the béchamel. It is made by melting butter to which flour is added. How long the roux is cooked results in varying degrees of colour. [Translator's note]

JARDINIERE

Green beans, turnips, carrots, spring onions, seasonal mushrooms, potatoes.

To serve: pre-cut the leg of lamb once lengthways, then five or six times across and present it whole. You may serve it with a serving spoon. Display the vegetables around the meat as a bouquet. Pour the sauce over the dish.

When you serve dinner at home, avoid all decorations resembling restaurant presentations – no cork-screw tomatoes, parsley bouquets, egg slices; no lace paper under your cakes or pastries; no embossed paper around your *petits fours*; no frills on the bones of your lamb chops; there should also be no labels or names on your cheeses – or vine leaves. And don't forget to remove the price tags from your wine and spirit bottles!

On the other hand, if you have called on the services of a *traiteur* to cater for your large cocktail party, do not interfere with any of the decoration; do not remove the lace or the embossed paper from the *petits fours*.

WELCOMING YOUR GUESTS

Punctuality is the duty of honest people. If you are going to be more than twenty minutes late, you must telephone to let your hosts know and to apologise.

Hosts, for their part, should be ready before the first guest arrives. It is entirely inappropriate for a hostess to appear after her guests have arrived. She needs to greet them as soon as they enter the salon, and even in the anteroom, with a pleasant word for everyone, showing her joy at their presence. Greetings, however, need to be reasonably brief so that the other guests do not feel excluded. If your guests sent flowers or brought chocolates, thank them warmly but discreetly so as not to embarrass the guests who came empty-handed. If there are only a few other guests, undo the gift-wrap in their presence, and if you have been offered chocolate or sweets, offer them to everyone at the end of the dinner. When I am hosting numerous guests, it is simply not possible to discover the content of their gifts in their presence, so I will thank them by telephone or in writing the next day.

During a trip to Turkey, a few years ago, I arrived at my hosts' home loaded with gifts, as local custom requires. And I was offered the customary return gifts; a dozen boxes of sweets. I did not have the time to open all of them.

On the day I left the country, I offered the hotel maid the few boxes I could not fit into my suitcase. She was delighted. But just as I was arriving at the airport in Istanbul, I heard the scream of police sirens, commanding the driver to stop.

Three policemen sporting what appeared to me as menacing moustaches walked towards me, one of them carrying a large box in his hands. Amidst the tender rose and pistachio Turkish delights, there was a Turquoise stone, larger than a walnut. The hotel maid had been tempted to taste the mouth-watering sweets as soon I had left, and she had alerted the director of the hotel, as soon as she had discovered the gemstones.

And so, thanks to her honesty, I was reminded that it is a duty to open gifts when we receive them. My own lack of *savoir-vivre* had almost caused me to miss out on the wonderful gift bestowed upon me by this oriental prince, out of the One Thousand and One Nights.

Useful advice

Don't forget that at a dinner party, you must introduce the youngest person to the oldest, men to women, French guests to foreign guests, your more familiar friends to the less familiar: "*Madame Morand,* may I introduce *Mademoiselle Tardy?*" or "*Madame,* Reinhald Traxl, an Austrian painter who is exhibiting in Paris".

By mentioning your guests' professional, social, artistic or political activities, you can facilitate connections and help initiate conversations.

It is most inappropriate to either call someone by the wrong name or to mispronounce their names. You must make the effort to memorize and pay attention to the names, first names and occupations of each of your guests.

When we gave dinners, when I was first married, I had to greet some people whose names I could not remember. Falling back on a trick of the theatre trade, I wrote their names in the palm of my hand.

If you are hosting thirty people or so, introduce the last person to arrive to the persons closest to the doors of the salon, or take them to a group of people they already know.

Men should introduce themselves, but it is customary to introduce women.

When one of my guests is more than twenty minutes late, I will ask my guests to the table, as I believe it is more impolite to require patience of those already present than it is to not wait for a careless guest.

To the few friends who are permanently late, I send an invitation with the time underlined twice and I make a point of writing 8:00 pm when I am expecting the other guests to arrive at 8:30 pm.

Cocktails and aperitifs

Cocktails and aperitifs are served in the salon before lunch or dinner, and before seating at the table.

To serve before lunch:

- Tomato or grapefruit juice (lighter than orange juice)
- Port
- Chilled Champagne
- Dry white wine (rosé in the country)
- Flat and sparkling mineral waters
- Ice cube (with ice tongs)

If your guests are English or American, you may serve them their favourite cocktails, for example:

GIN FIZZ
The juice of a lemon
A shot of gin
One teaspoon of sugar
Ice cubes

Mix the ingredients in a cocktail shaker, serve in a tall glass, with the rim iced with sugar.

DRY MARTINI
2/3 Martini dry
1/3 Gin
I green olive
lemon zest

Universally, your guests will appreciate the delicious "Star Cocktail" mixed from a variety of fruit juice (either orange, grapefruit, apple or pineapple), and vegetable juice (either celery, carrots or cucumber), to which you add fresh ginger before shaking.

PICK ME UP
(This one is my favourite when I need a pick me up)
1/ 4 cane alcohol
2/4 orange juice
1/4 ginger liqueur
A shot of grenadine

Add ice cubes and mix the lot in a shaker.
Serve in a cocktail glass, garnished with a mint leaf and a strawberry.

To serve before dinner

- Tomato juice (no fruit juice)
- The same drinks as before lunch with the exception of white wine and rosé
- The first red wine which will be served at dinner
- Bourbon and chilled vodka

To accompany the drinks:
Pistachio nuts, salted hazelnuts and almonds
Pealed quail eggs
Warm canapés (ramequins and cheese matches) as well as cold canapés as for example the following:

RECIPE FOR SHRIMP CANAPE
Shell the shrimps. Blend with butter. Add salt and Cayenne pepper. Lightly toast bread and spread the shrimp butter. Cut in small pieces.

RECIPE FOR WATERCRESS CANAPE
1 bunch of watercress
1 egg yolk
a quarter of a litre of vegetable oil
a sandwich loaf

- Remove the stalks from the watercress and put a few leaves to the side.
- Blanch the watercress in boiling and salted water (one second only).

243

- Make the mayonnaise.
- Drain the watercress. When all the water has drained and the watercress has cooled, cut it very finely and mix it in the mayonnaise.
- Season with salt, black pepper and cayenne pepper.
- Spread on the bread. Using a cookie cutter, cut the canapés into circles.

At a small gathering, avoid serving prunes with bacon, cocktail-size sausages, pizzas and quiches: these should be reserved for cocktail parties.

If your friends gather at your house before going to the theatre, offer them miniature *croque-monsieurs*, served piping hot, and which will keep them going until the end of the play.

Calling the guests to the table

If one employs a Maître d'Hôtel or a well-trained chamber maid, they will announce the traditional: *"Madame est servie"* [Madame has been served] to call the hostess and the rest of the party to dinner. If Madame has a nobiliary title, her guests will hear: *"Madame la Comtesse est servie"*. When hosting a minister or a sovereign prince, the Maître d'Hôtel calls out: *"Monsieur le ministre est servi"* or *"Monseigneur est servi"*. This Important Person then presides at the table and sits facing the hostess. When a minister or an unmarried ambassador hosts a dinner, the Maître d'Hôtel announces: *"Monsieur est servi"* and not *"Monsieur le Ministre..."* or *"Monsieur l'Ambassadeur est servi"*.

When a widower or a divorced man hosts guests at dinner, their oldest daughter acts as the hostess; in which case, the Maître d'Hôtel calls: *"Mademoiselle est servie"*. But when the hostess is a single woman who is no longer a young girl, the Maître d'Hôtel calls: *"Madame est servie"*.

Among traditional families and at official dinners, the host together with the lady who will sit at his right (at the place of honour) first enter the dining room. But in general, the hostess leads and her guests follow her.

TABLE MANNERS

One of my aunts found India fascinating. She once recounted to me that during one of her numerous trips at the turn of the twentieth century, she had forged a friendship with a Maharaja from Srinagar. On the occasion of his first visit to France, she invited him to her house to lunch along with two friends of hers, a married couple.[43]

For entrée, she served Brittany artichokes, bought fresh from the market, with a vinaigrette dressing. The maharaja, his face beaming, detached the first leaf, looked at it, bit it, found it to his taste, and with a large gesture, threw it over his shoulder. My aunt was speechless. But having soon recovered, and using her most charming smile, she copied the prince and threw over her shoulder the leaf she was holding between her fingers. Her friends, initially astounded, bowed to the novel etiquette and artichoke leaves were soon flying all over the dining room, while the four personalities remained seated on their chairs in all dignity.

My aunt believed that the Maharaja had wished to test the civility of his hostess. And he had found it excellent.

The actual truth of my aunt's speculations are not what is at stake in this anecdote, as they are possibly the reflection of her own complex mind. But I have retained from this story a magisterial lesson about politeness, which guides me whenever I host in my own home foreign guests whose table manners differ from ours. I never fail to bow to their etiquette.

---

[43] Note that arriving ten to fifteen minutes late is considered within the realm of punctuality. Arriving early is also impolite, but a more unlikely occurrence. [Translator's note]

Dos and don'ts of table etiquette

- Don't attach yourself to the table, stay fifty centimetres from its edge.
- Hold yourself straight when seated on your chair, but don't be rigid and don't slouch.
- Don't for any reason eat with your elbow(s) on the table; and do not lean over the table either your elbows, or your forearms, or even your wrists. If you are using your right hand to eat, do not take the opportunity to lean on your left elbow.
- Don't surround your plate with your arm, as though you are guarding it from your neighbour.
- Don't keep your hands on your knees.
- Unfold your napkin discreetly without making a slapping noise. If it is a large napkin, keep it folded in half, lengthwise and place it on your knees.
- A man should never tuck his napkin into his shirt collar, whatever animal he may be eating.
- One never lowers their mouth to one's plate. We all remember our parents famously and relentlessly admonishing us to "Lift your elbow!". You bring the fork or the spoon to your mouth, not the other way around.
- Nicole Hapland, who was one of the most famous French ambassadors to Washington, taught me that in during a meal, you should speak with the guest on your right at the first course and the guest on your left at the second, and at dessert time, you can speak with whomever you please.
- We eat noiselessly (without aspirating or slurping the soup, without blowing on it – just wait a few seconds for the liquid to cool).

247

- We do not incline our plate to recover the last drops, we just let them go!
- We eat with our mouth closed.
- We do not drink with a mouthful of food, and we wipe our lips before drinking from our glass so as to leave no trace of either food or make-up on the rim. And we wipe our lips after drinking.
- When the dish is presented to you, do not try out a few pieces before deciding which bit is to your satisfaction, and don't go fetching a piece at the other extremity of the dish. Choose from what is in front of you. If the cut is too big, don't cut it either when it is in the dish or once it is on your plate, ask the person who is serving to cut it for you. It is also simpler to take what is presented to you and not to hold up the serving of the food.
- Don't scrape the last shreds of meat from a bone and don't suck on bones, even if they are pigeon bones!
- Don't feel all the fruit just so you can find the ripest.
- Bottles of water can be placed on the table only at family or small dinner parties, where there is no serving staff. Water is otherwise always served in carafes. Men have the responsibility of filling with wine and water, the glasses of the women who are seated next to them, and without waiting for the women to ask. A woman should not have to help herself to drinks at the table.

Bread

Bread is eaten after the potage when the entrée is served. One should not eat bread as soon as they are seated at the table.

Bread is broken, not cut. It is never placed on the edge of the plate, but on the tablecloth, or a small bread plate. It is inappropriate to spread butter on a piece of bread. As it is eaten, the individual piece of bread is broken into a smaller piece, to which is added a dab of butter. The breadbasket stays on the table at a country dinner, or when having dinner with family and friends. In the country, it is also customary to present the bread whole and to break it at the table. Finally, we never mop our sauce with bread.

And Monsieur! If the woman sitting next to you begins to crumble her bread and to roll the crumbs into small balls, you may safely assume that you are being sent a message clear as a traffic sign: she is bored, and you need to find another topic of conversation.

As for the bread, it is recommended to serve several types with the meal: nut, rye, black olives, muesli, seven grain, bran loafs... without forgetting our unforgettable baguette: you are dining in France, where good bread is part of the national ethos

Service

All dishes are presented to the left and wines to the right. The first guest to be served is the woman seated to the right of the host, then the woman on his left, then the woman facing him from across the table and on the right of the hostess, and the woman on the left of the hostess; next is the second woman to the right of the host, then the second woman to his left, and so forth, moving from the host to the hostess who is the last of the ladies to be served. After the ladies, the gentlemen are served: the first is the man on the right of the hostess, and second the one on the left, then the man seated across from her to the right of the host. The little dance ends when the host has been served.

Plates and cutlery are removed from the left-hand side, and they are immediately and unfailingly replaced from the right. A dinner for twelve will thus necessitate two Maîtres d'Hôtel.

SERVING WINE

Wine is integral to our culture and holds the ascendant place in gastronomy. It is possible to have an unforgettable memory of a Grand Cru. It is therefore not necessary to advocate for the role of wine in the composition of a menu.

One of my cousins once invited to lunch an Israeli general, who was a long standing friend of her mother. Just before sitting at the table, guessing correctly that his hostess's kitchen did not conform to Kosher rules, he informed her in a quiet aside that he did not eat meat. My cousin was dismayed.

"Avram, you do eat shellfish, don't you?"

"No, no shellfish."

Seeing her problem, he added: "Two eggs will do me."

My cousin then made a charming gesture, she had her last bottle of Château-Laffite 1959 brought over to the table, a wine of exceptional vintage and equally exceptional year. When this venerable bottle was about to be open, my husband exclaimed: "Ah, no need! This wine is not Kosher."

The general smiled: "You are absolutely right, but I would commit a greater sin if I did not partake of this historical *Château*. God would never forgive my lack of taste."

The marriage of wine and food

The guiding principle rests with harmonising:

- The power of a wine with the richness of the food.
- The subtlety of a wine with the delicacy of a dish.

A dish should never crush a wine, thus we should never serve:

- Game with a white wine or a light red
- Dishes dressed with vinaigrette together with red wines.

Wine should not dominate a dish, hence

- A red Bordeaux is not served with a white meat.

One should not associate:

- Sugar and salt: to serve a Sauternes wine with oysters would be sacrilegious.
- Acids and astringents. Serve a red Bordeaux with a sorrel sauce and it is the wine that has been assassinated.

Be wary of slightly sour sauces based on raspberry and spiced vinegar; cider is only just suitable here. Sweet dishes are formidably difficult because it is so awkward to pair them with the right wine. Thus, duck *aux raisins* can be successfully accommodated with a not too powerful red wine, but pastries rarely go well with sweet wines. Champagne is the easy way out. A red wine, even a wine that is a little evolved can accompany a cake or a chocolate sauce to perfection.

A few simple rules

Adapt the strength of the wine to that of the dish:

- Light white... fish
- Full bodied white ....fish, white sauces
- Rosé...white meats
- Light red .... red meats
- Full bodied red..................................... game

An elementary rule marries greater wines to simpler dishes of the best quality.

Wine and cheese

- To go with a relatively neutral flavoured hard cheese, as for example Edam, serve a tannic red.
- With a full flavoured hard cheeses such as Beaufort, serve a light, fruity white; and match a Comté with yellow wine from the Jura region or with Xeres.
- Where fermented cheeses are concerned, serve a light white with soft cheeses, and an Alsatian wine with full flavoured cheeses, as for example a Munster.
- With goat cheeses, serve a dry white, or a cool tannic red.
- With a fully ripened creamy Brie de Meaux (without bitterness, and *fermier*), serve a well-rounded generous red.

I recommend an old Sauternes for a Roquefort: it is a sumptuous marriage, and an Apremont wine for a Beaufort cheese.

Other possibilities

- Cheese *soufflé*: full bodied white or rosé
- Fish – shad with sorrel: dry white
- Monkfish *paupiette*: full bodied white Graves
- Lamprey Borderlaise: powerful red Bordeaux
- Porcini mushrooms: red Bordeaux(Médoc, Saint-Emilion)
- Game: most great vintages (Burgundy, Châteauneuf-du-Pape, red Bordeaux)
- Baron of lamb: Médoc or Lafite 59 (impérial!)
- *Foie gras* soup: Clarke

You will find at the end of this section a detailed listing of Burgundy, Bordeaux and Alsatian wines.

A basic guide for serving wine at the right temperature

8 to 10 degrees: Dry whites
10 to 12 degrees: Full bodied whites
14 to 16 degrees: Light reds
16 to 18 degrees: Full-bodied reds

It is better to serve a slightly cooler wine than a wine that is too warm. Wine will have time to warm in the glass and to be drunk when it is just right. A warmer wine shows its flaws more easily than its flavours and subtleties.

Not to do:

- Leave a bottle of white wine more than forty-eight hours in the refrigerator
- Cool a red wine with ice or in the freezer (although a white wine might tolerate a similar treatment)
- Suggest to serve the wine with ice blocks.

Decantation

Decantation must be reserved for aged and great red vintages.

The first aim of decantation is to attempt to separate the wine from the precipitates which form during its ageing. Prior to decanting, a bottle should be stood up for twenty-four hours.

The second goal of decantation is to aerate the wine that has not been in contact with air for a long time. This operation should exalt the fragrance although it does, on occasions, have the opposite effect. Avoid decanting Burgundies, young and light wines.

When should you decant a great bottle of wine? Between one and three hours before serving, and so remember to think about the wine the day before you invite your guests for dinner.

At mealtimes, the wine must be ready, which is to say, the wine

- must be at the right temperature,
- rested,
- decanted (aged wines).

The art of serving wine

Unlike the dishes which are presented to each of the guests from the left, wines are served from the right. If it is a great vintage, the Maître d'Hôtel will inform each guest, in an unobtrusive voice, of the cru and the year: "Château-Pétrus 1969".

At an intimate dinner, it is the host who announces the wine but only when it is of excellent quality. The bottle should be held by the body, not the neck. Never pour wine with your hand turning backwards, and do not rest the neck of the bottle on the glass. To avoid staining the tablecloth while pouring a glass (never fill a glass to the brim), the Maître d'Hôtel turns the bottle slightly and catches the last drop in the white napkin folded in four, which he is holding with his left hand.

Red wine is served in carafes. White wines can be served in their bottle, as they are never decanted, but at home, we always serve white wine in carafes. Bottles are never laid in a wicker or woven silver basket as they are at the restaurant, they are placed on the table standing up.

The order of wine

- A white wine always precedes a red
- A young wine always precedes an aged wine
- A light wine always precedes a full-bodied wine

Note that tobacco smoke alters the taste of wine

The etiquette of wine drinking

A wine is discreetly inhaled, but it should not be kept in the mouth even if one is a connoisseur, nor should anyone have to throw back their head to swallow. The wine will find its way down without prompting, especially if it is enjoyed slowly for its savours, and drunk in small mouthfuls. The lips must be wiped before and after drinking wine.

If you do not drink wine, do not refuse it by placing your hand over your glass, but simply say: "*Non, merci*" to the person in charge of the service before they begin pouring, as one should not waste even a drop of a great wine.

Before leaving the table, do empty your glasses, your hosts will be appreciative, especially if they have served you a great wine. If you accidentally spill your glass of Bordeaux on the pretty white organdie tablecloth, you may flush with embarrassment, not knowing what to do next – indeed, there is nothing you can do, except apologise to the hostess, and let her remedy the situation. Since everyone has their own method and opinion on the removal of wine stains, do not rush to grab the saltshaker or reach for the bottle of white wine or Perrier to pour their contents on the table.

THE END OF THE MEAL

Leaving the table

The hostess rises, and after her, her husband and the other men, who then help pull the chairs for the women seated next to them.

You should not fold your napkin on leaving the table, nor let it drop on your chair or on the floor, nor throw it on your plate, but leave it in a loosely tidy state on the right of your table setting. The hostess leaves the dining room first, leading the women and the men into the salon. Her husband leaves the dining room last and closes the door.

Coffee and liqueurs

Coffee is served either at the dining room table or in the salon. At lunch, coffee is usually served at the table, especially if the conversation is lively and you do not wish to interrupt it. At dinner, the hostess serves coffee in the salon. Men drink theirs standing up, while smoking cigars and women seize the opportunity to absent themselves discreetly, and to adjust their make-up.

Chocolates, glazed chestnuts and *pâtes de fruit* are presented to the guests while they are drinking coffee. Coffee is served twice and should be as hot on the second serving as the first. If you use only half a sugar cube with your coffee, don't return the other half to the sugar bowl, leave it on your saucer.[44]

When drinking coffee, the saucer is held with the left hand, and the cup with the right. The coffee spoon is left on the saucer not in the cup.

Cognac and sweet liqueurs (blackcurrant [Cassis], blackberry, red currant, cherry) are served after coffee.

Since not all your guests will drink coffee, it is important to have a choice of teas. One of my favourite herbal teas *"Nuit angélique"* [angelic night] has magical virtues, and you will find that it is universally appreciated. Its ingredients are in equal parts: green anise, angelica, lemon balm, fennel, ginger, and cinnamon. This tea should be brewed thoroughly.

Cigars

Some men will tell you that nothing tastes better than a cigar after coffee. I like equally the man who smokes a pipe in my salon as the man who smokes a cigar, but it is true that the scent of a Havana cigar, like a good wine, leaves me pleasantly light-headed.

The rules of *savoir-vivre* require you not to keep your favourite cigar in your pocket when you are invited to dinner, since, in principle, you will be offered a cigar after coffee. However, I do not find it at all shocking when a guest refuses the cigar I am offering to him and remains faithful to his favourite brand. An old saying has it that the man faithful to his cigar is also faithful in love.

---

[44] In France, hot drinks (coffee, tea, chocolate, herbal teas) are sweetened with either white or brown sugar cubes. [Translator's note]

It is also in good taste for a man to ask the women in his presence, for permission to smoke his cigar – a permission which they are obligated to grant. He should, however, smoke away from them if smoke bothers them.

The etiquette of cigar smoking

According to my friend Monsieur Davidoff, the first rule is to leave the paper ring in place.

A cigar is cut either with a cigar cutter or with the teeth (with some subtlety). A cigar is lit with a match, not a cigarette lighter, and even better, an excellent cigar is lit with the leaf in which it is wrapped, and which is rolled up before being lit.

In former times, thoughtful women would prepare the gentlemen's cigars by holding them delicately above a flame. Today, professional cigar smokers feel nostalgic about the women, but not the practice.

A good cigar is smoked to the very end, not halfway, and should not go out. Should a cigar go out, it will not be lit again, but deposited in an ashtray. It is better not to offer cigars at all than to offer mediocre ones.

COCKTAILS AND BUFFETS

It has become common practice to serve a buffet when hosting large numbers of guests. But in fact, it is even more difficult to organise a beautiful standing buffet than a sit-down dinner. I have suggested below three buffets which I spent much time perfecting. I will leave it up to you, of course, to choose which dishes are best suited to your circumstances, the occasion, the place, the seasons and the guests you have invited. Remember that if you have called in caterers, you should not remove their decorations (lace paper, embossed paper, or the labels on the cheeses).

The Cold Buffet

For entrée, serve a variety of canapés, rustic bread or brioche, which are the specialities of good *traiteurs*.

Vegetables

- Vegetable salads with a tartar sauce, comprising radishes, celery, cherry tomatoes, red, yellow and green capsicums, cauliflower, Provence artichokes, mushrooms and hard boiled eggs.
- Artichoke salad.
- Mixed salad: rice, corn, tomatoes, capsicums, celery, grapefruit, green beans, and tagliatelle with basil.
- *Salade Martiniquaise*: spinach leaves, avocado, capsicum, pineapple, grapefruit, crab seasoned with Tabasco sauce.

261

- Potato salad, prepared the evening before.
- Lentil salad (don't forget the cloves).
- White bean salad.
- Legume terrines: carrots, celery, artichokes.
- Avocado mousse.
- Gazpacho.
- Pasta, served warm or cold, in various sauces: tomato, sage, seafood, aubergine, zucchini, gratin, salmon. The pasta is always thoroughly appreciated.

Charcuterie

Ham of Parma and York; capocollo; salami (saucisson); rillettes; andouillette; mortadella.

Poultry and Game

- Duck pâté, foie gras terrine, rabbit terrine, pheasant salad, partridge salad, *foie gras mousse.*
- Chicken *chaud-froid.*
- Duck with peaches or cherries; or glazed duck.
- Chicken in *gelée*, or chicken with ginger, lemon, or pineapple.

Meat

Roast pork (with sage); roast veal, roast beef (with *gelée* or Port wine) or leg of lamb with mint sauce.

Fish

- Marinated salmon with dill, salmon tartar, cold or smoked salmon.
- Nordic plate: Baltic herrings, smoked eel and trout, sprat, haddocks, halibut.
- Lobster, prawn, crab, scampi salad – or a seafood platter.
- Sole fillets in tomato sauce (served cold).
- Fish pâté (beware: it is generally tasteless).
- Bass with mayonnaise.
- Grouper in a Carribean or ginger sauce.

Cheeses

It is believed that there are four hundred and ninety three types (not brands) of cheeses in France. Evidently, you cannot serve all of them. In the country, serve the local cheeses. In town, two platters. On one, offer goat cheeses only, and on the other Brie, Munster, Vacherin or Reblochon in full: Don't offer portions.

Fruit

- A basket of seasonal fruit so long as they are ripe, and exotic fruit.
- A fruit salad prepared two hours before serving, perfumed with a fruit brandy (as for example: peach or mirabelle plum).

Entremets [sweets]

In former times, all the dishes served after the roasted meats were referred to as the *entremets* and this ensemble included sweet dishes as well as vegetables. From the fourteenth century until the seventeenth, the entremets was also a form of entertainment, an interlude presented half-way through dinner,[45] and during which wandering players, troubadours, danseurs and other artists performed before various stage sets – a fortress, a palace, a cathedral – constructed at great expense by specialist artisans. Today, the *entremets* consists only of sweet dishes served after the cheeses, for example:
- Chocolate mousse (with orange zest or coffee)
- Chestnut mousse (with Chantilly cream)
- Red fruit mousse
- *Crème renversée*
- *Oeufs à la neige* [46]
- Ice-cream
- Sorbets

and all the cakes in their innumerable variety.

---

[45] *Entremets* means literally "in-between-dishes". [Translator's note]

[46] *Oeufs à la neige* means literally "eggs *à la* snow" or "snow eggs". This perfectly delicious dessert consists of small clouds of soft poached meringues floating on custard. Note that the custard is always home made, and that custard in French is actually called *crème anglaise* – English custard. [Translator's note]

The Hot Buffet

A buffet is never entirely composed of cold or hot dishes, and the most pleasing is a mixture of both. If you are serving hot and cold dishes at the same time, keep the hot dishes on a dish warmer. At a very large buffet, fruit and sweets are placed on a separate table.

Include:

- Pizza, quiches (cheese, vegetables, fish, chicken, mushroom)
- Ham and cheese croissants
- Prunes or bananas with bacon.

Entrées

- Gratin potato *Savoyard* or a legume gratin.
- Seafood pasta, ravioli, lasagne, gnocchi, spaghetti bolognese, and so forth.

Rustic dishes

- *Potées* [stews cooked in earthenware pots – there are many regional varieties]
- Morteau sausages [*saucisses*] and potatoes
- *Boudins blancs* [white pork sausage] or black pudding inside baked cored apples [*pommes en l'air*]
- Cured pork shoulder in lentils [*petit salé aux lentilles*]
- Polenta rabbit

Meat and game

- Rack or leg of lamb.
- Beef fillet in a pastry case [*fillet de beuf en croûte*].
- Chicken with salt crystals [*poulet au gros sel*].
- Duck with turnips or in its own sauce.
- Partridges with cabbage.
- Grilled chicks.
- Duck breast with apples [*magret de canard aux pommes*].
- Goose with vegetables.
- Venison.
- Saddle of hare, with a celery purée or steamed potatoes.

Fish

- Lamprey Bordelaise [wine sauce].
- Monkfish Armoricaine.
- Grilled bass with fennel.

Desserts

- Apple strudel with Chantilly cream.
- *Tarte Tatin*.
- Warm fruit compote.

World Food Buffet

Today, all over the world, there are excellent Chinese, Japanese, Lebanese, Turkish, Moroccan, Italian, and other restaurants. Address yourself to their chefs for the buffet of your choice and your success as a hostess will be assured.

- Baba ghanoush
- Imperial dumplings
- Crab claw fritters
- Caribbean crab and Caribbean black pudding
- Scampi
- Lamb kebabs
- Mechoui
- Osso bucco
- Lamb or chicken curries
- Tabouli
- Mutton or chicken couscous
- Pastilla
- Moussaka
- Sushi and sashimi

Drinks

The best, and flowing! For a rustic buffet, wines and beers may be served from the barrel.

WINES

Burgundy wines

Grand Crus

Chablis

Vaudésir	Les Clos
Valmur	Grenouilles
Les Preuses	Blanchots

La Côte de Nuits

Chamberlain	Romanée Conti
Clos de Tart	Clos-Saint-Denis
Clos de Vougeot	Musigny
La Romanée	Grands Echezeaux

La Côte de Beaume

Corton	Montrachet
Chevalier-Montrachet	
Criots-Bâtard-Montrachet	
Bâtard-Montrachet	
Bienvenues-Bâtard-Montrachet	
Corton Charlemagne	

Grape variety

Reds and rosés: pinot noir and Gamay noir à jus blanc
White wines: Chardonnay, Aligoté.

Exceptional years

Red wines	White wines
1969	1971
1976	1976
1978	1978
1979	1979
1983	1985
1985	1986
1988	1989
1989	1990
1990	1992
1996	1996
1998	1997

Three years in particular deserve a special mention: 1978, 1988, 1990 and 1980 is a year worth re-discovering.
Millesimes of the last decade: 2002, 2003, 2005, 2009, 2010

Serving

– Do not shake the bottle before opening them, handle them with care.
– Red wines are served at room temperature (heat is a wine's worst enemy).
- 16 to 17 degrees for the great red vintages
- 12 to 14 degrees for the great white wines
– White wines are served cooled
- 10 to 12 degrees for young wines
- 12 to 14 degrees for vintage whites
– Burgundies are decanted at the point of serving. Decantation is not mandatory, and all depends on the age of the wine. Decantation can spoil wines that are over ten years old.

– Use tulip shaped wine glasses for white wines and balloon shape for reds. Fill the glass halfway, so that the wine has a chance to turn and reveal its savours.

– Sparkling white wines [*crémants* or *mousseux*] and Champagnes are delivered ready to drink.

– When you keep your wine in the cellar, let it rest for two or three weeks before drinking and two or three months if it is very old.

Food and Burgundy wines

Seafood, fish: Dry white dry
Charcuterie: Dry white or rosé
Omelettes: Rosé
Foie gras, poultry, white meats: Great white vintages
Meat: Light reds
Game, meats in sauce, not so strong cheeses: Great red vintages
For aperitif and at dessert: A sparkling white either natural or nuanced with a touch of *crème de cassis* or *framboises* (blackcurrant or raspberry).

Bordeaux wines
Grands Crus

Médoc
Château-Lafite-Rothschild
Château-Mouton-Rothschild
Château-Latour
Château-Margaux

Graves
Château-Haut-Brion

Sauternes
Château d'Yquem (white)

Saint-Emilion
Château Ausone
Château-Cheval Blanc

Millesimes

	DRY WHITE	DESSERT WINE	RED
1989	very good	exceptional	exceptional
1990	very good	exceptional	very good
1991	good	good	good
1992	average	average	average
1993	average	mediocre	good
1994	good	average	very good
1995	very good	exceptional	exceptional
1996	very good	exceptional	exceptional
1997	average	exceptional	very good
1998	very good	very good	exceptional
1999	exceptional	very good	exceptional
2000	very good	average	exceptional
2001	very good	exceptional	very good
2002	good	very good	good
2003	very good	exceptional	very good
2004	very good	average	good
2005	exceptional	very good	exceptional
2006	good	very good	gd/vy good
2007	good	vy gd/except	average
2008	very good	very good	exceptional
2009	exceptional	exceptional	exceptional
2009	exceptional	exceptional	exceptional
2011	very good	very good	good
2012	good	good	good
2013	good	very good	average

Alsace wines

Seven varieties of grapes

These varieties produce wines which have the right to *"appellation d'origine controlée"*, which is a copyright on local origins.
- Sylvaner (dry white, fresh and light)
- Pinot blanc (dry white, supple and filled with energy)
- Riesling (very dry white, classy, exquisite fruit)
- Tokay Pinot gris (dry white, heady, opulent and full bodied)
- Gewurztraminer (dry white, structured, powerful bouquet)
- Pinot noir (dry red or rosé, elegant bouquet)

Grands Crus

Altenberg de Berheim	Zozenberg
Brand (Turckheim)	Winzenberg
Kastelber (Andlam)	Wineck–Schlossberg
Kitterlé (Guebwiller)	Sporen

Schlossberg (Kayserberg and Kleintsheim)
Sommerberg (Niedermorschwihr and Katznethal)
And a special mention for Rangen (Thann).
Two rare and prestigious mentions may crown an Alsace grand cru of *appellation d'origine contrôlée*: *"Sélection de grain nobles"* [selection of noble berries] and *"Vendanges tardives"* [late harvest]. Issued exclusively from the Alsace muscat grapes, these "black pearls" are harvested in a state of hypermaturity and during exceptional years.

Exceptional years
1976
1981
1983
1985
1988
1989
1990
1992
1997
2005
2007
2009
2012

Serving

– Cool but not chilled, in an ice bucket cut with water (10 degrees)
– Do not let them linger in the refrigerator as this risks spoiling their arôme.
– Serve in a tulip shaped glass with a rounded side and coloured stem
– Alsace wines are drunk young, six months to five years after the harvest. Only the great vintages age happily.

Food and Burgundy wines

As aperitif: a Gewurztraminer or Muscat Alsace grand cru.
With *foie gras*: a Tokay Pinot gris Alsace grand cru.
With fish: a Riesling Alsace.
With shellfish: or a Gewurztraminer Alsace grand cru.

With poultry: a Riesling or Gewurztraminer Alsace grand cru
With meat and game: a Tokay Pinot frais.
With cheeses: a Gewurztraminer Alsace grand cru.
With dessert: a Muscat Alscare, or even better a "*sélection de grain nobles*".
For an exceptional meal: A Riesling Alsace grand cru.

<u>Champagne wines</u>

The symbol of celebrations, success, and seduction, Champagne is the wine of love and gaiety. Champagne creates waves of happiness and is the delight of hosts and friends.

However, finding one's way through the forest of houses, cuvée, and labels is essential.

For an apéritif, a brut of no specific year, or a special cuvée. The most famous are: Dom Pérignon, Cristal de Roederer, the Comtes de Champagne (Taittinger), Grand Siècle (Laurent Perrier), Belle Epoque (Perrier Joüet), la Grande Dame (Clicquot), la cuvée William Deutz. However, some high-end houses such as Krug, Bollinger, Pol Roger, Cordon rouge, Charles Heidsieck, Piper, Pommery, Lanson, Jacquart, Boizel, Henriot should not be overlooked. You may serve Champagne before the meal or with the first course if you are serving *foie gras*, fish or shellfish.

The great houses from Reims, Epernay and Tours-sur-Marne are a must for evening celebrations.

Champagne pleases the ladies. You may serve it at the start of the meal, halfway with the lamb or the fattened chicken, with red fruit desserts.

Champagne should be served at a temperature of 9 degrees and left in a bucket of ice blocks. It is savoured in flutes, never in a coupe. Never pour Champagne wine into a carafe, or shake you Champagne flute – you will kill it. When the party includes more than eight persons, Champagne should be served in a magnum bottle. A 750ml bottle of Champagne serves six persons.

Before serving, the hostess should ensure that the flutes were correctly washed. Detergents and chemical residue will annihilate the froth and the bubbles, which spells the death of the Champagne.

Champagne bottles cannot be re-corked once they have been open, and their contents must be drunk by the next day at the latest. Champagne bottles should be kept lying down, and in a cellar, and should never be placed in the freezer.

WHEN INVITING FRIENDS FOR THE WEEKEND

Having guests should be a pleasure even when we are inviting out of obligation. And your guests should share in your pleasure. You must take care of them and dedicate some time to them, while leaving them some personal space.

If you have several guests staying over, it is best that they share complementary or common interests. And indeed, forty-eight hours under a single roof can seem a very long time when you are sharing the space with persons lacking in *savoir-vivre*.

You may invite in writing or by telephone, about two weeks before the date. Provide a map with the most straightforward and simplest directions, and add your phone number, especially if people are coming to visit you for the first time. For a weekend visit, your guests may arrive on Friday night or on Saturday morning.

Bedrooms and menus

Before your guests arrive, inspect the bedrooms and the bathrooms they will be using. Nothing can substitute for the eye of the mistress of the house. Make sure that a previous guest has not left any clothes in the wardrobe and that everything is impeccable. In winter, turn on the heating in the bedrooms so that the beds do not feel humid and the air is not stale. As soon as your guests enter their rooms, where all the lights are lit, they will judge the importance and the pleasure which their visit holds for you.

Below is a list of the objects which you should provide for your guests:

In their bedrooms:

- A carafe of water and two glasses
- Sweets and chocolates
- Fresh and dried fruit (dates, figs, prunes, sultanas…) with a plate, cutlery set and a small napkin
- Writing paper, pencils and pens
- A pad of paper
- Postcards and a guide to the region
- Books
- Radio
- A gentleman's valet stand for Monsieur
- A light day rug.

In their wardrobes:

- Clothes hangers in a single colour
- A baggage carrier
- Extra blanket and pillows (for Madame's head in particular)
- A sewing kit
- A shoe-horn for Monsieur
- A wicker basket or a pretty box to tidy up jewellery and small objects
- Perfumed sachet or small sachets filled with lavender.

In the bathroom:

- A silk flower or a bouquet of silk flowers
- Unopened soap
- Bath salts or bath oil

- Cotton buds in a small wicker basket
- A box of tissues in a pretty fitted cover
- Aspirin, Alka-Seltzer, medical mint spirit with a few sugar cubes
- A hair-dryer
- Along with the bath towels and face washer,[47] a bathrobe is always appreciated.
- A shoe-shining kit (a brush, cloth and neutral shoe polish), or shoe pouches
- In winter, a hot water bottle in a cover.

If your guests arrive on a Friday night, plan on a late dinner so that they have time to settle, visit the house and familiarise themselves with their surroundings. Dinner may not last too long, as your guests will need a good night sleep.

Before they retire to their bedrooms, let them know that breakfast will be served in the kitchen or in the dining room, and between such and such time. Make sure they are lacking for nothing. And of course, if you employ domestic staff, have your guests' breakfast or at least their first cup of coffee brought to their bedrooms.

Planning activities

It is not enough to plan accommodation and menus ahead of time, you also need to think of fun things to do, such as a game of cards or other games, strolls or bicycle rides in the region, fishing, tennis, pétanque, golf.

---

[47] In France, the face-washer is a mitten rather than the square piece of toweling material used in Australia, the UK and the US. It is called a *"gant de toilette"*. [Translator's note]

When I have one or two guests in my small house in Quiberon, I organise a visit to the institute of Thalassotherapy to unwind and re-energise – for their well-being and… mine. In Megève, during summer, I organise golf and we usually end the day with a few laps at the pool, or a relaxation session at the Chalet du Mont d'Arboit.

If you are hosting children, try to give them a place of their own (a barn, attic or basement room) where they can have fun freely. If they are very young, if possible, try to hire a young person from the village to look after them during the afternoon.

Our shared weekends usually end around 6:00 pm. This gives my guests time to go home without rushing. Before they leave, we always have a copious *goûter* with hot chocolate (now famous), brioches, cakes, *tartes* but also cold meat and salads.

And so, *au revoir*!

Savoir-vivre with our friends and our friends' friends

Here is the situation: you have been invited to your friend Irene's where you have met a charming couple, and discovered that you have much in common. Naturally, you wish to see them again. Nothing could be more legitimate, but on one condition. The next day, you need to call Irene on the telephone to thank her for her invitation and for giving you the opportunity to have met the Nemours. You let her know that you intend to see them again then when you invite the Nemours to your house for the first time, you must also invite Irene and her husband. Furthermore, you should inform Irene of the date and event before anyone else.

If you do not proceed in this manner, your friend will be in her right to reproach you for being off-handed. We all feel a certain right of ownership for our friends.

BEING A WEEKEND GUEST

Respond to a written invitation promptly, thanking your host. Inviting friends to one's home to spend a whole weekend necessarily imposes extra work. Arrive on time, with an elegant and reasonable amount of luggage and in an elegant casual outfit.

Bring your hosts a gift which you give them when you arrive (not when you leave) and which communicates your happiness at being hosted.

As soon as you arrive, you ensure that you are the ideal guest: discreet, pleasant, courteous, smiling and light. As light as possible. Don't bring attention to yourself by waking up at the crack of dawn or staying in bed until lunchtime. Having breakfast after 10:00 am may bother your hostess. Moreover, bow to the habits and tastes of the majority.

If you share a bathroom with the guests in the next bedroom, don't linger too long. Rinse off the bathtub and the hand-basin, and tidy up your toiletry items. Use the cotton buds, not the towels, to remove your make-up. And keep your bedroom tidy. If there is no domestic staff, make your bed and hang your clothes in the wardrobe. Don't leave a mess in the room.

If you accidentally tip your cup of coffee on the sheets, or worse, on the bedspread, let your hostess know immediately. Don't try to hide your crime! And as soon as you get home, send flowers to show your contrition.

You may suggest going into the village to buy cheeses or desserts, helping with cooking, setting the table, or tidying up after the meal, washing up, making tea… in the evening, help put away the garden furniture and close the window shutters. Play with the children and avoid even a shadow of conflict.

On a Saturday evening, choose a dressier outfit such as a pretty pair of trousers and a blazer for your husband.

Before leaving, thank the staff with a small note placed in an envelope.

Do not take home with you a book or a DVD, either accidentally or because you feel like it. Do not borrow them either, as you could forget to give them back.

As soon as you have come home, and not a week later, write a pretty *lettre de château*, [48] even if you are a regular visitor.

If you have sojourned without incident, your hosts will no doubt consider you ahead of everyone else for a future extended stay.

---

[48] A *lettre de château* is a letter sent to thank one's hosts after sojourning at their home. [Translator's note]

THE ETIQUETTE OF FLOWER OFFERING

Giving flowers

Nothing is simpler and more complicated than offering flowers. Yet, everyone offers flowers: children, women and men.

Who offers flowers?

A child may offer flowers to all the women in his family: his mother, his grandmothers, godmother (and this is a wonderful habit that the child should not lose growing up), his primary school teacher. More rarely, a child may offer flowers to his secondary school teachers.

A woman offers flowers to either single or married women, but never to a man, no matter how old, unless he occupies a high public function. But of course, a daughter can offer flowers to her father, or another male relative. A woman employee may also give flowers to her female or male employer.

A man sends flowers to a young woman (preferably, he gives her the bouquet in person rather than having it delivered), to a married or single woman. A man never offers flowers to another man, with the exception of employees who may give flowers to their employers, and of sons who give flowers to their fathers.

When should we offer flowers?

As often as we wish and as often as we are able to. No one will ever complain of receiving flowers too often. And the most appreciated flowers are those which we send for no special reason, just to express our friendship or affection.

When must we offer flowers?

- When thanking our hosts for a dinner party
- On the occasion of a happy event: birth, baptism, communion, engagement, wedding, birthday, university graduation, a special award.
- When we are thanking people for their help.
- When we wish to apologise for a clumsy word or action.
- On the occasion of a funeral.

The art and etiquette of offering flowers

You can either send flowers or bring them yourself:
- Send flowers on the day of the ceremony to which you have been invited, always addressed them to the hostess not to the couple. Attach your visiting card with a few words of congratulations.
- If you have been invited to lunch or dinner, you can send flowers either the day before, on the morning of the chosen day, or the day afterwards, with your thanks.
- When a person passes away, a funeral wreath, cushion or bouquet is sent on the day of the ceremony

285

to the place where the deceased is collected for the final rites. On this occasion, it may be best to entrust your florist with the selection of flowers.

- When you are invited to family or close friends, you may arrive with a bunch of flowers in your arms (no need to attach a visiting card to the wrapping paper). My preference is for a round bouquet and flowers with short stems. If you have a garden, do not hesitate to bring your own roses, carnations or lupines, still fresh with morning dew. They are no doubt your pride and joy.

Choosing flowers

Choose flowers to suit the recipient of your gift and the circumstances.

To the young woman he is courting, a young man may offer:

- One or several white, yellow, or pink roses, never red.
- A round bouquet of pastel colours
- Violets
- A white gardenia
- A pot of daisies, which is more fun than the more traditional azalea (the pot has to be earthen, not plastic)
- A pretty box of mixed flowers.

A man may offer any flowers to a married woman, except red roses. But a man may send the unmarried woman he loves any flowers he likes and especially red roses or red peonies.

To a married woman he is in love with, a man sends a bouquet of pastel flowers. And if he cannot resist the temptation of sending a secret message, he places a single blushing rose in the centre of the arrangement.

For a ceremony (birth, baptism, communion, engagement, wedding), offer white and pastel flowers (lilac and lilies).

A woman sends another woman any flowers except red roses.

Don't forget that the women who have houses with terraces prefer potted flowers to cut flowers.

Flowers which we could never receive happily

Chrysanthemums;[49] and sad, long, rigid gladioli. And never offer an actress a carnation: she is bound to be superstitious.[50]

Flowers that will surely end a love affair

If you really want to break up once and for all, send your lover a big cactus plant in a plastic pot!

---

[49] When the French think of crysanthemums, they specifically think of the incurve chrysanthemums, which are placed on graves, and are therefore entirely associated with the dead. In Australia, and in the Southern Hemisphere more generally, the chrysanthemum is often given at Mother's Day since it blooms in May. In China, it is symbolic of autumn. [Translator's note]

[50] In the theatre, it was customary to deliver a bunch of white carnations to an actress to inform her of her imminent dismissal. The flowers were brought to her dressing room on her last performance. [Translator's note]

Week-end flowers

In winter, a bouquet of dried flowers, a bunch of lavender or a little tree of roses make a beautiful sight in a country house.

Flowers for friendship

When a foreign friend comes to your town, do not forget to send flowers to her hotel just before she arrives, and to attach a few words of welcome.

Saint-Valentine's day

On this day (14 February), a man in love should send the object of his passion the craziest bunch of flowers, to say again and again: "I love you".

Receiving flowers

When you invite people for lunch or dinner, have one or two vases ready before they arrive, as some of your guests will no doubt come with flowers in their hands. *Savoir-vivre* requires that you do not to leave the flowers waiting in the kitchen; you need to take the time to put them in water and to bring the vase to the salon where again, you thank the person who offered them to you.

If you received flowers in the morning, thank all the people who sent them to you as soon as you welcome them into your home. Their flowers should be placed in full view in the salon or at the entrance.

If you receive flowers the day after your party, write a word of thanks or use the telephone.

A few words of advice: If someone sends you roses just before you leave for your holidays, don't put them in water, leave them to dry by hanging them upside down in a dark place. Later, you can cut the stems just below the flower and detach the petals which you can then place into a cup or a basket. To create a perfume, add cinnamon sticks, cloves, peppermint and eucalyptus leaves. And now you can vaporise a few drops of your very own scent!

The art of the florist

Examining the display of a small florist shop, I find myself guessing at some personality traits.

The florist who tempts me to buy her or his flowers is (I am almost certain) eager, optimistic, alert, and happy with her or his profession – and no doubt, she is an extremely pleasant person. The florist who displays more shrubs than flowers may have a more cautious, more reserved temperament.

Still, we can safely assume that all florists are charming people with whom we have great pleasure associating.

The role of flowers

Ah! If men only knew how flowers can move a woman! And if they only knew how a single rose pleads in their favour...

When a woman detaches, in great haste, the visiting card attached to the bouquet she has just received, when she discovers that the flowers have come from her beloved, she is.... She is all of a sudden, so happy, so joyful, so young that she forgets everything, forgives everything, and she loves once again, just as she did on the first day.

THE LANGUAGE OF FLOWERS

The anemone says "Don't abandon me".
The cornflower "I will always be faithful".
The camellia "I will die at your feet".
The nasturtium pledges to love you madly.
The cyclamen brings you tenderness.
The geranium whispers "I miss you".
The gladioli shows cold indifference.
The hydrangea reproaches you your proud indifference.
The iris reproaches you your frivolity.
Jasmine covers you with caresses.
The daffodil declares you his first love.
Lilac tells you that your love is tyrannical and
the lily that your purity has seduced him.
The daisy says "I love you".
The lily of the valley says "I think of you".
The forget-me-not begs you not to forget him.
The carnation warns you, "Be careful, I may love you less".
The pansy says "My last thought will be of you."
The peony admits his shyness.
The sweet-pea says, "You are elegance personified".
The primrose suggests "Let us love one another for the
duration of Spring".
The white rose praises your purity.
The yellow rose accuses you of infidelity.
The pink rose honours the blossoming of your beauty.
The red rose swears, as Carmen in the Habenera factory,
"And if you love me, beware!"
The marigold worries about your jealousy.
The tulip promises you a sincere but bourgeois love.
The violet, subtle and delicate, blossoms under your charm.

VII

CUSTOMS

AND GOOD MANNERS

I have, you have, he has, she has, we all have good manners. Or at least this is what we believe. Although, when it comes to spelling out, defining, and putting our manners into practice, we find that I don't have, you don't have, and we don't have a very precise idea of what good manners are or what they should be.

So who has good manners?

To begin with, the person who grants their neighbours an absolute respect – respect for their territory, their private life, their tastes, their opinions, their behaviour, their friends.

A person who has good manners is never indiscreet, tiresome, annoying, or over-familiar.

A person with good manners knows the rhythm of things, the rules of harmony and is never out of tune. He respects the rules of ascendency, abides by the rules of courtesy, understands the multifaceted complexities inherent in the consideration and the respect that a man owes a woman. He is entirely knowledgeable of the rules of politeness (as for example, how to greet and how to introduce someone), and table manners hold no secret for him. Good manners cannot be dissociated from social behaviour: their complex

293

mechanism is triggered as soon as we are in the presence of others.

A feudal lord had to excel in the equestrian and martial arts. Today, cultured persons know what to say, write, and wear in all circumstances.

The Duchess of Sabran who knew better than anyone, the art of infusing aristocratic rigor with Mediterranean familiarity once spelled her own definition of feminine *savoir-vivre*: "A society woman is never hot, never cold, never hungry, and never tired. Whatever the ordeal she must face, she never complains and she never appears affected." And she concluded: "Dammit, let's have a little self-control!"

FORMAL INTRODUCTIONS

Introductions are founded on the rules of precedence governing gender, age and social status. A man is thus always introduced to a woman, "*Madame* Maury, may I introduce *Monsieur* Engoulevent?" And a young person is introduced to an older one; an employee to his employer; a sub-lieutenant to a general.

However, we introduce a woman, whatever her age, to a sovereign, a head of state, a royal prince, a minister, an ambassador, a prefect, or other eminent dignitaries (academicians, authors). We then say: "Your Royal Highness, or *Monseigneur*, or Monsieur le President, or *Monsieur l'Ambassadeur*, may I introduce *Madame* Charles Maury?"

In the same vein, a young woman is introduced to an elderly gentleman.

When introducing two women, the younger is introduced to the older, unless the younger woman has a significant social position as for example, she is an ambassador or the wife of an ambassador, or she is a well-known author or artist.

When introducing two couples to each other, introduce the younger to the older beginning with the women. To the older, you announce: "*Madame* Lavallière, do you know *Madame* Vernon?" The same goes for the men, and to the older you ask: "*Monsieur* Lavallière, I would like to introduce *Monsieur* Vernon."

When a man greets a person (woman or man) who is older than him, he should wait for the lady or the gentleman to extend their hand, it is not up to him to initiate the gesture. A woman who is seated should not stand when a man walks over to greet her, unless the gentleman is very elderly or a very well-known personality. A young woman, on the other hand, rises for everyone else except for a young man of her generation.

A young man, when introduced to an elder man or a superior, waits for the latter to extend his hand. And if the gentleman concerned does not, the younger man may simply give a discreet bow or incline his head slightly. It is also up to the person we have been introduced to, to initiate the conversation.

When women (and especially if they are older) are introduced, they should not respond with *"Enchantée, monsieur"* but simply say: *"Bonjour monsieur"* or *"Bonsoir monsieur"*.

A man abides by the same rules. To a young unmarried woman, he says: *"Bonjour mademoiselle"* or *"Mes respects, mademoiselle"*. The expression: *"Mes hommages, Madame"* is reserved for married women. The word *"Enchanté"* is to be banished from the rituals of introduction.

A man never introduces his wife as *"Madame* Bovary" but as *"mon épouse"*.

At a public meeting or a large party, men and women introduce themselves to each other, clearly enunciating their names and first names (one never supplies either title or rank). A woman says: *"Madame* Charles Bovary", a young unmarried woman: "Claire Mareuil".

Shaking hands

We are all in agreement that in France we shake hands too often, and thus abuse of the custom, however, none of us would risk moderating the practice. As a general rule, we should not extend our hand to a person we meet for the first time: A woman only needs to smile, and a man to give a slight bow.

Custom requires us to take off our gloves before greeting either a man or a woman. But it is accepted practice for a woman to keep her gloves on, especially when she is approached in the street. A man should then entreat her not to take off her gloves.

A handshake discloses a temperament or an emotion. A prolonged and insisting handshake translates an amorous intention or a deep affection. A crushing handshake is proof of vitality or authoritarianism, whilst a listless handshake betrays indifference, boredom, and melancholy. There are soft and warm hands which bring us together, and others sweaty and evasive that pull us apart. Note also that in English or French we use the metaphorical expression because we don't actually shake hands. In French, we do not say shaking but "squeezing hands" [*serrer la main*]. But while it is true that we neither shake nor squeeze people's hands, this is no reason to go extending a mean two fingers, unless you are suffering from acute arthritis.

When "shaking", meanwhile, smile discreetly and make eye contact, don't let your eyes wander left and right.

Professional introductions

When people attend a seminar today, they follow the American fashion and wear a badge indicating their names, first names, nationality, and the name of their companies. This largely means that introductions have become redundant.

On their first day at work, new members of staff do the rounds of the offices, either alone or accompanied by their superior who does the introductions. If you must take the initiative and you must introduce yourself, just give your name and first name followed by your position: "Antoinette Crespin, I am Monsieur Tournebois's new assistant." It is also good to smile and to add a few pleasant words.

Kissing a lady's hand: *le baisemain*

In the feudal period, liegemen kissed the hand of their overlords as a mark of respect and submission. Later the custom spread to the royal courts and the episcopate. Then, along with the romance epics and the rituals of courtesy, it became customary to kiss the hand of one's lady and ladies of high rank.

Today, the practice of the *baisemain* is limited to certain social milieus, as it never spread to the small bourgeoisie or the popular classes. Meanwhile, even men in possession of a nobiliary title commonly forget that one never kisses a lady's hand in the street or a public space – railway station, café, restaurant or a tennis court, and even less a beach. Also, a man should never lift the hand that a woman is extending to him, but bow towards it – even if he is suffering from backache. The man should only lightly touch the hand with his chin, never with his lips. During a reception held in Versailles, I had the opportunity to ascertain that among the hundreds of men present, those who knew how to kiss a woman's hand were very few indeed. The majority did not bow, but casually lifted the hand to their lips; some going as far as to deposit a wet kiss, others looking sideways while they were saluting me, and a few did not even bother to take their left hand out of their pockets!

If we had been in the Gallerie des Glaces... Madame de Pompadour would no doubt have thought that these characters dressed up as penguins had very strange manners

298

and Monsieur de Saint-Simon would have had great fun laughing at them.

At a reception, a man should not kiss the hands of all the women present, but only the hands of the hostess and older ladies. A man should not kiss a young woman's hand. As a general rule too, a man does not kiss a gloved hand, unless it is a dear friend's, but then the kiss is placed inside the wrist and it is a gesture of sweet intimacy.

Kissing a woman's hand is therefore contingent to place and circumstance, social rank, and tradition. A man may greet the wife of an employee with deep respect, but he will never kiss her hand. Neither should a man kiss the hand of a foreign woman who is unfamiliar with this custom. He should content himself with a respectful or friendly handshake.

Kissing

In France, not only do we shake hands, we also kiss. And have you noticed? The less we know someone, the more we seem intent on kissing them! Some kiss twice (a kiss on each cheek – which surely ought to be enough), others in their enthusiasm kiss three times as do the people of Brittany, and some even kiss four times, which adds up to four times too many.

Why do we generalise such unnecessary effusions? Why not reserve our kisses for those we truly love?

The formal *vous* [you] and the informal *tu* [you]

The use of the formal second person pronoun *vous* is a mark of distinction, a social attribution; it was once the rule in the aristocratic class to use the *vous* form between spouses and between parents and children. Only servants were addressed with the informal second person pronoun *tu*.

Today, in some families, parents still insist on their children addressing them with the formal *vous*. They are of the opinion that the *vouvoiement* [use of the *vous* form] maintains distance and therefore keeps disrespect and familiarity at bay.

Others use the *vouvoiement* to appear chic, and to pretend to a social rank so as to impose upon others. The *vouvoiement* in those circumstances becomes frankly ridiculous, especially in the regions of France where informality rules.

In Marseilles, a middle-class man who addressed his son with the *vous* form would become a laughing stock. To the contrary, in Lilles, the same behaviour may well augment his social prestige. At any rate, the *vouvoiement* has lost a lot of its social power, and has ceased to be the mark of a perfect education. In fact, switching brutally from the informal *tu* to the formal *vous* is an expression of contempt, even an insult.

On the other hand, for two lovers, nothing is more romantic than *vous*. The theatrical, the drama inherent in lovers' games finds a suitable expression in the excess of the *vous* form. With the *vous* form, lovers preserve a last veiling, an ultimate mystery, a secret garden where conquest and all its incomparable pleasures may last longer.

For its part, the *tutoiement* (the use of the informal *tu* form) is today an institution among the young who adopt it as soon as they are introduced. The not so young slip from *vous* to *tu* as soon as they are on more familiar terms. It is, as they say, "cooler".

In some professions as well, the *tutoiement* is virtually mandatory. Not to submit to its usage is perceived as antisocial.

However, should one of your friends be promoted to a high function position, you should never use the *tu* form in the presence of his colleagues, nor in the course of an official ceremony.

If a foreigner addresses you with *tu* at first meeting, do not look dismayed, and respond in kind, as it is evident that he or she does not understand this French custom.

To end with this topic, it would be wrong to think that the *vouvoiement* is automatically the mark of a good education and that the *tutoiement* leads to familiarity and carelessness. Everything depends on the circumstances, the tone, the nuance, the manner of speech.

After all, the prophets said Thou to God.

SAVOIR-VIVRE AT THE RESTAURANT

This evening, you are dining at the restaurant with some friends. No shopping, no cooking, it's playtime!

If you really want to have fun think of the following: make an effort to dress up. After you have left the university or work, go home and take a bath, relax, re-do your make-up and your hair and then, put on a nice set of clothes, freshly ironed. Don't forget to add a few pieces of jewellery, earrings and a touch of perfume.

And Monsieur, you must select a quiet restaurant, the best cuisines cannot accommodate noise. When you have to strain your ears to hear what the person sitting next to you at the table is saying, and raise your voice so that they can in turn hear you, there is only one thing to do: run away from the place, and well before coffee is served. There is no good meal without a conversation in which participants can engage in tranquillity. Invite your friends to a place where there is enough distance between the tables.

The restaurant is the only public space where men should enter before women. They enter and hold the door open. They help them take off their coats, which they entrust to the cloakroom and they also hold onto the ticket.

Women always sit first and on the bench seat. If you forwarded invitations, seat people according to your seating plan, as you would if they were guests at your house.

Even if the menu is sumptuous, do not spend an eternity selecting an entrée or a main dish. Don't hesitate too much or change your mind half- way through, and don't look disappointed when your plate arrives. If you have been invited, don't select the lobster as it is too expensive or the sardines which are too cheap.

302

A man always gives the orders to the waiter, and women always take over! The man also chooses the wine. A woman does not help herself to either wine or water but asks the man seated next to her to pour her drinks – indeed, he should have noticed her glass was empty and filled it without being prompted.

Unless you are too many and your companions ask you to start, wait until everyone is served before starting your meal. Certainly if you have ordered a cold entrée or a cold dish, *savoir-vivre* requires you to wait until the last person is served.

Don't strike a conversation with the Maître d'Hôtel, or call out for the waiter, or knock your glass with your knife for attention; wait until they are within hearing range and say "Maître d'Hôtel" or "Garçon".

When you are invited, refrain from indulging in disparaging remarks if the service is too slow or the sole is too dry, keep smiling. If you invited the others, simply strike the restaurant from your address-book without showing your discontent.

As for you, Monsieur, ask for "*l'addition*" and do not comment on its flaws or merits in front of your guests. While you pay the bill, the others continue to talk and look elsewhere.

While at the table, women should not take out their lipstick, their powder puff, or their comb, keep this for the powder room!

When you leave your seat, try not to turn your back to the people who are sitting at the table next to yours, rather move sideways and remain facing them .

Today, in some fashionable bistros, it has become customary to shake the hand of the owner of the restaurant if a man, and to kiss her cheek if a woman (and of course to

303

shake and kiss if they are a couple). Indeed, why not? Nonetheless, you should not shake the hand of the Maître d'Hôtel, when you take your leave.

Finally, have sufficient elegance not to ask for your restaurant bill to be printed with a tax invoice, come back to ask for this later, or ring the restaurant so that the management can post it to you.

A woman dining alone at the restaurant

There are in France about five million single women; among them, widows and divorcees who, although they are alone, do not suffer from loneliness. Yet these women often find it difficult to enter a restaurant on their own. Why?

Because restaurant owners relegate them to the back of the restaurant and serve them with a sour face.

Mesdames, do not pay attention, demand a good table, and all the more so, if you intend to order a real meal with a good wine. At any rate, a woman who is dining alone is unlikely to linger at a restaurant table.

On the other hand, a woman may be best advised not to enter a bar alone, but in the company of a man. You may sit on a stool, your companion stands next to you.

To reserve a table

It is advisable to phone ahead of time to make a table reservation, as it is always unpleasant to be told "We are full" when entering a restaurant.

The Duchess of Windsor while out in Paris in the company of a few friends, found herself in this very situation.

One of the men in her entourage suggested: 'Wallis, just tell them who you are, and they will no doubt find us a table."

She stared down at him "If I must tell them who I am, then I am nobody."

Inviting friends to the restaurant

When I invite friends to a fine restaurant, I always drop by in the morning to see the Maître d'Hôtel to ensure the success of the evening. I discuss with him the composition of the menu, a unique menu for all of us. I choose the wines and the composition of the floral central piece. I then have three or four individual menu cards written up, listing the names of the wines and their millesimes. This way, the pace and tranquillity of the service is assured. My guests feel as though they have been invited to my home, or at the very least, that they are the object of careful attention.

When a woman pays the bill

While it is entirely acceptable for a woman to pick up the tab for a man in the context of a professional dinner, and to charge the expense to her or their company, I find it perfectly inelegant that at a dinner between friends, a man should lose his prestige in order to save a few euros and under the pretence that he is bowing to ideals of sexual equality.

There are two types of men: those who grab the bill even if they have been invited, who would never allow a woman to reach for her cheque book, and the others, and there are too many of them, who can watch a credit card or bank notes pass in front of them without feeling a hint of either embarrassment or guilt.

Do you want to test the mettle of a so-called gentleman of means? Put him through the restaurant test.

Firstly, there is the choice of restaurant: will the gentleman invite you out to the small Chinese restaurant in his neighbourhood, a brasserie, or the latest restaurant written up in the Guide Michelin?

The next crucial moment: reading the menu and the wine list – if the gentleman begins with "We don't need an entrée, do we?", you can guess what will come next: you will be drinking water, or if you are lucky, tea. And of course, there will be no dessert for you!

Now, for the second scenario: he has taken you to a brasserie and you have chosen the sauerkraut. Your mouth is watering at the thought of drinking a nice cool glass of Riesling, and you hear him say: "*Garçon*! Two beers, on tap, please!"

And then, there is the true gentleman who believes that nothing is too beautiful for a woman, who insists on you tasting the oysters, the salmon, the duck and all the desserts. And who, from the very start of the evening, wishes for nothing else than to watch the golden gleam of a pink Champagne sparkle in your coupe and in your eyes.

SAVOIR-VIVRE AND DIETING

There is no such a thing as a happy slimming diet. If there were, I would have met it! But all the diets I have tried have left me with an indelible memory of a merciless and joyless struggle against self-screaming famine, desperate battles with food obsession, satanic visions of chocolate soufflés, spaggetti *alla rabiata*, bread and butter – all for a Pyrrhic victory, a fool's exchange, in which a few kilograms were bartered for gold with a feeling of deep injustice, an abyss of permanent frustration and ill-humour.

Have you noticed that there are even more books on slimming than there are cookbooks? Which goes to prove that while we have invented a thousand good recipes for cooking beef, we have yet to think of one single recipe that will make slimming enjoyable.

Those of us who, at the return of spring, attempt to return to our Sylphidic selves feel as though we are entering religious orders. For the diet has excluded us from the world of good living. Every morning, when the sun rises, you plunge into abstinence and punish yourself with a horsehair mitten[51] but no punishment can absolve you of the sin of gourmandise.[52]

---

[51] French women use a horsehair mitten to exfoliate the skin from the body. The author is being humorous, as the mitten recalls the hairshirts worn by religious penitents. [Translator's note]

[52] The words *gourmet* and *gourmand* have been adopted from French into English but they are often confused in popular English usage. In French, there are clear differences of degree and meaning. A gourmet is a connoisseur of food, a person who has a sophisticated and educated palate. A gourmand is a person who loves food and finds it difficult to resist taking a bite too many or a

Is there a *savoir-maigrir*? An art of slimming? In fact, there is, and here it is: feel free to diet so long as you do not subject others to your *régime*.

- Outside of your doctor, do not breathe a word to anyone about your weight issues and your diet, as this is most tedious and immodest topic of conversation.
- At dinner, pretend to eat just like everyone else, and leave what you are not allowed to eat in your plate. No one will notice.
- Watch your mood as closely as your weight: should your mood drop faster than your weight, reach out for a chocolate bar to balance the scales.

If you wish to eat well, not suffer from indigestion, acidity, a heavy stomach or bloating and you also want to lose weight, try the dissociated diet.

The rule is to never eat, in the same meal, proteins and lipids (meat, eggs, fish, cheese and milk) with carbohydrates (potatoes, rice, pasta, bread, legumes and pulses), their association being indigestible.

---

second helping. A gourmet is not necessarily a gourmand but a gourmand may well be a gourmet. The word *glouton* has the same meaning as the English glutton. In colloquial French, however, there is yet another degree below the glutton. The excessive glutton is called a *"goinfre"* which is a frankly insulting term, somewhat tainted with vulgarity perhaps by association. Its etymology may lie in *goufre* or *golfe* - meaning abyss and gulf respectively. The French love food and while they empathise with the gourmand, they are sincerely scandalised by the individual who lacks all discrimination regarding the quality of the food he is over-eating and who has no manners to boot. [Translator's note]

The way in which we usually plan a menu is often a cause of indigestion and weight gain by virtue of the fact that we eat at the same meal an entrée, meat and bread, vegetables and bread, cheese and bread, and a dessert made from some sort of grain and sugar. From the perspective of digestion, meat does not mix well with either bread or cheese, and cheese does not mix well with bread. Finally, fruit can seriously interfere with digestion.

Therefore, the best way to proceed is to compose a menu with three elements: a vegetable salad, cooked vegetables, and only one other food type, either protein or carbohydrate. Fruit are not eaten at mealtimes but on an empty stomach in the morning or in the afternoon between 4:00 and 5:00 pm. Fruit should be eaten as a meal in its own right, and never with either lipids (fat), protein or carbohydrate. Melons should likewise be eaten on their own, as a meal.[53]

A few rules for healthy eating

Firstly, eat only when you are hungry, and never eat to the point of saturation. And in the course of one meal, refrain from eating:
- Acidic fruit and starchy foods
- Protein food with and high carbohydrate foods
- Fats with protein
- Sugars with protein

---

[53] Note: The author makes a special point about melons because, more often than not, small rock melons are eaten as an entrée in France. Thus, the French do not regard the melon as other fruit, as for example, apples, pears or grapes which are eaten as dessert or snacks. [Translator's note]

Avoid drinking milk on its own, and don't mix it with other foods. And so as not to dilute gastric acids, do not drink half an hour before meals and during meals. Drink two hours after you have eaten.

Finally, never eat pastries or confectionary – the only exception to this golden rule is chocolate with 99% cocoa.

On Being Vegetarian

Some years ago, when I was in Marrakesh at a conference attended by bankers and their wives, I met a young Nepalese couple from Kathmandu. They were both very beautiful. The husband was dressed in Western style, and the wife wore a sari which further enhanced the youthful grace of her figure and the extraordinarily delicate beauty of her face. I was no doubt attracted to their charm because I found myself seated at their tables during the many wonderful banquets which punctuated the conference. I quickly noticed that their plates were almost always empty and that they ate practically nothing. I then learned that they were Buddhists and strict vegetarians. They ate neither meat, fish nor eggs. Neither could they eat the vegetables that had been cooked with either animal flesh or fat.

The Moroccan buffets were virtually collapsing under the weight of the dishes – Imperial couscous, royal sea bream, the mountains of tagines and cakes – but save a few radishes, there was not a single vegetable in sight, either raw or cooked. I suggested asking for an aubergine or tomato salad on their behalf but they protested that all was perfectly fine with them. Their discretion, their modesty, and their determination not to bring attention to themselves enchanted me.

Unfortunately, our own Western vegetarians are not all non-violent. Among them are a few, eager to voice in loud condemnation their disapproval of the carnivores they have a tendency to confuse with cannibals. Like all people committed to political or ideological struggle, their position slides towards extremism and they become antisocial, refusing to eat in non-vegetarian restaurants as though the latter were dens of vice or damnation. Yet, their own table may be so meagre, so sad with its bits of seaweed, its sesame seeds and its fifty-seven varieties of soy, that even their friends run away from it. Such people have become members of a sect, and fallen prey to all the usual failings.

GOING OUT

Savoir-vivre and the theatre

One should always arrive at the theatre dressed for the occasion. Making the effort to dress well is a politeness we owe to the actors. A beautiful audience adds to the pleasure of the performance. Next, one must arrive on time. Nobody appreciates the latecomers who unseat a whole row of spectators and distract the audience from the author's lines. And finally, silence is golden. A polite audience does not comment on the play or the acting, lean towards the ear of the person sitting next to them, crunch on lollies, or fiddle with paper wrappers. And of course, if you do not like the play, do not get up to show your disapproval. Wait until half-time to leave.

Savoir-vivre and the Opera

The breadth, the majesty, the splendour which Opera deploys across the stage and from the pit of the orchestra, creates in the audience a rush of emotion and intense aesthetic pleasure.

We express our gratitude and admiration for the singers, the divas, the conductor and the musicians not only with long-standing ovations but with the special care we take with our personal presentation. An evening at the Opera would cease to be a feast if we were not at one with the beauty of the spectacle – and this means: refinement from head to toe. Which, however, does not mean that we should be dressed for the stage – an elegant, pretty dress and a dark suit will do. In former times, a woman was expected not to

312

wear a dress exposing her back. Was it for fear that it may agitate the gentleman sitting behind her?

Whatever the state of your knowledge, or no matter how much you love Opera, do not sing along with the great arias. Opera lovers have come to hear a diva and nothing less than a silence worthy of a church service will do.

If you have come to the performance as two couples, the two women seat in the middle, each next to the other's husband.

If you are two women and a man, the man will sit in the middle. If you are two men and a woman, her knights sit on either side of her.

The cloakroom and purchasing the program are usually the men's responsibility.

SAVOIR VIVRE IN SOCIETY

Listen to how Europeans say no: No, Non, No, Ne, Na, Nein, Nèt, Nem. And how this chorus diversifies when it is time to say yes: Yes, Oui, Si, Ano, Ya, Hej, Igen, Ha, Tak! One is tempted to believe that saying no is a fundamental trait of human nature and that yes is a sort of luxury with shallow linguistic origins. Whatever the case, the fact is that where each of us is concerned, knowing how to say both yes and no requires a certain strength of character.

There are invitations, weddings, baptisms which you cannot refuse, and obligations which you must accept. And no matter how much boredom these constraints may inflict upon you, you must answer yes clearly and loudly. And under no circumstance, may you cancel at the last minute.

On the other hand, should you be invited to partake in a project that does not interest you, should you be asked for a favour you are not able to do, should you be asked to lend an object you have no desire to either lend or give, do have the courage to say no, frankly and honestly. Don't tread down the difficult path of lying, either by looking for a plausible excuse or entering into a maze of prevarication. And to be fair to the other party, do not wait until the last minute to say no.

We had among our friends a forty year old bachelor, Charles, who was also an incorrigible playboy of limited financial means. One day, to the great surprise of all who knew him, he announced his engagement to the heiress of a cement fortune. The jet set arrived in Cannes for the wedding: crowned and uncrowned heads landing from helicopters and stepping out of Rolls Royces in an uninterrupted dance with mobs of photographers and

314

journalists in tow, and television channels ready to broadcast the most glamorous society event of the year. After much pushing and shoving, the protocol was finally underway and the guests began filing into the town-hall.

Only the groom was still missing... Five minutes passed, then ten, and then twenty-five. The bride, in a magnificent lace dress, lost in metres of train and veils, was waiting on her father's arm. The audience became agitated, people began to move to and fro in greater and faster numbers. Some came in, others went out. Tongues were beginning to wag, each and everyone proposing a theory. At last the groom arrived. In all evidence, he had drowned his bachelor's life the evening before, in a barrel of Champagne.

Thoroughly irritated by this late arrival, *Monsieur le Maire*, cut the speech he had prepared for the occasion, cut to the chase, and went straight to the requirements of the Civil Code.

"Monsieur Charles T., do you take Mademoiselle Catherine B. to be your wedded wife?"

"No."

The mayor was speechless. In the surrounding icy silence, he repeated the question in a faltering voice. The guests then heard a resounding "Non. Non et non!"

When no is no, late may be better than never, but consideration for others requires us to think before we commit to a yes that we will have to retract.

Laughing and smiling

There are many ways to laugh and smile. One can laugh like a hyena, like a drain, laugh on the other side of one's face, laugh in the face of, or laugh at the expense of others; we can

315

burst out laughing or have fits of laughter; we can roar with laughter and cry with laughter...

Laughter when it is light and straightforward, communicates good mood, gaiety. But there are also crass and loud laughters that annoy, irritate and exasperate us beyond endurance. True, it is important to know how to laugh, neither too loudly, nor too long, neither inappropriately or at any opportunity. Laughter needs to be subtle and brief, and always express an authentic joy or pleasure, or a response to a comical situation.

A sincere smile works as a charm because it communicates your trust, your desire to please, your affection, your acceptance, your simplicity. A smile catches the eye, disarms criticism and reproach. A smile is a peace proposal. The smile is also said to be a symbol of femininity – the mystery of the Mona Lisa lies with her smile; the mystical passions Dante felt for Beatrice, and Petrarche for Laura, were born of smiles that were almost divine...

For common mortals, however, it is enough to know that our smiles are the privileged ally of our *savoir-vivre*. Let us be weary of tight smiles, forced or silly smiles, haughty smiles and provocative smiles, pitying smiles... For every personality has its own way of smiling, and a smile is a message which we can learn to decode.

Laughing at ourselves but not at others

Some situations or incidents are so comical that they provoke laughter, and at times they provoke uncontrollable and irresistible laughter – it makes you laugh, it makes everybody laugh! But to laugh at other's discomfiture, at their weaknesses, their mistakes, their inadequacies, or their lack of intelligence, is facile and nasty.

316

There is no glory in looking good by making someone else look bad; in belittling others to show off our wit, just because we cannot resist a clever joke; and the more ferociously so when the victim of our humour is incapable of repartee. Montesquieu said: "When you chase after wit, you catch foolishness" – add to this scorn, if not contempt.

To offend a sovereign, a party boss, a strong personality may be proof of courage because we are taking risks. But to wound or humiliate an inferior is the antithesis of all *savoir-vivre*, the fundamental rule of which is tolerance and above all respect for others, and for all others.

On the other hand, we are all free to laugh at ourselves and to exercise our brilliance and intelligence in self-deprecating humour! The corollary of "Know thyself" is very possibly "Laugh at thyself!"

Savoir-vivre and getting angry

Of all the emotions which agitate us, anger is undoubtedly the most powerful; it comes in a wave, submerges us, cutting us off from our means of control; the machine goes mad, breaks down and our good education is suddenly blown to smithereens like the lid of a volcano.

A significant setback, indignation born of an interlocutor's bad faith, and here we go, momentarily disconnected from our cerebral cortex, the seat of reason, to fall under the empire of our limbic system, the seat of emotions. Our face changes colour: we become white with rage or red with anger, our voice trembles; our facial muscles contract; our cardiac rhythm accelerates and we begin to feel painful palpitations; our breathing is also altered, we are short of breath, panting. Finally, our skin temperature rises, and we feel hot, suffocating, hence men loosen their ties, unbutton their shirt collar, open the windows... All these reactions are the result of a discharge of the stress hormones – adrenalin, acetylcholine, noradrenaline... Under the influence of these hormones, we are no longer ourselves. We will say anything, and more often than not, we will say horrible things; and then we might do anything, we feel murderous! And that feeling can be so powerful that it may actually kill us! For anger can kill.

Happily, this accident is rare, and the storm passes, the crisis is resolved and calm and reason return.

Can we avoid getting angry? Yes and no.

Yes, so long as we can engage in a double investigation, which is to say:

- We can analyse the reasons underlying our anger: what provoked it? Was it a sentiment of injustice, envy, jealousy, humiliation, the desire for revenge, or fear of failing?
- We can also analyse why certain personality traits or certain behaviours irritate us. Is it something to do with physical appearance, or an attitude, that remind us of someone we do not like?

Yes, you can avoid getting angry if you dissect each of your crises to get to their objective causes (the causes that are outside of yourself), and to their subjective causes (the causes lying in your own unconscious). You are then able to know what part of responsibility can be attributed to the person who made you angry, and which is your own part. It is on the part that belongs to you that you have the power to act.

Should we control our anger? Yes and no.

No because sometimes, anger is salutary. It allows one to vomit a poison that would "turn the blood".

318

And yes because we cannot allow ourselves to do or say things which, even if they are not unforgivable, are so hurtful to the other, that they are bound to damage our relationships. And this is especially so if the other is our spouse, a family member or a close friend.

And how should we act when someone becomes angry?

We should stay calm, wait patiently for the storm to blow over, and refrain from adding fuel to the fire. We should not attempt to say or do anything that risks being misinterpreted. Remember that a person who is angry is not thinking straight. Overall, we must try not to show disapproval, and rather give the angry person enough to understand that we are on their side, that we believe they are right...

How do we deal with anger after the fact?

Firstly, it is good to do something physical, something hard and quick. Go running, kick a football or hit a tennis ball, vacuum the house, do anything that allows you to expel the toxins produced by the adrenalin. If not, they will clog your arteries, and your heart will be at risk.

Once the physical damage has been repaired, however, you need to address the emotional damage. You have to apologise for your anger. The path of caution is to write a letter with a few lines explaining your remorse and your regrets. On the telephone, or in person, you take the risk of saying something that will ignite the conflict all over again. Make a conscious choice to renew with courtesy. And finally, look into yourself and try to uncover the motor of your passions. Self-analysis is a fascinating process. Finally, never make a decision in a fit of anger: anger is the worst of advisors.

We should not however confuse anger and indignation. The first is a blind passion and generally speaking an egotistical one, the second may arouse the best in ourselves, may push us to say no, and whatever the risks, to refuse or denounce a despicable or unjust situation. Indignation, not anger, drove Voltaire and Zola to accuse, to defy royal abuses of power and republican injustice.

Indignation belongs to *savoir-vivre*.

Giving up smoking

A man or a woman who, as soon as they wake up, reach for a cigarette and inhale smoke as a drowning man would a breath of air, who live with their heads in the clouds and their feet in ashes and cigarette butts, who burn holes in tablecloths, sheets or even bath towels, and whose hair, clothes, and home reek of tobacco, are difficult to live with. If you are not a smoker, your spouse's smoking habits become an act of aggression, their cigarettes like smoking guns aimed in your direction, killing you slowly. Smokers, it is true, often do not respect non-smokers. Is it because they are lacking in *savoir-vivre*? No: it is because they are subjected to a need they cannot control. I once saw a friend, at the cinema, put a cigarette in his mouth without lighting up, until finally unable to resist, he rushed to the bathroom to inhale the nicotine fix his body was screaming for.

Today, smoking in public places is prohibited. But how much private space should smokers be allowed to claim? Non-smokers sometimes act towards smokers as Crusaders pursuing the Infidel. Could they not show a little more understanding?

The conflict between smokers and non-smokers in a couple tends to explode when the smoker decides to quit smoking. Life then becomes a nightmare, and clean air unbreathable! It is as though you were treading on dynamite: the words barely come out of your mouth before your partner blows up!

The man (or woman) in need of nicotine develops nervous tics, becomes obsessive, desperately seeks a substitute, sucks on sweets, empties the refrigerator, gains weight, climbs the summits of irritability and poisons his entourage. A few weeks later, he returns to his tobacco. Before facing the ordeal of detoxification, smokers must be sure of their motivation so that they will put themselves through it only if they are certain of victory.

To leave the people around him uninjured, the smoker needs a place to retreat to, or he needs to isolate himself in the country, or even travel – in other words, the reformed smoker must change his habits. If not it may be wiser to spare the useless struggles for his sake and others' and to be content with taking shorter breaks, like refraining from smoking one weekend per month, so as to clean his lungs. Small gains are better than a Pyrrhic victory.

There are, of course, those who are able to quit smoking out of sheer will, craving yet without ever looking back, not unlike some men who leave the women they no longer love and yet can never forget them.

A few years ago, in Quiberon, as I was walking past the hot pool, a man with water up to his neck and a swimming cap on his head, called out to me. At first, I did not recognize him because his face had become very round. It was our most beloved Jean-Pierre Hutin, the producer of the famous television program: *30 million d'amis*. [54]

---

[54] Jean-Pierre Hutin (1931-1996) was a Syrian born French journalist. *30 million d'amis* [thirty million friends] was a television program dedicated to the welfare of animals, mostly

That same evening, he explained to me over a glass of wine, that he had given up smoking, gone from four packets a day to nothing, virtually overnight. And he had experienced the descent into the last circle of Hell.

"Why did you do it?" I asked.

"Because of Mabrouk Junior" he answered matter of factly. "My smoking was affecting his breathing."

And he stroked the head of the dog sitting next to him. Mabrouk Junior was his German shepherd dog, the true star of the television program. The bond between this man and his dog was extraordinary. Jean-Pierre never left his Mabrouk, preferring to have lunch in a bistro with Junior than to eat in a three star restaurant where his dog was not allowed entry. To stop smoking for the well-being of an animal, now that is a story worth telling.

The art of not talking too much about ourselves

Like all of us, I have, in my circle of friends, a woman whom I will call Hélène, who is, and unfortunately I am not exaggerating, a caricature of egocentrism. In appearance, she is entirely fulfilled. She is beautiful, rich, and social. However, no one would like to trade places with her. Why not? Because her egocentrism is such that it has made not only her three husbands, but all the other men in her life as well as her friends, run away from her.

And unfortunately, with every new heartbreak, her egotism leaves the harbour, full sails into the wind. When she is on the phone, she even forgets the elementary greeting: Hello, how are you? For years, her well-being and her states

---

companion animals. Jean-Pierre Hutin was also the founder of the animal welfare society of the same name. [Translator's note]

of mind have been her only topics of conversation; and in every conversation, there is only space for her, and her only.

To speak only of oneself is the height of rudeness. Over time, this flaw in Hélène's character has negated all of her qualities and I know that one day, I too will jump ship just as others have done.

Savoir-vivre means that in our friendships, we take interest in our friends before we talk about ourselves.

The art of not writing

To write about one's life when the latter is not extraordinary, to narrate an experience when it is not so different from one's neighbour's, to revisit a journey which is anything but epic, to evoke encounters of no consequences, to publish one's childhood poems, the fruit of one's reflexions or one's memoirs, somehow has become an obligation, a must do. It is the *maladie* of the century. "What? You don't write? Why not? You have not published anything?" we are told in the most reproachful tone.

Is writing a book mandatory? Rainer Maria Rilke answered this question in his *Letter to a Young Poet*. "Ask yourself in the most silent hour of the night: Must I write? And then ask yourself again: Would you die if you were forbidden to write?... To my mind, it is enough to feel that we could live without writing for us to refrain from writing."

Well, so much is clear: if we transgress this injunction, it is simply to satisfy our vanity. Indeed, it is easy enough to ascertain the uselessness of our writings – you only need to step into the first bookshop. In September, there is a deluge of novels, both epic and short; in April, there is the rush of best-sellers, and in both April and September, there is a tidal wave of guides, illustrated books, biographies and essays!

323

And of course, every book published implies the felling of a tree. Having read these lines, you are perfectly in your right to ask whether I am not seeing the straw in my neighbour's eye. *Vanitas vanitatis...* all is but vanity...

But there are worse people than the people who write books: There are those who talk about the books they have written, who pitilessly turn every social encounter and reduce all topics of conversation to that unique spot where their *oeuvre* must shine. Without blushing, without even a hint of shame, they add to this the flatteries bestowed upon the "most beautiful," the "most prophetic" book of the year! And then, there are even worse people than those who *talk* about their books, there are those who *read* their books to you! Here you are, innocently going to dinner at their house, and before you have removed your coat, they are already serving you the "most sublime pages". And caught in this mortal trap, you now curse all of literature.

To write or not to write...

Ageing

Women who were not, in their youth, splendid creatures have an advantage over those who were so. They age well, because they have not lost in mid-life, a gift they never possessed: beauty. Free from the stresses of having to appear attractive or of the frustration of not being able to do so, they acquire a serenity, a contentment, an even temperament, envied by former beauties.

Beautiful women who are able to acquire wrinkles, who can accept that they are no longer the focus of men's attention without feelings of bitterness or regret are very few. For most, the compliments, the eyes turned towards another feel like so many poisoned arrows.

324

And so, in order to recover this precious possession which every day drifts further away, they begin a frantic and pathetic race against time and sagging muscles, in the desperate hope of winding back their biological clock. In this impossible up-hill battle, even the most adventurous may plunge into deep dark depression. Some women prefer to lose their lives than to lose their beauty – and not only movie stars die of ageing.

Edmond and I once knew a woman who had a facelift every time her lover failed to divorce his wife. She did not understand that his wife's wrinkles held more comfort and security than her false youth.

Savoir vivre, knowing how to live, is also knowing how to age. Ageing well requires that we construct a value system that is not founded solely on appearance. Intelligence, culture, moral qualities, courage and determination (the Roman *virtus*) grant a woman a more beautiful beauty than beauty itself. This is what we call charm.

Now, I am not advocating that we renounce physical beauty, nor am I suggesting a return to grey hair and rough skin. To the contrary, I admire women who take care of themselves with an exemplary discipline to the end of their lives.

During a trip to Brussels, on the way to the airport, I began a conversation with the taxi driver, and this charming man talked to me about his customers. He much preferred to give lifts to women than to men because he found them more open, friendlier and more surprising. Then, he told me this story. The evening before, a lady had called on the phone. He arrived at her front door and waited for her to get into the car. As she was not moving, he realised that she was blind, and he got out of the car to help her.

"Where would you like to go, Madame?"

"You are not my usual driver? 28 rue de l'Amigo."

325

When they stopped in front of a beauty salon, his first thought was that he had driven her to the wrong place.

"Indeed, we are at the right place, Monsieur. I come here once a month, to take care of my face. At my age, this is a courtesy I owe to others as much as to myself."

And the taxi driver to conclude: "Now, that is a real woman! You know, she is also eighty years old!"

The real danger lies in taking care only of one's body, to live only for it because one day, inexorably, our bodies will abandon us. We need to moor ourselves to solid foundations that prevent us from drifting away, and this as soon as possible. We build such vital foundations with children and grandchildren, our friends, our interests, service to others, and our hobbies: going to the cinema or the theatre, travelling, playing bridge, gardening, reading...

"We must cultivate our garden" said Candide. Let's cultivate the gardens of our passions, so that they may grow and blossom, and allow us to grow deep roots into a happy present.

Knowing how and when to lie

'In Paris, an honest man lies ten times a day, an honest woman twenty times, and a gentleman a hundred times. It is impossible to count how many times a day a high society lady lies." So wrote the clever gentleman, Hippolyte Taine, at the end of the nineteenth century.[55]

---

[55] Hippolite Adolphe Taine (1828-1893) was a French critic and historian, proponent of the French school of naturalism, sociological and historicist criticism which stresses the importance of context in the interpretation of knowledge. [Translator's note]

We simply could not live in society, nor in our marriages, without lying – this we all know. But actually, why do we lie? Because we do not want to hurt others or be seen in the wrong light. In fact, we lie not to displease others. Can you imagine yourself telling a friend that the dress she is so proud of wearing makes her look ridiculous! We also lie to protect ourselves, to protect others and to avoid unnecessary confrontations. Imagine that your husband is jealous of your distant cousin Paul and that he becomes unpleasant in his presence. You decide to see Paul on your own, and to say nothing about it to your husband. This is lying by omission. And it is the kindest and most generous of lies. After all, he suffers in Paul's presence as from an allergy, and you love him too much to be the cause of an attack.

We lie out of vanity – perhaps the most common of all lies. We take credit for non-existent successes, we report a compliment we did not receive, we exaggerate our possessions, the price of our cars or our dress, all this for a little more appreciation!

The politician lies to seduce and in this domain, inflation can be such that politicians too easily forget that the electorate is intelligent and that you cannot fool intelligence indefinitely.

We lie out of laziness, to avoid telling too long or too complicated a story. We take the path of least resistance, so that we sometimes lie also because a lie appears more believable than the truth. Yes, sometimes we lie just to be credible! For we can encounter such incredible coincidences that we find ourselves in the frustrating position of not being able to tell the *real* story.

And we lie because of the excesses of our imagination, for the pleasure or embroidering, or embellishing, or adorning the truth with more vibrant colours. This is the aesthetic lie, a magnificent lie that charms and enchants us

327

partly because this lie doesn't fool anyone, neither the teller nor the listener; everyone floats between fiction and reality, we are in a novel.

I have noticed (and no doubt, you have too) that we also tend to lie most to those we love. Thus, I wish you a happy life, with many, many little white lies between you.

Knowing when to tell the truth

To tell the truth is both very easy and very difficult because some truths would be easy enough to tell if they were not unbearable to hear. Should I speak out, or should I not? Do I unload a truth that is too heavy to bear on the other, or do I bear it alone?

It is courageous and honourable to cover the truth for the sole end of protecting someone from hurt. On the other hand, not to confess one's own wrong doing, failings, failures, weaknesses, sins or crimes so as to preserve one's own comfort, or the image we wish to give to others, without a thought for the duty we owe others around us is worse than cowardly, it is utterly inelegant.

To conclude, let me recount this exchange with my husband: "If you don't want to know the truth, don't ask me questions, and I won't lie to you." And he answered, "Fine, but on the condition that you don't ask questions either".

Clumsy people and savoir-vivre

Imagine that you have been invited to afternoon tea at a friend's. As you put your cup back on the table, it slips from your hands and breaks – Was it myopia? Were you feeling a little distracted? Or are you perhaps a little clumsy? Or, another scenario: You are spending the weekend at a colleague's and, inadvertently, you break a trinket, a lamp or a vase. Or maybe you break a window kicking a football in the garden.

You dissolve into a flood of apologies, which indeed is the least you can do. But you cannot be so casual as to stop there. You cannot put this incident to rest until you have made reparations and replaced whatever it was that you broke. Sometimes this is simple enough, and at other times, it is almost impossible. The cup could be an antique Sèvres porcelain, the vase a Gallé or Lallique. Still, *savoir-vivre* demands that you take responsibility.

You must insist that your hostess provide you with the address of an antiquarian who will be able to find a replacement for the broken object, or to find another of equivalent value. And you must not wait for time to go by. The faster you pay off this debt and the more appreciated you will be.

Some advice: when visiting friends, if you are short-sighted, wear your glasses; your friends would rather be deprived of the pleasure of looking into your beautiful eyes than be deprived of their dearest curios, which are after all the apples of their own eyes.

I was invited to Rome by the French ambassador in his Palazzo Farnese, the most beautiful embassy in the world,[56] and I found myself sitting next to a young architect who had just been awarded the Rome Prize. When dessert arrived, we were engaged in a lively exchange about modern art. We were served profiteroles. And I noticed that the

---

[56] The Palazzo Fernese is among the best examples of High Renaissance architecture in Rome. It has been an inspiration for other buildings around the world, including the Chief Secretary's Building in Sydney. [Translator's note]

329

young man had not removed the white organdie napkin from his plate, after removing the finger bowl. Amused, I waited for what was bound to come next. The brilliant architect poured three large spoonfuls of hot chocolate over his three profiteroles. From the corner of my eye, I then saw him battling with his fork and knife; and looking anxiously at the plate of the woman sitting next to him, then at mine and the other guests'. Everyone was pleasantly eating their desserts. Not understanding, he decided to cut this Gordian knot by hitting the profiterole with his fork. The profiteroles resisted the shock, but his plate broke and sent the napkin, the chocolate and the choux pastries flying into my cleavage.

There followed a brief, but profound silence as the whole table stared at us. Then, to avoid bursting out laughing, everyone followed the ambassador's example and acted as though they had seen nothing. The moment passed as a dissolving scene in a movie.

Meanwhile, the beautiful prize winner peered through his beautiful green eyes. I comforted him the best I could: "It's nothing. You just forgot to remove this from your plate." And I showed him the guilty napkin which I held between my thumb and index finger.

"But where does it come from? I didn't see it!"

"Maybe you should wear your glasses?"

He had sinned on account of a coquettish instinct. As for me, I had been punished for playing a prank on him.

Savoir vivre with a *faux-pas*

If you are in the habit of talking too much, of speaking off the cuff without considering the weight of your own words, one day, your lack of caution will catch up with you. There are *faux-pas* which are irretrievable, irreparable, and to use

330

Paul Claudel's beautiful phrase, *faux-pas* that are met "with a deafening silence". In such situations, nothing can be done and nothing can be said.

I will never forget my embarrassment when one day, I asked a man with whom, it is true, I was not closely acquainted: "How is your wife? Is she here tonight?"

"No… I am sorry, Madame, she is still dead…."

And I remembered a little later that I had even sent him my condolences a few weeks before. I mumbled a few words of apology: "I am sorry… I cannot believe that she is no longer with us".

Hypocrisy

Claws drawn behind a smile, backbiting dissimulating as flattery are common currency in all social milieus and at all ages. Behind the mask of the friend lurks an enemy whose game is so subtle that a great deal of time may pass before the mask is dropped.

What can we say to hypocrites, save that theirs are short-term goals destined to eventual failure. Hypocrites practice a fragile *savoir-vivre*, an illusion with a limited shelf-life.

Flattery

Flatterers are more intelligent and more well-meaning than hypocrites by virtue of the fact that their weapons are limited to praise and compliments. And they have an excuse – the unfathomable weakness, the unfathomable credulity, vanity and pride of those who do not notice the exaggeration in the toadying they are the object of. If we possess neither modesty nor wisdom enough to beware of unwarranted praise, we are not in a position to bear a grudge against those who heap their flatteries upon us. Let's learn therefore to keep the right measure of things.

Familiarity

It is usual for American radio and television presenters to address the person they are interviewing by their first names even when they are meeting them for the first time. Even in the presence of the First Lady of the United States, they behave in the same familiar manner. Across the Atlantic, the practice is customary: It is found in the street. Taxi drivers, waiters, salespersons will cover you with sweet words: "Honey, darling, sweetheart..."

In France, journalists are not quite so off-handed, yet they will say Catherine Deneuve rather than Madame Catherine Deneuve, and even Jacques Chirac, rather than Monsieur le président de la République. Why this loss of respect for good manners? Why not wait until we actually know people before addressing them by their first names? Why not familiarise ourselves before we give ourselves license to use or abuse of familiarity?

Borrowing

There are very few if any valid reasons to ever borrow anything. To ask a friend to lend you either an evening dress, her country house or a beautiful car for your daughter's wedding procession may provide an easy solution to a problem but it goes against *savoir-vivre*. You ask someone's help because it is convenient for you and saves you an expense. In other words, you place your comfort and convenience ahead of others.

Between relatives, borrowing is permissible. It is enough for everything to go well, not to make a habit of it, to be aware of certain facts, and to respect the sacrosanct law of reciprocal exchange. When you borrow something, you need to return something. Therefore, if you borrow a dress, you will need not only to return it but to send it to the drycleaners before-hand (even if you have not stained it, for there always remains a trace of perspiration or sweat). When you return the borrowed dress to the person who lent it to you, bring a bunch of flowers or a box of chocolates along with a thank you card.

If you are house-sitting or spending time at a friend's country house in their absence, ensure that you take the greatest of cares to follow the instructions you have been given. If you break an object or a piece of furniture by inadvertence, replace it or have it repaired. As for the telephone, either use a phone card or your mobile. Before leaving, inspect the rooms, not forgetting the corners, to ensure that everything is in perfect order – even if this was not the case when you arrived. In the kitchen, remove all the small leftovers (butter, jam, salads, fruit), and leave only un-opened products. Replace the tea, coffee and all that you have consumed. Launder the bedding and other linen, including the tea towels, which you used during your stay. Finally, before you close the door for the last time, check that all the taps are closed, the lights are out, and the radio and television are turned off. Except for the lovely present and accompanying thank you note you have left for your hosts, there should be no trace of your passage.

If you have borrowed a car, return it clean, with a full tank of petrol, and a small card and a little gift.

Borrowing money

We should never borrow money from anybody, except the bank and our parents. Asking for money, even if it is a minor sum, from a friend or a close relative, risks straining your relationship. But why should borrowing money be either riskier or more reprehensible than borrowing an object? For a thousand reasons, which are not always evident. To begin, borrowing money implies that you are in need, and this is a thing as difficult to confess as to hear. Then, borrowing money is to dispossess others of a good which you spend in their stead, and which they accept to lose for the time being with no real guarantee of recovery in the future. Therefore, before borrowing something which no one likes to lend, it is essential to ensure that there is no other way and to take necessary precautions. If for example, you borrow a thousand euros, on the day the loan is made to you, hand over a cheque written up with the same value to your lender, and agree on a date at which he or she will be able to cash it. If you need to repay the money in instalments, prepare three cheques, the first and the second to the sum of three hundred and fifty euros, the last for three hundred. In this manner, there will be no need to discuss your debt again before you repay it. Should the loan you have requested be a large one and the settlement date at a significant distance in the future, you should suggest adding an interest payment.

If you are the one lending, and you know that the person asking for the loan will have great difficulty repaying you, suggest making them a gift of half or a third of the sum requested instead of lending money which they are unlikely to repay. You will then be in a position to refuse further loans. Did you know this repartee attributed to Henry de

Montherlant: "He began to nurture the greatest admiration for me the day I refused to lend him money."

To know not to borrow, either a dress, a country-house, a husband (you risk never giving him back), or money is one of the golden rules of *savoir-vivre*. And coming a close second: Ask for favours, services or a recommendation as rarely as possible.

SAVOIR-VIVRE AND THE GOOD CITIZEN

Voting

Voting is a civic duty from which many shrink on the grounds that they are not interested in politics, that all political parties are as bad as one another, that electoral promises are all lies... thus forgetting that their vote does have power. Because politicians *will* change tack when they become conscious and concerned that they have lost their credibility. Our ballot can compel them to do so.

Whether we like it or not, we are all concerned with politics.

I know a woman who calls herself a feminist who is proud of the fact that she has never been enrolled to vote, that she has never voted in her entire life, and that her son and daughter have followed in her footsteps. When you ask her for reasons and explanations, she throws herself into an advocacy of individual rights, and challenges the myth of universal suffrage. Voting, she says, gives us the illusion of liberty, the illusion of having power. She finds no inspiration in the historical struggles women waged to win the right to vote: "Politics have remained a man's world."

Such words may be spoken by certain intellectuals and persons in alternative social milieus but good citizens fulfil their duties to vote, even if all they do is hand in a blank vote.

Did you know that in the past, long before women had the right to vote, men used to remove their hats before casting their ballots?

Savoir-vivre and the environment

Seas turned into rubbish dumps, beaches polluted with oil, poisoned seaweed, acid rivers, wild fires, unbreathable cities, mad cows, sheep culled for foot and mouth disease – is this the world we wish to leave for our children? The younger generations more sensitive to conservation turned my generation into environmentalists. We are all Green when the ozone layer is torn asunder.

We know that we risk in the future to become short of water, the most precious resource of our planet. Our first duty is therefore to save it. We must teach our children to turn off the tap when they brush their teeth rather than allowing the water to continue flowing, to turn off the light when they leave a room, to dispose of waste paper and empty bottles into the appropriate recycling bins.

People in Scandinavian countries and Switzerland, where I live, show much greater civic responsibility in this respect that we do in France. Severe penalties punish those who do not respect environmental rules.

It would be a good thing to conduct classes in civic education in the field rather than in the classroom.[57] The sight of birds trapped in an oil slick, of seaweeds suffocating marine life, and first hand experience of a devastated forest

---

[57] In France, civic education is a compulsory subject of the national curriculum, taught from primary school and through to the end of secondary school. In lower secondary school, it is delivered by history-geography teachers – history and geography being compulsory subjects from primary to the end of secondary school. In the *lycées* (upper secondary schools), civic instruction is delivered as a weekly thirty minute discussion class, by teachers from a broader range of subjects. Civic education includes a knowledge of law, political institutions, social issues, ethics and so forth. [Translator's note]

337

would teach children more effectively than our speeches, make them aware of the dangers threatening our planet, and of the necessity to take action.

And of course, adults must provide children with good models of behaviour.

And then, there is noise pollution! In some municipalities, mayors have installed loudspeakers in pedestrian malls, which broadcast deafening music from morning to night, thus affecting the health of small children and ours. Our streets are filled with noise pollution: from the backfiring of car mufflers, to noisy engines, screeching police sirens and screeching car brakes, jack-hammering, and then passing cars pouring out flows of loud music. We live in a field of stridency – the culture of the decibel. And yet, it is high time to address the problem, for the toxic effects of noise pollution have long been documented and denounced. Please, *Mesdames* and *Messieurs* Mayors, we need to recover the art of silence.

And I would like to add a last request: In summer, the number of men who walk down the streets in shorts and sandals and inflict upon us the sight of their hairy calves is increasing. But recently, they have also insisted on imposing upon us the sight of their bare chests and their pot-bellied paunches… Could we not impose a mandatory minimum dress in town: a shirt or tee-shirt? Tourists ought not to escape the rule either. A shirtless middle-aged man wearing a crumpled pair of shorts and dusty sandals in the Gallerie des Glaces, the Louvre or Vézelay abbey is enough to shock even the most open-minded citizen.

338

VIII

SAVOIR-VIVRE

AND

LOVE AFFAIRS

THE UNFAITHFUL HUSBAND

An infidelity committed one single evening is an adventure. Two evenings, and it is already an affair.

Messieurs, a love affair is an accident or an incident – sometimes happy and sometimes not – that can happen to any one of you. And it can happen even when you are in love with your wife.

No doubt, you may not be quite as in love as you were in the first days of your marriage, but a thousand bonds unite you to the woman you have shared your life with for many years. And yet, you have felt the (nearly) irresistible need to give yourself over to the pleasures of an extra-marital affair. Why?

You reply that there is no truer thrill than seduction, and especially when the woman you desire is (or seems) inaccessible – a top model, a princess, a movie star, a virtuous woman… You say that the man who has the capacity to seduce a woman finds it near impossible to resist that temptation. Desire, and the emotions that go with it, are tantamount to recovering the ardour of youth. Nothing flatters our virility and our pride like seeing a beautiful woman who is content in her marriage capitulate to our flirting.

To have a mistress is to escape the routine that settles in a couple after several years of marriage. But a love affair is also a means of fulfilling the unfulfilled needs, which all of us, men and women experience.

The husbands I interviewed on the matter provided me with more specific reasons. Some cheated on their wives because they were too possessive, others because they were absent too often; some even because their wives were always depressed. But the men were in agreement on one point: A man cheats on a wife who has stopped telling him that he is beautiful, and stopped telling him that she loves him – a wife who no longer lays admiring, desiring eyes upon him, but also a wife who may be ageing, gaining weight, neglecting her appearance and herself. And then, they invoked a taste for adventure. Since they cannot play Tintin in Tibet, they face other perils, running the gauntlet where their lies and petty betrayals have thrown them.

Caution and wisdom

- Messieurs, take a mistress who has the same constraints as yourself: a spouse, children and a job. In this way, neither of you will wish to endanger their respective marriage. Or at least, this is what you will tell one another. You are on equal footing, and subject to the same obligations, both of you must act with caution and not make anyone suffer. You both wish for nothing more than a simple adventure (as though it were possible!) which will last as long as your mutual desire, or for the duration of your choosing.
- If, however, your mistress is not married, then announce from the start, unambiguously and without beating about the bush that you will never divorce your wife, that you love your wife and that you will never risk the well-being of your family: in other words, no secret weekends, no crazy nights spent away from the conjugal bed. Put your cards on the table: your liberty is limited to the traditional "five to seven" which today may well have become "1:00 to 3:00 pm", and your playing field has boundaries. The neighbourhood where you live, the places where you

go as a couple, where your spouse works, where her mother and her best friend live are out of bounds. In a small town, in truth, this does not leave a lot of space for your escapades and secret meetings.

- Finally, learn to lie, well and quickly, and with the greatest innocence. And so that you are never caught inadvertently, have a few scripts at the ready, and whatever happens, even if you are caught in the act, deny everything.

The signs that betray your infidelity

The more involved in your affair and the more clues you are likely to leave around you, perhaps quite unconsciously – all of which are bound to alert your wife.

- You are more preoccupied with your appearance than when you were young. You are aware like never before of the crease of your trousers, the colour of your shirt. You make sure that your collar has been pressed, and now you are choosy about your ties (and you have just bought several new ones – indeed, a dangerous move!). In the morning, standing before the mirror, you look at yourself front on, then side on, you puff out your chest, you suck in your stomach, you brush your hair ten times, trying to cover a small area of receding hair. In the evening, hiding in the bathroom, you try for the very first time a face cream, and then you cover it up with lashings of aftershave. Worst of all, you are now colouring your greying hair!
- Next, you start to diet. You only liked *cassoulets* and goose *confits*, cream sauces or spicy foods, and now

you are eating grilled fish, steamed vegetables and you have swapped your Bordeaux for mineral water.

- You hated exercise and you are working out, lifting heavier weights by the day.
- Great thundering typhoons! You have bought a motorbike, a helmet and a leather jacket. You ride everywhere on your rocket while your car gathers dust in the garage. You can't stop talking about the thrill of riding unhindered through traffic. Think about it: if this is not enough to warn your wife, it is because she has decided not to see the blindingly obvious.
- You come home later and later in the evening, blaming your tardiness on meetings that begin at 6:00 pm, one after the other. And this morning, you are leaving especially early – "Do you have another meeting, Dear?"
- You hate Sundays. Now, that's new! Why such brutal change of taste? But Sundays have become empty never-ending boring days. You are walking to and fro, checking your mobile phone ten times, twenty times, switching it on and switching it off, and finally you find an excuse to go out alone. You are running like a thief caught red-handed.

… Well, it is not easy to lead a double life.

Breaking up a love affair

One day, you discover as Swann did, that your mistress is not your type. Like Swann, you are now wondering what you ever saw in her. You have only one desire: to break up. But what do you do if she does not want to let go? Discourage her? Yes, but be gentle. You simply cannot break up an affair overnight. You need to explain, with remorse, that both of you have strayed into a dead-end street. If you are truly desperate for a way out, tell her that your wife and children have discovered your affair and that you have promised them that you will break it up.

When two couples are friends

Let's imagine that you rented a villa in Spain together with a couple with whom you are friends. The constant intimacy from dawn to dusk, the semi-nudity in the heat of summer, a sudden desire to... Before you know it, and what a disaster! You find yourself the lover of your wife's best friend. By mutual consent, you just fell into each other's arms.

Why, of all the possible scenarios, did you opt for the situation with the greatest potential for destruction? Does the thrill of danger sharpen your sense of pleasure? To stand on the edge of a precipice may tempt those whose lives are too quiet. Or does the feeling of power, the power to make your partner suffer, fill you with satisfaction? Don't deny it, the capacity for revenge lies in all of us, and we can at times hate those we love most. The thought of seeing your wife, so frivolous, so self-assured, break into pieces allows you to play God. Your power brings you a certain felicity.

Cheating on a spouse means having the upper hand, even when this superiority leads to tragedy.

If you are a man who must give into some of your passions, do not give into all of them, be a responsible man.

While you remain under the same roof, in Spain, you must control your passions if you do not want scandal to explode. Nothing in your behaviour should give your wife and your mistress' husband reasons to be suspicious. Should they discover your crime, committed virtually in their presence, there would be no end to their resentment and anger.

As soon as you have returned home, if your affair continues, avoid meeting as a foursome, and invent a pretext to break off the four-way friendship. If your children are friends, find reasons for them to see each other less often, and do not host the children of your mistress in your own home.

Avoid writing to her, in particular avoid writing compromising letters, or to leave any proof of your infidelity: photos, gifts (don't keep the ties or *pochettes* women in love are so fond of offering, leave them in the bottom of the last drawer in your desk).

Now, let's imagine what is likely to happen. Eventually, your spouse discovers that you are cheating on her, and with her best friend. Tragedy, screams, anger, insults follow.

In her indignation, your wife makes a grave error. She tells her friend's husband (who would never have guessed it if it were not for her) of the betrayal to which they have both fallen victims. You are now accountable to two persons who hate you. Imagine now, that this other husband, in a fit of anger and humiliation decides to divorce his wife.

On the other hand, imagine that your own wife, who is a sharper customer, avoids adding oil to this infernal fire and contents herself with overwhelming you with reproaches. "And under the same roof" she repeats through her tears, "How could you have done this to me?"

"Oh, darling, forgive me… I couldn't help myself, I was always left alone with her in the house."

Thanks to your declarations, the sincerity of your remorse, the despair which the word divorce arouses in you, she finally puts your adventure into perspective and slowly, tragedy abates. Your marriage has been somehow strengthened by this ordeal, but in your wife's heart, you are no longer the knight in shining armour.

When your mistress is older than you

When you were a young man, charming a woman ten or fifteen years older than you seemed a far more difficult and exciting enterprise than going around with a girl your own age. Facing this challenge sharpened all your faculties. Do you remember when you were a student, shy, inexperienced, gnawed by the fear of failing? You had barely left your parents' home and your imagination was filled with the women you dreamt of conquering. Nurses in particular had a special appeal: Was this on account of all the movies you had seen? But it was not only a matter of charming the women: in your own casual words, it was to make it to the next step. And at the thought of wavering, you suddenly panicked.

The mistresses of your youth taught you everything. They revealed to you certain feminine mysteries and gave you confidence. Being older than you, they transmitted to you aspects of their precious knowledge and thus sent you on the path to glory. To them, you owe your sentimental education. And at the memory of the prestige, and the sense of fulfilment their conquest lavished upon you, you have kept for these tender, forgiving mistresses and these whirlwind love affairs a feeling of boundless gratitude. That was the Golden Age!

You are now a married man, sure of yourself, enterprising, and you find yourself the lover of an older unmarried woman. How much older than you? You do not know, and of course, you should not attempt to find out. Whether she is eight, ten or fifteen years older than you, who cares? If she has

345

charmed you, and you have charmed her, isn't this what matters?

Have the sensitivity to allow her to feel that in giving into your advances, she has granted you a privilege. From a married man, she expects only what he can give – and that is not a lot. And in return, she gives gaiety and lightness, her independent, and sceptical spirit. You have engaged in an affair with no expectations other than pleasantness; a relationship sheltered from reproach, from resentment, tears and remorse. Lucky man!

You start a second family

As the CEO of a multinational corporation, you travel often, for example to Africa, where you often remain for extended stays. Tired of living in a drab hotel, you take up residence in a house surrounded by a garden scented by frangipani. Your evenings are a little brighter. And we can guess the rest. In the mould of those African men who, as soon as they have an opportunity, open what they call a "second office", you now have a mistress. And little by little, habit and pleasure lead you to start a second family. So long as your wife knows nothing about it, you are able to control the situation. But if she discovers the truth, the sky falls on her head.

You have two choices: either you break up your affair and save your marriage; or, and especially if a child is born out of your adventure, you manage to convince your wife to accept the situation, cruel as it is for her. If you are sincere and eloquent, you may succeed in explaining to her the reasons that brought you to break your solitude. So much bonds you to your lawful wife: your children, the years of common life, your roots and culture, and economic interests, that she will possibly come to terms with the situation. So be it, she is then in her right to request certain guarantees. The words: "I love you, you are my life" may still make her heart beat. If she is sure of your love, she will forgive you, but she won't forget. There will be a compromise, but exoticism will also wear out.

Masculine thoughtlessness and fickleness have accustomed us to such misdemeanours. Illegitimate children have longed ceased to be the privilege of princes.

Your own children, however, will accept their half-brother or sister with relatively few difficulties.

You are the lover of your daughter's best friend

Caroline has just sat her *baccalaureat*, and she has invited her best friend Isabelle to spend the summer holidays at your country house in the Ardèche. It's a beautiful summer. The two young women stroll through the house in their bikinis, spend hours at the local pool with you; you swim, you play volleyball. Isabelle is joyful and charming from morning to night, her body is gleaming with youth, golden as a brioche. It quite dazzles you, or rather it blinds you to the fact that Isabelle is your daughter's best friend, that she is twenty-five years younger than you, that she is under your roof and that you are with your family.

One afternoon, the thought of this spring chicken makes you lose your head. You set things up so that you are alone with her. And you commit an error the dimensions of which only become apparent after the disastrous fact. And now, you are panicking. Your family will hate you. You don't know what to do. You are eminently guilty, and conscious of it, but it is too late.

Since you cannot repair the irreparable, you must strive to contain the damage. For fear that either your wife or your daughter might suspect something, you must ask Isabelle (who is no doubt just as astounded as you are by what has happened to her) to find an excuse to leave immediately. Make sure that she will not say anything to your daughter about what has passed between you. When you return home, you must never again see Isabelle, and nothing must betray the attraction you felt for her.

Should your daughter discover your secret, her disillusionment would be immense. Firstly, she would lose her friend; and secondly, the love and admiration she has for you would suffer tremendously. As for your wife, better not even imagine what her reaction might be. *Bonjour tristesse!*[58]

---

[58] *Bonjour tristesse*: Hello sadness. The phrase recalls the title of the novel by Françoise Sagan (1935-2004), who borrowed the words from a poem by Paul Eluard (1895-1952). It evokes love triangles with fatally tragic consequences. [Translator's note]

THE UNFAITHFUL WIFE

One evening, when you are feeling blue, you succumb to the charms, the declarations, the daily attentions of a man you met several weeks ago at the supermarket. You were turning into the next aisle, your trolleys collided, and your knee had a nasty scratch. Embarrassed, worried, the man stood by your side, and he helped carry your bags all the way to your car. As he appeared eager to follow up on your wounds, you made the mistake of giving him your name, your address or your phone number – after which, you began to receive phone calls and invitations. And then on a certain evening, you fell into his arms. Since that moment, your heart has been in a tumult and has known no peace.

If your lover is married, you may feel somewhat reassured by the fact that he is no freer than you are. But if he is single, then how should you manage your affair?

First discovery: as the days pass, you become conscious that you love two men – your husband and your lover. You feel infinite tenderness and affection for the former, while curiosity, attention and desire draw you to the latter.

Savoir-vivre and infidelity

Unfaithful women are like unfaithful men: they use the same words, fall back on the same reasonings, they experience the same situations, and take the same risks. When it comes to infidelity, men and women have the same behaviours.

If your lover is single, and appears animated by great passion, inform him of your intentions from the first day: you do not have any wish to divorce, nor do you wish to endanger your family.

At home, if you do not want to betray your secret, keep to the same habits, and remain yourself. If you spread clues about yourself, even the most inattentive of husbands will end up suspecting something. What clues, might you ask?

Imagine that one evening, you return home with your hair cut short and dyed blond, looking like a movie star. Your husband and children were so taken aback, you made them scream – scream in alarm.

Imagine that you are by nature quite lazy, and you like staying in bed as long as you can in the morning, or you like to nap in the afternoon or simply lay about. But now, out of the blue, you have become a bundle of energy, you are almost neurotic. No longer do you spend hours on the phone, you are running from one errand to the next, and you are renewing your lingerie (the clue of all clues). You are renovating the apartment, moving the furniture around, re-upholstering the armchairs, then you move onto the bedspreads and you hang brand new curtains at your windows. Your need for renovation is as eloquent as a confession. Your crazy desire to tidy things up, to clean out your cupboards from top to bottom, is equally revealing.

Let's now imagine that you are perfectly house-proud. When your husband discovers that you have forgotten to make dinner twice in a week, and that the refrigerator is desperately empty, he may just begin to wonder.

If your oversights continue, if you appear disinterested in the things that usually preoccupy you, your spouse will no doubt ask himself: "What is she thinking?" He is almost on the point of discovery… watch out!

You used to do needle work, but you have thrown away your embroidery and taken up reflexology. All of this eventually leads to the conclusion that you find new pleasure in new hobbies.

Are you sure that you have what it takes to lie to your husband, to answer his questions without faltering, without flinching? Should you blush, search for your words, have sweaty hands and heart palpitations, you better renounce putting him and yourself at greater risks.

At last, the fatal blow arrives: you have replaced the good old conjugal bed with rigid, cold twin beds.

If your husband does not object to physical separation, it is because he has decided to remain blind to your escapades. Some men refuse to see the obvious. Why? Is it pride? *I am not the kind of man his wife cheats on...* Is it to avoid conflict? To avoid a pain too awful to bear? To deny the danger that should be confronted? To avoid a divorce?

Your unconscious has been tricking you, giving away the clues your husband needs to discover your subterfuge. But beware: there is danger!

What should you do, if your husband discovers your affair?

Deny everything. Play indignant: "Your jealousy is leading you astray! How could you doubt me?" And assure him you love him. Your family is worth the lies and deceit which will return you to peace, smiles and perhaps renewed passion.

If there is irrefutable proof of your affair, and you do not want a divorce, then you must prove to your husband that it is with him you want to live. Your adventure was only an interlude, a passing fancy, nothing more. If you assure him that you will put an end to it, you may calm his furore but you will need to do more than this to heal his pain. Imagine how you would feel if you were in his place!

351

What does a woman look for in an affair? To feel attractive – just like men who cheat on their wives – to feel desirable. To be filled with new energy, to feel the desire to begin something new, to give and be open to the world; to be young again, to enjoy lightness and feel irresponsible, to be carried away. To desire and be desired in return. To love and be loved, and to be charmed.

You are single and your lover is married

Why did you choose, or accept, to have an affair with a married man? Why would you reside in what the English call the "back street", or the Spaniard, "la casa pequeña" [the little house], or as the Africans say "the second office". In France, indeed, bourgeois hypocrisy does not even have a name for this!

Is it because bachelors are hard to come by? Because the man who charmed you was impossible to resist? Or is it because you are too attached to your freedom and do not want to complicate your independent life?

If your affair is pleasant and enduring, you certainly run the risk of becoming attached to this man, to find yourself needing his daily presence, to want to make plans together, or indeed, more... And at this point, things will become complicated. The affair which was only lightness and pleasure becomes a source of pain and trouble. And you are no longer willing to honour the contract which you committed to, implicitly, when you became the mistress of a married man.

Savoir-vivre requires that you show unalterable and unshakable discretion, and that you submit to a multiplicity of constraints:

- Do not demand to see your lover, who is married and a father, more than he is able to see you. This indeed excludes weekends, public holidays and vacations. Do not become an agent of scandal. Do not demand that he take you to Belle-Ville or Prague on a business trip, and especially if he has small children, on the pretext that he is attending a conference on his own. He may be travelling without his wife, but he still has his colleagues to take into account.

- You have to come to terms with the fact that you should meet your lover in neighbourhoods that are at a distance from his own home, and you must avoid meeting in public spaces, which are by right his wife's territory. A mistress, do not forget, is a woman of the shadows. Your lover will share his worries and troubles with you (you are such an attentive and caring listener…) but he will never associate you to his celebrations. The day he will be awarded the Légion d'honneur, you will not be among the guests. But his legitimate wife will, and she will be the one he introduces to his friends. None of this should surprise you. From the first day, your relationship (and a relationship with a married man is among the most difficult of all relationships) was established on an evident power imbalance.

- Do not try to meet his wife, to see what she looks like, or for that matter to meet her friends. Do not start going to her hairdresser's, or to the cafés, the restaurants, or the shops where she usually goes.

- Do not seek to meet your lover's children in the hope of rallying them to your cause. They should know nothing of your existence. One of my friends, a mature man, was for many years an inconsolable widower, until he met a woman, at a charity dinner, in

353

Genève. This woman made him lose his head. He asked her to move into his home, showered her with every care and attention, and satisfied all her desires: travel, receptions; society events… She then began to behave as though she were the mistress of the house, which failed to endear her to his children and grandchildren who soon put a stop to the situation. All her subsequent efforts to charm and seduce them left them cold as marble, and before long she had to depart with tears in her eyes and suitcases in hand, and leave the man she had been weak enough to want to possess too quickly and too completely.

- Never call your lover at his home on the telephone. And do refrain from calling at night for the sole purpose of disrupting his conjugal sleep. If your number were to show up on his screen, you would be so quickly discovered. And what would you look like then?

- Don't ask your lover about his wife: what she wears, what she likes, what she does.

- Don't ask any question relating to their private life and their conjugal intimacy.

- Don't change your habits, keep the same friends, and never sacrifice an evening out in the hope of hearing your lover knock on your door. Give yourself over to projects of your own, if not, you run the risk of limiting your life and sinking into depression. If you spend your evenings and your weekends waiting for his call, you are wasting your time, and your life – which is always all too short.

- Don't try to make either the date or the place of your vacations coincide with your lover's, for he will go on vacation with his family.

- Never lose your independent spirit. Remember, it was one of the qualities that attracted him to you in the first place.
- Whatever your age, whether you are divorced or a widow, with or without children, the desire to live with a man whom you love, to share every moment of his life, to build a life together, endures in you no matter how you may wish to deny it, and even as you proclaim your desire for independence. Independent? Yes, but alone? So, do not opt for difficulties and trouble by having a long-term relationship with a married man with small children.
- Safeguard your own equilibrium by placing no hope in your lover, and by seeing in your relationship nothing more than short-lived happiness, always threatened yet delicious: a woman's happiness.

And remember: bachelors may be hard to come by in the city, but they are plentiful in the country areas. A word to the wise will thus suffice!

You have several lovers

I have a friend who is divorced, and lives at Magny-en-Vexin – I am not too sure why. As soon as evening falls (and in winter it falls very early), she barricades herself in her bedroom and lives in terror of being burgled, invaded or physically aggressed. She has had bars installed on her windows and alarm systems at her front and back doors, but to no avail. Nothing seems to allay her fears. Nothing, except for human (usually masculine) warmth.

Having failed to secure one man, she has, over the years, acquired several lovers, one for each night of the week.

One of her lovers is Belgian and comes over to France at regular intervals to take care of business. The second is Italian and a sales representative for Panzani pasta. The third works as an anaesthetist at the local hospital, and thus invents himself night duties, in more ways than one evidently. The fourth is a member of the Republican Guard at Matignon[59] but his family resides in the Limousin. The fifth is a professional bridge player who is not only adept at shuffling cards but also at confusing the issues. The sixth has the fallback position, he is Scottish and sells wild salmon, his trips to France are dependant on the catch, and his clients' orders.

According to my friend, each of her lovers believes himself to be the only one who steps onto the Persian rug in her bedchamber. Each has his own wardrobe with his pyjamas, running shoes and toiletries. Her house is like Blue Beard's: There are doors one should resist the curiosity of opening.

Your children have discovered your affair

When your partner finds out that you have a lover, expect all manners of scenes and arguments, for these are inevitable. Even if your children do not witness your fights, they feel the surrounding threat, the danger lurking around them, because the entire atmosphere of your house has been altered. The silences, the permanent tensions, the irritability, the closed

---

[59] The "Garde républicaine" is a branch of the Parisian police, whose duties include maintaining security at official sites as well as providing honour guards and mounted police at special events. Matignon is the French prime minister's residence. [Translator's note]

faces plunge them into the depths of anxiety. You barely answer their questions if at all, and they are now sick with worry. What did Mummy do to Daddy for him to be so angry?

If you happen to exchange harsh or violent words with their father in your children's presence, don't pretend that they did not hear or that they somehow misunderstood. Even a newborn would be in need of re-assurance under the circumstances. Rather, as soon as you are able, you should have a conversation with your children and tell them the truth: just as children do, you too sometimes feel angry, impatient, or jealous, but the conflict between their father and you has nothing to do with your love for them, who are and will always be and unconditionally so, your treasure. If you no longer love your husband, tell your children, and explain to them that conjugal love can sometimes change, decline or even stop altogether, unlike the love a father and a mother have for their children. Because what is really terrifying for a child is not so much that his parents no longer love one another, but that they may then stop loving him as well. This is why your child needs you to re-affirm your love for him every minute of the day.

If you decide to divorce, you need to have separate conversations with each of your children. Explain to them that they will now have two homes. And since they will hold you responsible for the break-up of their family and the ensuing chaos, they will condemn your actions. Be prepared for their reproaches, whether or not they are voicing them aloud, and be prepared to bear their disapproval. Don't run from your responsibilities.

If you really want to know what your children's thoughts and feelings are regarding the situation, you may ask them directly or through a third and neutral person. Take their feelings utterly seriously.

Above all, behave as an adult, and don't criticize and tarnish the image your children have of their father and of their mother.

Don't take your children hostage or use them as currency exchange.

If, after you have divorced, you plan on living with another man, don't force your children to make his acquaintance. Give them the time to get used to their new life, to find a balance, before asking them to accept a person who will under no circumstance play their father's role. Let your children know of your relationship, but do not impose it on them too quickly because there will be much work to do, on your part and theirs, before they are ready to accept this revolution, in which they are the victims.

Savoir-vivre and breaking up

Beware! Breaking up with a lover is not to be left to improvisation! Breaking up demands a sense of humour, an acute sense of elegance, a taste for scripting and staging. The end of an affair should be prepared like a conspiracy, it should be ripened like grapes under the sun, and it should explode into the open only after the risks of reproach, resentment, revenge, and the telling of truths that are never good to announce, have been placed at a safe distance.

Ah, if you could only arrange a little ballet performance so you could leave on tippy-toes, like a ballerina on points, after one last entrechat!

Indeed, writing the famous last letter, restrained as you may feel at the time, may not always save you from spilling a certain bitterness, regrettable as it may be. Would it not be better to write something as below:

Jean-Pierre,

In a few days, we will have known each other four years. Did I await our anniversary to celebrate our separation? A break up several times announced and as many times withdrawn?

Tonight, I am leaving you. I will not come back.

I am leaving you because we have no common goals, not even this separation.

True, we had our small arguments, which came and went like the seasons: clear skies, cloudy skies, morning fogs, storms, excellent conditions. With always the same causes: low pressure in your hemisphere, and high tension in mine. And no equator, no neutral zone where our climate could settle in equilibrium.

I will remember you in black and white images: the white of desire and the black of absence.

White, black, white-black in our kaleidoscope too quickly turned our lives to grey.

Tell me, my dear sir, is grey the colour of life?

I am leaving you for none other. I could have waited for an opportunity to exchange you, but such barter would be undignified. I am leaving you for myself.

You were not free to love me, and so I could not love you. We were not lovable. And this is, in a few words, the story of our brief encounter. This story would have been even shorter, if I had not so loved the illusion of loving.

N.

SAVOIR–VIVRE AND HOMOSEXUAL LOVE

In France, the law granting homosexual couples the right to marry was promulgated 18 May 2013. It was followed by numerous mass demonstrations of opposition, as right wing and extreme-right political parties ferociously countered what the French call "marriage for all". Nonetheless, homosexual couples may now be married as all couples are in France, by the officer of the Republic of the municipality in which one of the partners has his or her residence. In addition, the marriage law guarantees same-sex married couples the right to adopt children.

We certainly have come a long way from the disapproval, the contempt that was once meted out to homosexual couples. Yet, we may be surprised, when we attend a gay pride parade to see that along with the joyous displays and a taste for frivolity, there may also be a certain helplessness and at times even a certain despair. Indeed, in spite of the cultural transformations and social and legal evolution of the past decades, to live openly as a homosexual can still be fraught with difficulty. And although homosexuality is perfectly acceptable in our great cities, it is still broadly rejected in the rural areas.

The savoir-vivre of same-sex partners

If homosexuality presents a challenge that your parents refuse to come to terms with, so long as you live under their roof, you should not make your preferences too obvious either by dressing flamboyantly, or wearing showy jewellery, or having exclusive friendships. When you are with your partner, it is best to avoid open displays of affection that could shock them. In fact, there is no need to supply them with information that they are not asking to know. Some parents may have an idea that their children are homosexual and at the same time be afraid to have their intuition confirmed.

However, you should have no issues with confiding in your siblings. It should not be difficult to discuss your sexual preference with them, all the more so that it is now socially acceptable and legally ratified. And unlike your parents, your brothers and sisters are not likely to feel responsible or guilty for your sexual drive.

With your friends, you should live openly. Introduce your partner or partners to them. If they look embarrassed or bothered, you may either wait for them to get used to the fact or seek friends who are liberated from outdated prejudice. The times when the poet Paul Claudel accused his friend Gide of "abomination" are now long gone.

In the workplace, there is no need for you to feel obligated to say anything to anyone. On the other hand, there is also no need to provoke by dressing ostentatiously or by holding a dubious discourse.

Women (and this is true of my girlfriends and myself) often seek friendships with homosexual men. Why? Because these friendships are free of all ambiguities. Besides, homosexual men often show women more care and attention than many a skirt-chaser! Those who believe that homosexual men are misogynistic are wrong – they are proponents of yet another prejudice we need to oppose!

As for men, there are married men who have friends who happen to be homosexual, and with whom they have no need to compete for women's attention, and who perhaps confirm their own virility. Others run in the opposite direction. Why?

Gay men sometimes have a very different conception of fidelity compared to straight men and women. Many homosexual couples accept, or at least tolerate more easily, their partner's infidelities. There are homosexual couples who can openly maintain two or three extra-conjugal relationships for many years. When having multiple partners is an acceptable norm, there is no need for lies.

You are bisexual

Let's imagine that you are a man, and you have been married for some years and your children are now grown up. Your dissatisfaction is bordering on depression. You have experienced a profound change, and you now find yourself attracted to men. Your sexuality, perhaps suppressed since childhood, is now being felt, affirmed and freed.

You must inform your wife, who no doubt is aware that your relations have cooled and who is suspecting an altogether different explanation for what she believes is your indifference. She is imagining you in the arms of a voluptuous brunette. The truth will not be less cruel, but it will at least safeguard some of her self-esteem. You will need to decide on your future jointly. Perhaps your wife cannot bear to lose you and will accept the "cohabitation". But this decision risks being not so simple and may not turn out to be the best option. Perhaps you will decide to separate, on the spot, and as fast as possible, before screaming matches and resentment destroy yours and your spouse's emotional well-being, which are already shaken. You will need to inform your children, best after attending some counselling sessions with a psychotherapist. They will need to learn the situation, and you have to avoid traumatising them with half-truths.

Savoir-vivre and female homosexuality

Since Antiquity, homosexual women have suffered relatively less social opprobrium than homosexual men. They have caused fewer scandals and been at the receiving end of less abuse. No homosexual woman was ever incarcerated or condemned to forced-labor as was Oscar Wilde.

Interestingly, the short hair and trousers which once upon a time were the distinctive signs of the tomboy, have become the norm for all girls and women aged between seven and seventy. Outside of sporting, artistic, or intellectual milieus, the likes of women such as Gertrude Stein, Romaine Brooks, Marguerite Yourcenar, Amélie Moresmo who never married and had no children, are rare. Many lesbians have had husbands, children and lovers.

Homosexual women have come out alongside the feminist movement, daring to affirm their difference and to demand their rights. However, they represent a very small proportion of the population, less than three percent, which combined with their bisexuality, goes some way to explain their political moderation and the fact that they do not constitute a distinct cultural group within our society.

Unlike homosexual men who tend toward sexual over-activity, lesbian couple are often examples of conjugal fidelity.

A homosexual woman should observe the same rules of *savoir-vivre* as an heterosexual one: elegance, discretion, and respect for others are the rule.

A few rules of savoir-vivre

Should you invite a homosexual couple (either men or women) to stay with you one weekend, and whose

363

relationship is not as yet public and out, you should send two invitations, addressed to each person, even if they share the same house. And if they have not informed you of their relations, you should not suggest that you suspect these two friends to be a couple.

IX

SAVOIR TRAVELLING

Today, you may go to Bora-Bora or Patagonia and you will no longer be an object of wonderment. Nowadays, everybody travels, and everyone wants to travel to the farthest corners of the earth.

I completed my first world tour when I was eighteen. Nothing could have prevented me from leaving. I was burning with the desire to see whatever was going on on our planet, and I wanted to see if America was like the movies. During four months, I travelled by any means of transportation, including rickshaws in Singapore. I heard every language spoken, and walked side by side with every race and nation; and appreciated just as many smiles and good attentions. I did take a few risks and I had a few hair-raising experiences, but when I came home, all I could think of was to leave again. Travelling is like an incurable virus. Once caught, you will journey together from now on! The pleasure of a departure never lessens – on one condition, of course, that we know how to travel.

THE ART OF LUGGAGE

At fifteen, there is no choice – one must bow to the backpack. Once we reach adult age, however, we love our comfort, and when possible, we also love luxury.

Perhaps it is the dream of every woman to travel with her trunks in tow, but only queens (sovereign queens that is) can still afford to travel in such style.

The more clothes and familiar objects a woman packs into her suitcase, the more she satisfies her femininity, recreating her familiar universe wherever she happens to set foot. She believes that should she be deprived of one particular garment, she would also be deprived of her power of seduction. However, it is well known that husbands hate luggage, and are always threatening: "No suitcases!"

Split between my husband's demands and my own desire not to lack for anything, I learned over time to pack a suitcase as if I were planning a menu for a festive dinner: everything, in small quantities.

Packing my suitcases[60]

I lay out all the clothes I have decided to take in my dressing room, along with matching handbags, shoes, stockings, gloves and jewellery.

Inside the suitcase, I first place my lingerie, scarves, gloves, handkerchiefs all packed in organdie or plastic

---

[60] Author's note: the following section was first published in *Heureuse and pas fâchée de l'être* [*Happy and glad to be so*] by Nadine de Rothschild, J-C Lattès, 1997.

garment bags. After which, come the woollens, blouses, dress-suits, dresses, and finally, the evening dress. I usually stuff the sleeves of my dresses with tissue paper to avoid creases. All my clothes have been hung on very light, velvet covered coat-hangers and placed inside clear plastic garment bags.

As a final act of fastidiousness, I cover everything with a small sheet of satin before fastening the straps.

TRAVEL CHECK LISTS

For women

Clothes
Pantyhose (light, dark and black)
Stockings (light, dark, and black)
Garter belt (white, black)
Pants and bras (white, black)
Slips
Nightgowns
Dressing gown
Slippers
Handkerchiefs
Neck and headscarves, shawls, gloves, belt
Pants
Blouses
Woollen jumpers
Dresses (for day wear and evening wear)
Shoes (running and dress shoes, including evening shoes)

In Summer, add:
Swimming suits
Sandals
Beach dresses and pants
Scarves (silk, cotton)
Shorts, pareos, tee-shirts
Sunglasses
Beach bag
Sun hat
Turbans
Swimming cap (mandatory in swimming pools)
Flippers

Toiletries
Cleanser and cotton balls, eau de toilette or perfume, face creams, body moisturiser, soap, face washer, deodorant, cotton buds, toothbrush, toothpaste, shampoo, tanning cream, multisocket adaptor, comb, hairbrush, hair dryer, hair rollers, pumice stone, ear plugs, magnifying mirror, manicure set, nail polish and nail polish remover.

Other small essentials
Mobile phone
Fun jewellery
Passport or identity card
Foreign currency
Credit cards
International driver's license
Visiting cards
Diary
Glasses
Camera
Travelling steam iron

368

Medications and supplements (aspirin, vitamins, tablets, etc.)
Sewing kit
Books

    – Whether I am travelling or out for a weekend, I always take my usual cosmetics in a smaller packaging.

    – I also bring with me a few small nylon bags in which I will store various purchases.

    – I stick something on my suitcase to help me recognise it, as for example a red dot, or I wrap sticky tape of two different colours on the handle.

For Men

Clothes
Pyjamas, dressing gown, slippers, underwear, shirts (sport, day and evening wear), cufflinks, ties, scarves, *pochettes*, handkerchiefs.
Belts
Socks
Suits (city, sport, dressy)
Shoes (city, sport) and shoe-trees
Coat and raincoat
Hat

In Summer, add
Swimming trunks
Sandals
Shorts
Tee-shirts
Sunglasses
Toiletries
Shaving cream
Razor (hand or electric), razor blades, multisocket adaptor
Aftershave lotion, eau de toilette, deodorant
Soap
Hairbrush
Cotton buds
Toothbrush
Toothpaste
Small essentials
Mobile phone
Passport or identity card
Credit card
Foreign currency

International driver's license
Visiting cards
Diary, document holder
Glasses
A spare pair of glasses (because it is so easy to lose them!)
Camera
Binoculars
Ear plugs
Books
Photos of the children!...

If your husband is a sport lover, don't forget to pack his tennis racket, his flippers, his golf clubs, his hunting or fishing license, club membership cards. If he likes a game, pack his cards.

Lately, although we now all have luggage on wheels, porters have made a come back in the railway stations. Charming and helpful, as well as highly visible in their red uniforms, porters also know which train departs from which platform before the information is officially announced.

Unpacking my suitcases

As soon as I arrive, either at the hotel or at my friends', I go into the bathroom and turn on the hot water tap over the bathtub. Then, I hang my dresses above, and the steam immediately removes all the creases.

After this, I hang my clothes (already on their own coat-hangers) in the wardrobe, and I put away the bags with the lingerie and accessories in the drawers. The whole thing takes less than fifteen minutes.

Savoir-vivre and travelling without luggage

Imagine yourself spending three days finessing the contents of your suitcase, taking count of what you need to dry-clean, wash, iron, so that you will take your best clothes and keep them in a state of perfection. You have even stored them in garment bags so that they will not crease. And you are so happy to be leaving, to go abroad, perhaps very far away.

You have now left the plane, and your head still spinning from the many hours of flight, you look on as dozens of pieces of luggage pass before your eyes; then suddenly the carousel stops and your luggage is no-where in sight.

You have a choice of two reactions.

You can throw a fit, call the airline by all manners of vile names, blame your husband for … never mind what: he has to be in the wrong since you don't have your luggage and he has his… Well, you would be quite a sight – everyone is looking at you, and you do not look so pretty because, think about it, whoever is responsible for this mistake is not here, but several thousand kilometres away. Nothing more can be done beyond searching for your missing suitcases.

Or…

You lose your smile (which is fair enough) but not your cool (which is fantastic). Indeed, you are aware that it is at this precise moment that others may form an opinion of you. If you care about how other people see you, you manage to overcome this truly annoying discomfiture. You state in a clear voice: "Well, it is not tragic." And you immediately meet with universal approval. Years later, you will still be remembered with admiration and someone, somewhere, will be thinking: "What a woman!"

A few years ago, I was travelling alone to preside at a charity dinner in Seattle, in the back of beyond in the United

States. I landed at dawn at the end of an exhausting flight and worrisome turbulences. You have guessed the rest: "No suitcase, Ma'am."

And the reception was for the evening. I now had to do without my beautiful Pierre Cardin dress, made especially for the occasion. And I did not have my shoes or my bag. In fact, I had nothing – nothing beyond my professional experience as an actress, for the advantage of that profession is that it teaches you how to overcome all manners of catastrophes: forgotten lines, an acting partner who has forgotten to come on stage, a misstep…

After several hours, the suitcase was finally located in Paris. It would be at least another twenty-four hours before it would arrive in Seattle.

I went to the hotel, and before even indulging in an American style breakfast and a long hot bath, I handed over the clothes I had been wearing for fast pressing. When I was laying in the bath, I reflected on my predicament and concluded that in the space of only a few hours, I was unlikely to find a suitable evening dress. If I am to believe American saleswomen, I am too "typically French".

Thus, I purchased the best toothbrush available, a superb make up kit, a pair of black pumps, and you will never guess what happened next: … A few safety pins and six metres of a flaming pink material with which I draped myself, as I would a sari. With a ravishing piece of jewellery bought at the local drugstore and a strong dose of self-confidence, I then stepped onto the stage, under the photographers' flashing cameras and before the crowd of guests seated in front of me. To the question: "Who designed your dress?" I answered, "Pierre Cardin, *of course!*"

TOURING AND SAVOIR-VIVRE

Car travel

Traffic rules are edicts intended to facilitate driving, they are the *savoir-vivre* we need to conduct ourselves well on the road. The principle rules of traffic regulation are concerned with the following:

- The state of the car. Although women often drive more cautiously than men, they can easily forget about car maintenance. However, an untuned engine, tyres in poor conditions, crooked or missing headlights, faulty windscreen wipers can also cause a road accident.
- Respecting priorities and road signs. If one fails to slow down when entering a built up area, an intersection, or when approaching a school, tragedy may ensue.
- Excessive speed and alcohol consumption are the first causes of road accidents.

Why should the French sadly claim first place among Europeans for road accidents? Certainly, neither our car makers nor our road infrastructure are to blame. So? Could it be that we are less responsible, less cautious and less civic minded than our European neighbours?

How should we drive a car? It may be a little complicated to answer this question, but it is simple enough to know what we should and should not do to conduct ourselves well when driving in a car.

If you are the driver

Take into account the taste of your passengers regarding
- The choice of itinerary: should you take the *autoroute* [freeway] or departmental back roads?
- Your speed: if your passengers are grasping at the armrests, it is likely that they are afraid of your driving, slow down and drive more smoothly, without braking suddenly or taking off at neck breaking speed. If you enjoy feeling like a racing car driver, wait until you are alone in the car.
- Smoking: before you light up, ask your passengers if cigarette smoke bothers them. Even if they are very polite and obliging, don't indulge in cigar smoking, unless your sole passenger is your wife and she is willing to put up with it. Don't drop your ash outside the window: the wind will throw it directly back at the passenger sitting in the back. Use the ashtray which is close at hand.
- The temperature: if you lower your window or the air-conditioning make sure that the person sitting behind you is not shivering with cold, and conversely, when driving with the windows up that they are not lacking for air.
- Music: you may like to drive while listening to classical music on France-Musique or perhaps you prefer something a little more rocky, but do your passengers share your tastes?

The seat of honour in a car is in the back, on the right hand side, and this is where the oldest passenger should be seated by right.

If you are driving in the city in the rain, you need to slow down before you hit a puddle and splash the pedestrians on the pavement. Don't drive down the laneways reserved for buses and two-wheeled vehicles. If a hoon overtakes you on the right or smashes into your car, brake as hard as you can, but don't fly into a rage and start yelling insults. Self-control and courtesy are rare qualities in a car driver, and those elevate him or her above the rest.

If you are dropping off a woman passenger, stop your car in front of her home. Before opening the doors, check that no one is coming on either side. Step out of the car to say goodbye and leave only after she has closed the door of her apartment building.

One must admit that Parisians do not shine on account of their sense of civility. When invited out for dinner, they forget to suggest dropping a woman home and indeed some would almost resent dropping her off at a taxi station.

When parking in the street

In the big cities, choking on ever denser car traffic, bus drivers, taxi drivers and other hurried people are put to the test on a daily basis by thoughtless drivers who double-park their cars, or park on a narrow street corner or in front of a driveway, or on the pavement, or where-ever, when-ever, and how-ever they feel, and thus block traffic. Not to respect street parking rules is another French disease.

In New York, which boasts of the greatest number of cars in the world, there are no street parking problems. Why not? Because the fines for illegal parking are steep and given on the spot, and no one can have a fine dismissed. A car parked in an illegal spot is removed within fifteen minutes.

376

Hence, drivers make sure they park in authorised parking lots and use taxis and the subway to circulate in the city.

Why could we not have electric minibuses circulating through the city, as in Rome?

If you are a passenger

Observe the same rules of civility as the driver. Even if you are the driver's spouse, refrain from criticising the itinerary once you are engaged in a direction. "I told you, you should have taken the bridge on the right, but as usual, you don't listen to anything!". This all too frequent argument is especially painful for the other passengers since it can degenerate into a full-blown domestic scene. In the same vein, refrain from critiquing the driver's driving style: Remember that the driver is Captain on board! If the driver is not speaking, refrain from distracting him or her, and maintain a fluid conversation on topics that are unlikely to unleash controversy.

Think of taking chocolate and sweets with you for the ride. I like to keep tissues, mint cordial and aspirin in the glove box of the car.

As a passenger, keep your luggage reasonable, avoid large objects that are difficult to store or multiple bags of awkward shapes and sizes. Also don't overdo your perfume. You do not want to force the other passengers to travel with their noses outside of the car windows.

When being dropped off at home, suggest being dropped off at a bus or taxi station rather than all the way back to your residence. As the Arab proverb says: "If your friend is made of honey, don't eat him all at once!"

377

Savoir-vivre and touring by coach

When travelling with other people, stay with the group, share in the general conversation and don't retreat into your own corner. Show courtesy to your travel companions, offer them sweets, candy, newspapers; offer your seat to an elderly person who happens to be sitting in a less convenient spot, or to a child sitting apart from his parents. When the coach stops, help the elderly and mothers with small children and luggage, step down onto the pavement. When getting back on the coach, don't let others wait for you, try not to be the last one to return to your seat.

On arrival, think of discreetly tipping the tour guide and the driver.

Savoir-vivre and the art of motorcycle riding

Women are catching up on lost time. Wearing helmets and leather, they sit astride heavy cylinder motorcycles and, elated by the power of their machines, they speed across the world. If this gives them happiness, why not? But would it be too much to hope for, to suggest that women riders show more sensitivity than their male counterparts regarding the various pollutions their passion produces?

Firstly, there is noise pollution: surely it is simple enough not to rev up your engine for half an hour before taking off? Could you not just start your motor when you are ready to leave? It is no doubt a lot of fun to play with the accelerator handle, but it also shows a total lack of consideration towards others. And it is also polite, in the night-time, not to go about the neighbourhood backfiring one's engine and waking up the population. Remember to change exhaust pipes on a regular basis, this will avoid polluting the airwaves as well as the air itself.

And one last word, when parking your bike, take care not to obstruct either pedestrian traffic or car traffic.

Savoir-vivre and train travel

In the train, men help women lift their luggage. Every time we leave our seats, we must excuse ourselves to the people seated next to us and those whom we are inconveniencing. We may take off our coats, but not our shoes, and we do not place our feet on the empty seat opposite. Rather than reading the magazine over our neighbour's shoulder, better ask to borrow it when he or she is done with it.

When using a mobile phone, it is polite to move away so as not to bother the other passengers. There is a special place in all TGV trains reserved for the use of mobile phones.

When taking our own food on the train, it is important to exclude foods with strong odours, as for example, mayonnaise sandwiches and smelly cheeses. In the same vein, it is best to stay away from juicy fruit which is difficult to manage eating with elegance. Passengers must also dispose of their paper cups and napkins in the bin provided near their seat.

Remember to bring a few toys, exercise books and coloured pencils to entertain your children so that they will not become restless. If they start to cry or throw a tantrum, it is best not to get into a power contest with them – on this one occasion give in, so as not to bother the other passengers.

Keep your dog or your cat on your lap, or better, if the trip is not too long, in their carry baskets.

When travelling at night, ask the people sharing your compartment if they would prefer your berth. This will establish courteous relations from the start. Before switching your light off, bid them goodnight, and wish them a good morning when you wake up.

In the dining car

Well, Madame, there is no order of precedence: everyone is served in turn. In the old days, it would have been unthinkable to speak to the man seated next to you if you had not been formally introduced. But, unlike our great-grandmothers who were so easily scandalised, we may not only engage in a conversation with a courteous gentleman, but should he offer us a glass of wine or a coffee, we are free to accept graciously,

When entering and leaving the dining car, it is polite to nod your head slightly in order to acknowledge fellow passengers in your immediate vicinity.

Savoir-vivre and plane travel

It may seem unfair, unacceptable and intolerable to have to wait for five hours in the worst of the August heat to board a plane between London and Paris, all because the French traffic controllers are once again on strike. But why become violently vindictive? Why should you pour your anger on the ground staff who have nothing to do with this? Surely, it would be more efficient to express your discontent in a letter addressed to the director of the airline, or even better to the union responsible for the chaos. But how can we make the best of these long hours of waiting? The best course of action is to not give into ill-humour and to try spending the time as pleasantly or perhaps more realistically, in the least unpleasant manner, as you can manage. Go sit in a café, and if you must go on waiting, buy a detective novel, a real "noir", so that your own situation appears a little more rosy.

When things go as per usual, why not just get on with the formalities required by immigration and customs with a smile?

During the flight, avoid moving about the aircraft without good reason as space in the aisles, especially in the economy class, is very restricted. Also, when seated in the middle or window seats, we should minimise the number of times we ask the persons sitting next to us to stand up to let us through.

If you are travelling with a dog who weighs under six kilos, you may keep him next to you in the cabin.

During the flight, don't bother the flight attendants to enquire about arrival-time, the name of the cities you are now flying over or because the turbulences are worrying you. If the meals are frankly mediocre or too small, once again, there is no point in complaining to the cabin staff. Write a letter to the company. Generally speaking, if we want a complaint to have a chance of reaching its goal, it is best to address it to those in charge rather than to intermediaries.

When disembarking, don't forget to smile back at the cabin staff.

Well-prepared women who travel long distances include in their hand-luggage sporting gear, or in summer, a comfortable cotton dress, a small toiletry kit (face cleansing and make up, add a small spray-bottle of mineral water for refreshing the face), a pair of soft pumps, and a shawl because airline blankets are very thin.

Where I am concerned, as soon as I have boarded the plane, and well before the meal is served, I change my clothes and remove my stockings, and I am ready for the night. I eat a light meal and drink a lot of water. I wake up early, before breakfast, with plenty of time to dress and to apply my make up – almost as if I were at home.

Savoir-vivre and sea travel

There is nothing like a few square metres of living space on a yacht to reveal an individual's true character and his level of culture. The observance of *savoir-vivre* becomes an absolute necessity when we find ourselves in confined spaces. Our dream boat quickly turns into the gallows from hell when one of its occupants appropriates the territory, the drinking water, the fruit, the cool drinks and the mattress in the sun, without even a thought for the desires or the comforts of others.

A cruise in a yacht is a pleasure trip when we travel with a group of energetic sporty people, capable of team spirit, or with courteous people who know how to share and offer.

If you share a cabin, you need to remember that in this narrow space where you will be sleeping several nights, you must be doubly vigilant. You must not leave your clothes, your swimming suit, your glasses or your sun cream lying around. Also, don't impose your nudity on your fellow travellers or take over the bathroom. On a boat, we strive to be models of discretion and to be in a good mood. Here, making others laugh is what *savoir-vivre* is all about.

On a skiff, it is imperative to bow to the commands, the discipline and the rules of safety demanded by the crew.

On a cruise ship, life is easier, since we can move about in a much larger space. During a cruise, we ought to be sociable, to partake in the entertainment organised on board, and to have fun. The sad-faced passenger, the loner, the man of a few words who, with haughty eyebrows and disdaining stiff upper lip, looks down on his travelling companions

382

moving on the dance floor, is no gentleman. Being intelligent is also about discovering the intelligence of others.

On a cruise, the dress code requires us not to wear evening dress on the first and last day.

If I had all the time in the world, I would go on all the musical and cultural cruises available, and this for several reasons. On a boat, everything is like a dream: the grandiose seascape, the sunsets, the starry skies, the reddening moon, the reflection of the water, the sweetness of nocturnal breezes. On a boat, we are cut from our past, and all that counts is the present moment when anything can happen. The crew and the captain, superb in their white uniforms, have taken charge and surround you with a thousand gestures of care and attention, discreetly courting you. The passengers are elegant, the entertainment is of great quality, and the service is refined.

On a boat, in this restricted and closed space surrounded by infinite space, to be single is an advantage. Meeting people is easier, conversations are lighter. Everything is as though served in a Champagne glass. Indeed, on a ship, if we are romantic or adventurous, we are likely to enjoy ourselves more, if we are on our own than if we are travelling as a couple.

SAVOIR-VIVRE AND THE HOTEL STAY

Reservations and cancellations

If you make a reservation over the phone, you will usually be asked to confirm your dates of arrival and departure in writing – by letter, email or fax. If you are sensitive to noise, don't forget to specify that you would like a quiet room giving onto a courtyard or garden, and do keep a copy of your written request. If you already know the hotel because you have stayed there before, you can request a specific room, as for example, room 22 which has suited you in the past.

If you cancel your vacations or change dates, let the hotel know in sufficient time so as not to be an inconvenience and join the ranks of unreliable customers.

On arrival

Will you arrive late at night? Expect limited service and help the night watchman get your luggage to your room. Avoid making noise or speaking loudly in the corridors, slamming either the elevator or your bedroom door. If you turn on the radio or the television, lower the volume.

Now, let's suppose your room does not suit you. Of course, it is a bother but it is not a tragedy. Armed with your most beautiful smile, ask the management to give you another room as soon as one (which pleases you more) becomes available. There is no point in recriminating. Also, avoid criticising the hotel in front of other patrons, wait to be face to face with the manager. If a hotel maid helps move your things to the other room, don't forget to thank her personally.

Your hotel stay

We must behave in our hotel room as well as we would behave at home: we don't drop our ash or cigarette butts, or our cotton balls on the floor, but use the ashtrays and the bins. Hence, remember to empty your bathtub and don't drop your towels in the bath water. Put away your clothes and shoes in the wardrobes; don't leave your jewellery, watches, glasses, or change laying around: you will find them more easily if they are inside the drawers. In addition, this shows consideration for the person who has to clean the rooms and who is expected to finish her work before lunchtime. Also when leaving the room, we switch off the lights and the television.

The more respect we have for hotel staff, the better we are served; their smiles adding to the pleasure of our stay.

In the dining-room

When entering your hotel dining-room, acknowledge the people sitting at nearby tables with a slight nod of the head. Don't stand out on account of some extravagant dress, loud laughter or noisy conversation, or by voicing criticism or other negative comments for all to hear.

At lunchtime, it is entirely inappropriate to enter the dining room in a swimming costume, shorts or bare feet. In the evening, dress up a little. Your husband may wear a jacket, and a scarf instead of a tie (a requirement in winter).

385

Keep to lunch and dinner hours, don't arrive either too early or too late. In some hotels, there is a special service for children, and it is a good idea to let your children lunch or dine before you do, for the peace and quiet of your fellow guests, and your own. If your children are very young, remain with them to ensure they behave and that they eat their meals as they should. If there is no such service at your hotel, you must ask your children not to run between the tables, not to throw tantrums, and generally speaking, to be well-behaved – and if they don't like meat or fish, don't serve them any, it will make dinner go more smoothly.

Don't forget your drops, tablets or liquid medications on your table; bring them out, and take them back with you to your room. In fact, you may prefer to take your medication in your room so as to keep your health matters private.

In the sitting-room

It is not polite to claim the best seat in the sitting-room by leaving one's knitting or newspapers on it. It is also a mark of over-familiarity, and highly intrusive, to expect to join in a game of cards before being invited.

Checking-out

Let the hotel management know that you are leaving, the day before your departure, and when you leave remember to thank the room service staff, porter, and concierge, and all those who have served you. Service is included in your bill, but there is no law against leaving a tip. When taking your leave, thank the manager for the care and comfort of his establishment. He will immediately think of you as a model customer!

Luxury hotels abound in temptations: piles of soft thick towels in the bathroom; face washers whiter than white; the silverware sparkling on your breakfast tray; and the porcelain ashtrays on the table. The temptation to take home a little souvenir may well be hard to resist. The temptation, nevertheless, must be resisted. After all, if you were staying at a friend's, you would not take anything home with you, would you? So, act in the same way at your hotel. Tell yourself that the cost of your room does not include the coffee spoon that you would so love to keep. Don't put yourself through the humiliation of receiving a bill for the bathrobe you packed in your suitcase ... by accident. Before you close your bedroom door, ensure that you have returned to Cesar all that belongs to Cesar.

I have kept an unforgettable memory of my first stay in a luxury hotel. It was in New York City, in the Sherry Netherland on Fifth Avenue. I had been asked by Jérôme Bière, the director of Unifrance-Films, to represent France for the release of the movie, *A Hair in My Soup*, in which I co-starred alongside the great Louis de Funès. We were scheduled to stay three days in New York and to return to France on Christmas Eve. But for some reason, I had in mind to spend Christmas Eve on Broadway and, unfortunately, between my desires and reality stood an empty purse and the exorbitant cost of the hotel.

What was this young hopeful to do?

She could charm the service lady in charge of her floor. So, I told her my story in a rather theatrical manner, and explained how I just had to stay one more night, just one little night, and how I did not have money to pay for even the smallest room in the cheapest hotel. Ten minutes later, I was happily leaving my luxurious room, suitcase in hand, and I soon found myself in a storeroom, a small space of only a few square meters piled with dirty laundry, without even a window and serviced by a dumb-waiter with loud creaking pulleys. But who cared! And as I walked through the splendid and glittering streets of New York that same night, mesmerized, a hot dog in one hand and a Coca-Cola in the other, I thanked Father Christmas for not forgetting me!

SAVOIR-VIVRE AND VACATIONS

Savoir-vivre and the holiday rental

Whether you have rented a chalet, a provençal *mas*, a country house or an apartment, for one or several weeks, remember that you are only a temporary tenant and that you must not act as though you actually own the place. You may re-organise the furniture and the home decorations to suit your taste, but when you depart, you have to put things back in their original places. During the course of your stay, imagine that you have let your own apartment, and then behave as you would like your imaginary tenant to behave. So, if your children have drawn all over the walls, you will need to wash them clean. You may also have to clean the curtains.

A broken object, a burned tablecloth can all be replaced, and a garden must be cared for, and the plants watered. If your landlord's orchard abounds with apples or apricots, it is fine to eat the fruit but not to make jams or jellies with it. Consume the fruit, not the usufruct!

On the day you sign the rental contract, you will be handed an inventory list, read it carefully (don't leave it for later) and make sure that the sheets, the cutlery, the plates, and the pots and pans all suit your purpose. You need to talk and ask for additional supplies before you move into the accommodation, not afterwards.

In France, house swapping with persons abroad, especially persons in the United States, is becoming a growing trend. For example, if you have a chalet near Grenoble, you can swap it, through the use of an agency, without any money being exchanged, for a house in Los Angeles or any other city in the United States. On both sides, the swap initiates an explosion of courtesy; not only do people clean, repair, polish and embellish their interiors, but they fill the refrigerators with drinks, the vases with flowers, and they put the prettiest sheets on the beds. In this way, people act as though they are lending their homes to their most treasured friends. And no one ever forgets to leave a thank you letter in the home they have occupied.

Savoir-vivre and the beach

The sea, the sand, the air are all polluted. This is one more reason not to relax into general complacency. The rules of *savoir-vivre* are even a greater must for all those who care for the environment. We must never leave on the beach, drink bottles or sun cream containers, nor paper – nothing at all. Before leaving our spot on the sand, we must collect everything we find into a rubbish bag and deposit the bag in a place provided for the purpose.

Let's have the good taste of not bringing a music box to the beach. Holidays provide the perfect opportunity to teach us the value and pleasures of silence.

Do you enjoy playing football or volleyball? Wonderful! But can you play without screeching every time you score a point? And if your neighbour has left their sun umbrella unattended, do you really think this is a good reason to invite yourself to sit underneath it? That is being bad-mannered. Also, remember to shake your beach towel, far away enough from others so as not to spray sand all over them.

No one should dress or undress in a public space, even if you happen to look like Venus emerging from the waters; when in a bathing suit, it is in good taste not to engage in excessive amorous embraces, and when going shopping in the village, to wear appropriate clothing that will not shock the local people. Dishevelled tourists, especially in Muslim countries, are often perceived as cultural aggressors.

Savoir-vivre and the vacation club

In a vacation club, hundreds of people find themselves thrust together in a bubbling bath of gaiety and familiarity. So, avoid dampening the atmosphere by making odious comparisons with holidays you spent in other places. If you are vacationing at Cap Skirring, don't go on that "Phuket was so much better!"

Here is the portrait of the perfect clubist. Up at dawn, he goes drumming at his neighbours' doors to drag them in the loudest possible manner, to a fishing party, a tennis game, a jog around the neighbourhood, a skiing treck, or some other excursion... From morning to night, all everyone hears is the sound of his voice. At lunchtime, he raids the dishes in the buffet, smacks everyone between the shoulder blades, calls across to his friends sitting at various tables, and engages everybody in conversation all the while using the "*tu*" form indiscriminately. Unstoppable, he can dance all night long. He sports an array of shirts adorned with flaming parrots, which he leaves open over his hairy chest; he grabs the microphone and fancies himself a crooner, or he tells off colour jokes, believing himself to be irresistible.

Should you come across this character, do not feel obliged to put up with his assaults. With a smile, you can let him know that you are an awful loner and that you have all intentions of remaining so.

Certainly, you must not abandon good manners, discretion, and courtesy, for *savoir-vivre* requires us not to make those who are lacking in *savoir-vivre* know that they have no *savoir-vivre*. In other words, let's not elect ourselves as judges of good manners. Nothing in our behaviour needs to show our disapproval, neither a critical look, nor an ironic comment. In the presence of a tiresome other, we should not show impatience, even as we grab the first opportunity to disappear.

Savoir-vivre and the caravan park

It is even more difficult to observe the rules of *savoir-vivre* in a caravan or camping park than in a vacation club, since people are living in even closer proximity, and comfort is minimal. In a camping park, there are no services at our disposal.

Under the circumstances, tensions can flare up easily, and so beware of domestic arguments which can ignite as fast as the pine forest surrounding you. As soon as you arrive, stick to this double negative:
- Don't bother your neighbours
- And don't spoil nature and the environment.

Evidently, one should never throw paper, cans, broken glass or bottles into a ravine or hide rubbish behind a tree.

Taking care of trees is of paramount importance. We should never break off branches or strip bark from trees. Above all, we must never light a campfire in a pine forest as this could ignite a tragedy. The well-being of rivers has become very fragile and any rubbish has the potential to pollute. The days of the washer-woman are well over. We should never wash clothes in a river, even if we refrain from using detergent.

Savoir-vivre and the perfect traveller

What not to do when travelling in a group:

- Make ourselves obvious by dressing either in a negligent or in an overly sophisticated manner, or by our behaviour or our comments,
- Speak loudly or sing at the top of our voices,
- Tell Belgian or Corsican jokes[61] at every conversation,
- Gorge at meal times, or the opposite, starve so as to make the point that the food is not to our taste or standards,
- Constantly request an alternative to the existing menu,
- Complain about the climate, about the lack of comfort at the hotel, about the service, the departure timetable, the guide, the excess of museum tours, or the dearth of,
- Forget either a suitcase or a piece of clothing at each stop of the tour,
- Insist that all the suitcases and bags in the luggage hold be taken out so we can make sure that our little case is on board,
- Act as the local judge or behave as a know all,
- Divide the group into hostile clans,
- Criticise or scoff at our travel companions.

---

[61] The French equivalent of the Irish joke. [Translator's note]

What we should do:

- Smooth the tensions that inevitably arise when people are in a group,
- Pay attention to our fellow travellers,
- Have a sense of humour in the face of difficulties or when things do not go as planned,
- And run from vulgarity.

Firstly, we are always judged on our appearance: a run in a stocking or chipped nail polish, a worn heel in our shoes, dull hair, crumpled blouses, flashy jewellery, heady perfume... All this risks leading to the conclusion that here goes a careless or unrefined person. Our choice of clothes certainly reflects our personalities. The ambitious woman wears black and red; the romantic wears grey; the infantile woman, wears pink or light blue; the coquette wears skirts split up to the thigh; the provocative woman sports a plunging décolleté where men may drown their eyes... But if you are truly elegant, then it is impossible to describe your style of dress because refinement and subtlety go together. And then we are also judged on our manners. Our gestures express who we are, and have a way of speaking that is immediately eloquent. Vulgarity is the one fault of character which no quality, no matter how exceptional, can ever redeem. But vulgarity is not a fatal flaw: remember how in Bernard Shaw's *Pygmalion*, the little flower merchant with an awful Cockney accent was transformed into a woman whose deportment, posture, and tone were those of a queen.

Some people are born, live and die in a state of vulgarity. Others have the intelligence and the will to remove themselves from vulgar circumstances. Yet, there are also others who acquire vulgarity through purposeful study and application, in reaction to an education which they believe was too strict or too oppressive, thus temporarily taking revenge on their parents. But everyone, of course, is free to evaluate the consequences of their life choices.

We can lose our name, our fortune, our social rank or our status but there is something that can never be taken away from us, and that is a good education.

How do we recognise, at first sight, that a person is "well educated"?

- At the tone of their voice and their manner of expression,
- At the way they dress,
- At the way they hold themselves,
- At their discretion in all circumstances,
- At their courtesy and their thoughtfulness,
- At their self-control,
- At the equanimity of their temperament,
- And finally, and above all, at their self-respect and the respect they have for others.

To travel is to go elsewhere, to look for exoticism and discover something else: Other landscapes but also other and different cultures. To travel is to experience a change of scenery and a change of life. When we travel, we carry in our luggage, history books and guides, but we also carry with us our *savoir-vivre* so that we may respect others' rules, customs, particularities and not least their sensitivities.

When speaking with a Scotsman, let's not talk of England but of the United Kingdom; in Sub-Saharan Africa, let's not go on about Picasso's invention of primitive art; let's not feel obligated to discuss the wars of religion in the Vatican, or the Inquisition in Spain; and in Morocco, we don't have to take the lead in criticising the monarchy.

We should also not remain strangers in the countries we visit but live with the local people, share in the festivities, the rituals, the customs. As Montaigne advised us several centuries ago: "Sharpen your wits against the wits of others".

Surely you have been asked this question a thousand times: If you were to move to a distant island, what would you take with you? I know of only one indispensable piece of luggage and that is courtesy.

We have travelled around the globe, visited the great capital cities, and on every continent, we have admired the wonders of the world. Travel has enriched our cultural capital and our imagination. We have made friends in all the places we have visited. And yet, everywhere and as far as we have gone, what have people talked with us about? Notre-Dame, the castles of the Loire Valley, Saint-Paul de Vence, the Mont Saint-Michel, the cathedral of Rheims, the pyramid at the Louvre, the Eiffel Tower…

The Italians have exclaimed with surprise: "What! You have visited the Roman catacombs and you haven't seen the caves at Lascaux?"

The Thais told us: "You strolled alongside the canals of Bangkok, but you haven't seen the gorges of Verdon?"

The Tibetans laughed: "So, you know the monasteries of Lassa but not the Abbay of Véselay?"

All added incredulously: "And yet, you have the good fortune of living in France!"

And so, what if we were to follow our foreign friends' advice, and set out on a discovery of our own country?